The Tragedy of Pious Antigone (1580)

Medieval & Renaissance
Texts and Studies

Volume 555

French Renaissance Texts in Translation

Volume 1

The Tragedy of Pious Antigone (1580)

by Robert Garnier

Translated, annotated,
and with an introduction by

Phillip John Usher

Arizona Center for Medieval & Renaissance Studies
Tempe, Arizona
2018

This publication was supported by
The Center for the Humanities of New York University

Arizona Center
for Medieval &
Renaissance Studies

Published by ACMRS (Arizona Center for Medieval and Renaissance Studies)
Tempe, Arizona

Library of Congress Cataloging-in-Publication Data

Names: Garnier, Robert, 1544-1590, author. | Usher, Phillip John, translator.
Title: The tragedy of pious Antigone (1580) / by Robert Garnier ; translated, annotated, and with an introduction by Phillip John Usher.
Other titles: Antigone. English | Medieval & Renaissance Texts & Studies (Series) ; v. 555. | Medieval & Renaissance Texts & Studies (Series). French renaissance texts in translation ; v. 1.
Description: Tempe, AZ : Arizona Center for Medieval & Renaissance Studies, 2018. | Series: Medieval & Renaissance Texts and Studies ; volume 555. French renaissance texts in translation ; volume 1
Identifiers: LCCN 2018053274 | ISBN 9780866986137 (hardcover : alk. paper)
Subjects: LCSH: Antigone (Mythological character)--Drama.
Classification: LCC PQ1625.G2 A6313 2018 | DDC 842/.3--dc23
LC record available at https://lccn.loc.gov/2018053274

∞
This book is made to last. It is set in Adobe Caslon Pro,
smyth-sewn and printed on acid-free paper to library specifications.
Printed in the United States of America

For my mum, Sue Usher;
and in memory of my dad, Den Usher (1935–2015).

Contents

Acknowledgments

Work on this translation began in a small apartment on the *Quai de la Tournelle* in Paris, in July 2010. The immediate goal was to produce an English rendering of the French text that I could teach in a new Comparative Literature course, "Tragedy Translated," to be offered at Barnard College, Columbia University, in Spring 2011. Numerous texts suggested themselves for inclusion in the syllabus, which was to feature Ancient Greek tragedies alongside later translations and adaptations from Ancient Rome, Early Modern Europe, and the present day. The trajectory thus stretched from Aeschylus up to writers such as Bertolt Brecht, Wole Soyinka, Griselda Gambaro, and Sylvain Bemba. As I planned the class, I quickly discovered that hardly any tragedies from sixteenth-century Renaissance France, my primary field of study, were available in English—with the notable exception of two translations (also taught in the class) realized by Richard Hillman, of François de Chantelouve's *The Tragedy of the Late Gaspard de Coligny* and Pierre Matthieu's *The Guisiade*. The present project thus sprang from a desire to respond to the fact that, in the Anglophone history of tragedy, the plays of the French Renaissance are somewhat underrepresented—and to begin responding in the most concrete way possible, with a translation to be read by students. Thanks must be addressed to Helene Foley, of Barnard College's Department of Classics, an expert on Greek tragedy and on its later translations/adaptations and most recently the editor (with Erin B. Mee) of the volume *Antigone on the Contemporary World Stage* (2011), for her advice and encouragement back when I was putting together the initial "Tragedy Translated" syllabus—and indeed, for allowing me to teach it! I thank Peter Connor, Director of the Barnard College Center for Translation Studies, for his college-wide promotion of translation, without which I would not have taken up the joyous challenge of creating such a class in the first place. Thanks are also addressed to all the students who took the "Tragedy Translated" class, for our stimulating discussions on all aspects of tragedy across the ages. Further thanks are due to all members of the Humanities Forum on Violence (2013–14) at the University of Pennsylvania, especially its director Karen Beckman and my respondent Sheila (aka. Bridget) Murnaghan, for their support of, and feedback on, my work on Robert Garnier's plays. Progress on this translation and edition would not have been possible without the collegial and scholarly communities of Barnard College, Columbia University, and of New York University. Progress was greatly helped by a generous Barnard College Presidential Research Award, for which I thank Debora Spar and the members of the Grants Committee. I should like to thank Robert Bjork, Roy Rukkila, Susan Dash, and everyone at ACMRS for welcoming this volume and ushering it into print with professionalism and good humor! Most importantly of all: this translation would not have evolved into its present form without the intelligence, dedication, and generosity of my wife, Penelope Meyers Usher.

List of Illustrations

List of Abbreviations

Beaudin	Robert Garnier's *Antigone*, edited by Jean-Dominique Beaudin (see Garnier 1997)
BHR	*Bibliothèque d'Humanisme et Renaissance*
BnF	Bibliothèque nationale de France, Paris, France
Butler	Butler Library, Columbia University, New York, USA
CP	*Classical Philology*
EEBO	Early English Books Online
EMF	*Early Modern France*
EurPhW	Euripides's *Phoenician Women* (see Euripides 1959)
Frank	Commentary on Seneca's *Phoenissae* by Marica Frank (see Frank 1995)
Fr.	The French language regardless of period
Gallica	Online library of the BnF (gallica.bnf.fr)
HO	Horace, *Odes* (see Horace 1994)
HSCP	*Harvard Studies in Classical Philology*
Lebègue	Robert Garnier's *Antigone*, edited by Raymond Lebègue (see Garnier 1952)
LIMC	*Lexicon Iconographicum Mythologiae Classicae* (see under title in 'Secondary Sources')
LS	Lewis and Short's *Latin Dictionary* (see Lewis and Short 1879)
ML	Middle Liddell, i.e., Liddell and Scott's *Intermediate Greek-English Lexicon* (see Liddell and Scott 1900.
Mouflard	Marie-Madeleine Mouflard's *Robert Garnier 1545–1590* (see Mouflard 1961–64)
Od	Homer's *Odyssey* (see Homer 1995)
PCPS	*Proceedings of the Cambridge Philological Society*
PEP	*Princeton Encyclopedia of Poetry* (see Greene et al. 2012)
Pinvert	Robert Garnier's *Œuvres Complètes*, edited by Lucien Pinvert (see Garnier 1923)

Propertius	Propertius's *Elegies* (see Propetius 1916)
RHLF	*Revue d'Histoire littéraire de la France*
RP	Ronsard's *Œuvres Complètes*, edited by Jean Céard, Daniel Ménager, and Michel Simonin (see Ronsard 1993–94)
RL	Ronsard's *Œuvres Complètes*, edited by Paul Laumonier (Ronsard 1937–83)
SenAg	Seneca's *Agamemnon* (see Seneca 2004)
SenHerc	Seneca's *Hercules furens* (see Seneca 1917)
SenOed	Seneca's *Oedipus* (see Seneca 1917)
SenPhW	Seneca's *Phoenician Women* (see Seneca 2002)
SenTBL	Seneca's *Tragédies* (see Seneca 2002)
SophAnt	Sophocles's *Antigone*, edited and translated by Hugh Llyod-Jones (see Sophocles 1994)
SophAntDG	Sophocles's *Antigone*, edited and translated by David Greene (see Sophocles 1991)
SophOedDG	Sophocles's *Oedipus the King*, edited and translated by David Greene (see Sophocles 1991)
STFM	*Société des textes français modernes*
StTheb	Statius's *Thebaid* (see Statius 2003)
TAPhA	*Transactions of the American Philological Association*
TDR	*The Drama Review*

Introduction

With four suicides and a total of six deaths, *Antigone, ou la Pieté* (1580), a title I translate as *The Tragedy of Pious Antigone*, is Robert Garnier's longest—and bloodiest—tragedy.[1] It begins with one death wish (Oedipus's): "Give me my death, make my death a cruel and bloody one" (32–34[2]); and ends with another (Creon's): "Put an end, I pray you, to my pain and to my life" (2736). Drawing on various classical sources (especially Seneca, Statius, and Sophocles), the five acts that separate these two moments of suicidal despair capture—as if in a long, drawn-out, and over-exposed close-up—a family (the Labdacids) at the exact convulsive moment when suffering, reaching its private and political paroxysms, obtains its final expression and ultimate annulment in death.[3] As this brief death-to-death summary already makes clear, Garnier's *Antigone* tells not (just) the story of Antigone's celebrated stand against Creon. We thus cannot watch or read the present tragedy—as Hegel read Sophocles—as a conflict between two opposed ethical claims (i.e., Antigone's and Creon's).[4] While the title foregrounds Antigone and highlights her main ethical stance—she stands for, and is ready to die in order to defend, *piety*—Garnier's play extends the *tableau* backwards in time to include another female voice, that of Antigone's mother Jocasta. It is Jocasta who first cries out in hopes of changing the course of events: "My child," she shouts to her son, "may your tensed hand re-house that odious sword in its sheath. Cast your club far off into the land. Take off this great shield that protects your chest" (686–89). This juxtaposition of the voices of Jocasta and

[1] The only contemporary French tragedy longer than Garnier's *Antigone* is Pierre Matthieu's *Esther*.

[2] Unless otherwise noted, all line references to the play are to the present translation.

[3] As one scholar put it: "nous sommes dès les premiers vers plongés dans l'horreur et dans le désespoir" (from the very first lines, we are plunged into horror and despair) (Gras 1965: 138); as Jacques Morel notes more generally about Garnier's tragedies, "il s'agit toujours de morts affreuses et inévitables" (they always involve horrible and inevitable deaths) (Morel 1964: 17).

[4] "The original essence of tragedy consists then in the fact that within such a conflict each of the opposed sides, if taken by itself, has justification, while on the other hand each can establish the true and positive content of its own aim and character only by negating and damaging the equally justified power of the other." (Hegel 1975: 1196).

Antigone best characterizes Garnier's bloodstained play—*Antigone* is a lamentation on the horrors of war and a resounding call for peace.

Garnier, of course, did not *invent* the various episodes he recounts—but his choice of where to begin and where to end his tragedy reveals his aim to have us reflect on the destruction caused by civil war and to hear, amidst the violence, the voices of a mother and daughter who call for peace. For those readers or spectators who lived through the bloody Wars of Religion (1562–98) that pitted Catholics and Protestants against each other, the five acts of this *Antigone* would have had immediate resonance—not as a play extolling or defending one side or the other, and thus to be appreciated only by members of that community, but as a seemingly non-partisan and earnest lamentation on troubled times.[5]

1. The Dawn of French Tragedy

Replacing the earlier French tradition of mystery and morality plays and preparing the way for the much more celebrated seventeenth-century works of Corneille and Racine, French tragedy was born in the 1550s. The watershed moment is usually marked either by Protestant Théodore de Bèze's *Abraham sacrifiant* (published 1550), a biblical tragedy about Abraham's sacrifice of his son Isaac, or by Etienne Jodelle's *Cléopâtre captive* (performed 1553), a retelling of the story of Cleopatra. One early staging of Jodelle's *Cléopâtre* took place at the Collège de Boncourt in Paris, demonstrating that early French tragedy—often referred to as "humanist theater"—was nurtured particularly in educational (rather than public-performance) settings.[6] There was no Globe theater, nor anything like it, in sixteenth-century Paris. While we know few details of the staging of these performances, Etienne Pasquier, who attended Jodelle's *Cléopâtre* at the Collège de Boncourt, describes a robust audience for the performance: "toutes les fenestres estoient tapissées d'une infinité de personnages d'honneur, et la Cour [était] pleine" (all the windows were filled by an infinite number of honorable

[5] As one critic phrased it, "Garnier n'a jamais imité pour le plaisir d'imiter [. . .] C'est son pays, ce sont les horreurs de la guerre civile qui l'ont poussé à écrire" (Garnier never practiced literary imitation for the pleasure of it [. . .] What pushed him to write was his country and the horrors of civil war) (Gras 1965: 138). Another wrote, "Garnier, patriote fervent, veut détourner les Français de leurs guerres fratricides" (Garnier, a fervent patriot, wants to turn French minds away from their fratricidal wars) (Lebègue 1973: 557).

[6] The fact that early French tragedy is so closely bound up with the task of translating and interpreting ancient texts and that, based on the current state of knowledge, it was likely in educational settings that such tragedies were read or performed, has had a lasting impact on how critics write about this corpus of texts, to the extent that the field can at times feel somewhat anti-theatrical. See section 5, below.

persons, and the courtyard [was] full)."[7] Over the next few years, other tragedies followed: Jodelle's *Didon se sacrifiant* (written c. 1555) which transformed Virgil's epic account of Aeneas into a lament on the death of Dido,[8] and Jean Bastier de la Péruse's *Médée* (published posthumously in 1555), which different critics have seen as either a "servile imitation" of Seneca's *Medea* or else as something much more original.[9] Many more authors followed suit, producing both translations/adaptations of Ancient plays and imagining new ones, thus paving the way for the authors of the next generations, namely Jean de la Taille (c.1540-c. 1607) and Robert Garnier (1544–1590).

Theory *about* tragedy was not particularly important, generally speaking, to early French tragedians.[10] Although Aristotle's *Poetics* was available in print

---

[7] See Etienne Pasquier, *Les Oeuvres* [. . .] *contenant ses Recherches de la France* (Amsterdam, 1703), vol. XII, p. vi.

[8] On this play, see the excellent edition by Jean-Claude Ternaux (Jodelle 2002). Among the key studies are Godenne 1969, Lazard 1990, Ducos 1990 and Ternaux 2002.

[9] The diversity of opinions regarding la Péruse's play offers insight into just how confused critics have been regarding the relationship of French Renaissance tragedies to their Ancient models. la Péruse's *Médée* was for a long time thought to be little more than a servile translation of Seneca's version of the same story. Such was the opinion of Emile Faguet: "La *Médée* de La Péruse est la *Médée* de Sénèque" (La Péruse's *Medea* is [nothing but] Seneca's *Medea*), placing his discussion of the play in the category of those "imitations serviles de l'antiquité" (slavish imitations of Antiquity) (Faguet 1883: 81). His fuller analysis is as follows: La Péruse "a appliqué à l'œuvre latine un système d'imitation qui consiste tantôt à traduire, tantôt à abréger, tantôt, mais très rarement, à délayer" (applied to the Latin work a system of imitation that consists sometimes in translation, sometimes in abridging, sometimes—but rarely—in padding out) (91). Elliott Forsyth, for his part, noted that the play is "beaucoup plus qu'une simple traduction de la *Médée* de Sénèque" (much more than a simple translation of Seneca's *Medea*), but he nonetheless concluded that all its elements are "d'inspiration purement sénéquienne" (of purely Seneca inspiration) (Forsyth 1962: 149–50). Nicholas Banachévitch's view is more nuanced—for him, the play "n'est pas une simple traduction de la *Médée* de Sénèque" (is not a mere translation of Senecea's *Medea*) but "elle n'en reste pas moins trop assujettie à son modèle pour ne pas marquer un pas en avant dans l'asservissement de l'art dramatique du XVIe siècle" (it nevertheless remains so greatly subservient to its model that it is another step towards the enslavement of sixteenth-century dramatic art) (Banachévitch 1970: 93). Thankfully, James A. Coleman has undertaken the serious scholarship necessary to make things clearer: "la *Médée* de 1556 est loin d'être une simple traduction ou une imitation servile de son modèle latin" (the 1556 *Medea* is far from being a mere translation or a slavish imitation of its Latin model) (Jodelle ed. Coleman 1985: ix), a statement based on his exhaustive study of the play's sources (Jodelle ed. Coleman 1985: Appendix 2). Coleman shows that while much of the play is based on Seneca, Euripides is also important, as are La Péruse's own inventions, notably Creon's monologue in Act 3 and the *canticum* in Act 4. For one possible political reading of the play, see Usher 2013.

[10] See Mathieu-Castellani 1984.

editions, and although it received a certain amount of attention in Renaissance Italy and elsewhere, it was not particularly central to discussions of tragedy in France at this time.[11] The period's (quasi-) theoretical writings on tragedy do not provide a unified definition, but do afford us a glimpse of key concerns and understandings. Several years before *Abraham sacrifiant* and *Cléopâtre captive*, Thomas Sebillet in his *Art Poétique français* (published 1548) asserted—rather strangely—that Greek and Latin tragedy still existed in France in the form of the French morality play, because both deal with "faits graves et principaux" (grave and important matters) (Goyet 1990: 127).[12] A year later, Joachim Du Bellay took a radically different view in his *Deffence, et illustration de la langue française* (Defense and Illustration of the French Tongue). Although Du Bellay judged epic to be much more important than tragedy,[13] he nonetheless allowed that France's future poet, his addressee, *might* want to write a tragedy in order to restore the genre's former dignity which, he says, had been "usurpée [par] les Farces, et Moralitez" ("usurped [by] farces [and] morality plays," by turning to Ancient models.[14] Hardly a call to arms regarding the tragic genre, Du Bellay's manifesto nevertheless captures, when compared with Sebillet, the moment at which tragedy based on Ancient models dethrones, in France, the idea that morality plays already *were* tragedy.

Several years later, Jacques Peletier du Mans became the first to dedicate a whole chapter to the genre, in his *Art poétique* (1555). Peletier defined tragedy as treating "Rois, Princes et grands Seigneurs" (kings, princes, and important lords), as being "luctueuse et lamentable, horrible à voir" (embattled and lamentable, horrible to see), and as depicting "occisions, exils, malheureux, définements de fortunes, d'enfants et de parents" (killings, exiles, misfortunate individuals, losses of fortune, children, and parents) (Goyet 1990: 279–80). Peletier is more specific about literary models and about their suitability to the French context: Sophocles is essential, but for France he should be made "plus grave de style et plus hautain" (graver in style and more haughty); Euripides is also essential, but should be modified to be "plus sentencieux et plus philosophique" (more

11 See Javitch 1999.

12 Despite the fact that Sebillet offers such a comparison, he also underscores difference: "Et si le Français s'était rangé à ce que la fin de la Moralité fût toujours triste et douleureuse (sic), la Moralité serait Tragédie" (And if the Frenchman decided to make the end of morality plays always sad and upsetting, than the morality play would indeed be a tragedy) (Goyet 1990: 127).

13 See Usher 2010: xvi–xx.

14 "Tu sçais où tu en doibs trouver les Archetypes" [you know where you should seek out the primary models] (Du Bellay 2007: 137–38). Du Bellay's sentence echoes Sebillet's statement that: "L'églogue est Grecque d'invention, Latine d'usurpation, et Française d'imitation" (the eclogue was invented by the Greeks, usurped by the Latins, and imitated by the French) (Goyet 1990: 126).

aphoristic and more philosophical); and Seneca, finally, although judged "guère magnifique" (hardly magnificent), is at least "sentencieux" (aphoristic) and "imitable avec jugement" (imitable, as long as judgment is used). In other words, Peletier argues that French tragedians should seek out Greek models—and make them more aphoristic, like Seneca.

Close, chronologically and conceptually, to *Antigone* is the "Art de la Tragedie" (Art of Tragedy) by Jean de la Taille (c. 1540-c. 1607), published in 1572 in the same volume as the latter's *Saül le Furieux* (Saul the Furious).[15] Moving between technical and thematic concerns, La Taille's text indicates that by the 1570s tragedy could no longer be discussed purely in terms of literary renewal or imitation—it has by this point become vital, pertinent, and controversial, i.e., meaningful in a more immediate way. La Taille affirms, among other things, tragedy's relevance to, and complicated connection with, contemporary matters. He evokes "les piteux desastres aduenus nagueres en la France par nos Guerres ciuiles" (the piteous disasters which have occurred recently in France because of our civil wars) and notes that "il ne faudroit ia autre chose pour faire des Tragedies" (nothing else would be needed for the writing of tragedies) (La Taille 1572: 2^{r}). And yet, just as quickly as he connects the Wars of Religion to tragedy, he suspends that connection, proclaiming that "pour ne remuer nos vieilles & nouuelles douleurs" (so as not to stir up our old troubles, nor to provoke new ones) he would rather "descrire le malheur d'autruy que le nostre" (describe the misfortune of others rather than our own).[16] But La Taille, who fought in, and was injured during, the troubles and who can be ideologically aligned with the moderate position of the *politiques*, wrote tragedies that *did* take up and reflect upon the Wars of Religion.[17] By simultaneously advancing and suspending the

[15] A brief introduction to this treaty is provided by Lebègue 1998: 26–28. For a fuller presentation of this text, see the introduction provided by Frederick West in his edition (La Taille 1939). For a bibliography of studies dedicated to Jean de la Taille, see Bellenger 1998.

[16] On the vitally important question of memory and forgetting in the Wars of Religion, see the valuable essays in Laguardia and Yandell 2015, as well as Frisch 2015.

[17] The most convincing and sensitive reading of this relationship is offered by Noirot-Maguire 2010. Noirot-Maguire argues in particular that La Taille's tragedies, not unlike the theater of Artaud, show dissemination of evil in order to articulate (perhaps paradoxically) a call for peace and for goodness: "Contrairement à une tendance globale de la littérature pamphlétaire des guerres de religion, il n'y a chez La Taille ni innocents, ni bouc émissaire, ni Antéchrist désigné. Le gentilhomme lettré au service de sa nation malade, déchirée par les guerres de religion, ramène ses nobles destinataires à leur conscience. [. . .] L'horreur des guerres civiles plonge le peuple dans un monde d'avant la Rédemption, engendrant un théâtre de la cruauté qui pour l'humanisme chrétien n'a pas lieu d'être, puisque seules l'omniscience et la justice divines peuvent trancher entre bourreaux et victimes" (In contrast with the general tendency within the pamphlet literature of the Wars of Religion, in the works of La Taille, no one is innocent, there is

association between contemporary history and tragedy, he foregrounds and problematizes the tenuous nature of that relationship, as too will Garnier.[18] However Garnier is different from his predecessors, it is difficult to read his *Antigone* without appreciating the steps they took to introduce the tragic genre into French literature. The shift between Du Bellay's timid avowal that one *might* wish to write a tragedy and La Taille's extended and bold reflection on the genre's relevance to contemporary troubles establishes a trajectory that leads to Garnier.

2. Robert Garnier: France's First Career Tragedian

Robert Garnier (1545–90) has frequently been called France's first career tragedian. Not its first tragedian, but its first author to produce a tragic *œuvre.* Whereas Jodelle published just two tragedies (*Cléopâtre captive* and *Didon se sacrifiant*) and whereas La Péruse died at age twenty-five having written only one (*Médée*), Garnier wrote seven tragedies and a tragicomedy. Garnier's first work, a "Chant royal en allégorie" (1564), while not itself a tragedy, contains much of what would later define his tragic *œuvre.* This "Royal Song in the Form of an Allegory" expresses an earnest longing for political and religious peace and argues that such peace is only possible under a strong monarch. Poetry, religious peace, political systems, and the rights and duties of a country's rulers are the defining characteristics and concerns of Garnier's life and works. After studies in Toulouse, Garnier became an *avocat* in the Paris Parliament and then, several years later, a counselor at a judicial tribune called a *présidial* in Le Mans.

Garnier published his first tragedy in 1568: *Porcie, tragedie françoise, representant la cruelle & sanglante saison des guerres Ciuiles de Rome: propre & conuenable pour y voir depeincte la calamité de ce temps* (Porcia, a French tragedy, which displays the cruel and bloody season of Rome's civil wars, in which we can rightly and appropriately see depicted the calamity of our own times). As La Taille would advocate in his "Art de la tragédie" (1572), discussed above, *Porcie* talks of "others' troubles," those of Roman civil war, in order to mirror the French "calamity" of the Wars of Religion. The main female character of the play calls for peace—unlike her literary models, *this* Porcia criticizes Brutus for his involvement in the assassination of Caesar. Better to have one tyrant, she

no scapegoat, no designated Antichrist. The lettered gentleman in the service of his sick nation, torn apart by the Wars of Religion, directs his noble dedicatees back to their own conscience. [. . .] The horror of the civil wars plunges the population into a world that predates Redemption, giving rise to a theater of cruelty that, for Christian humanism, should no longer exist, for only divine omniscience and justice can make the distinction between executioner and victim) (136).

[18] On the various theoretical influences on La Taille's treatise (Horace, Aristotle, etc.) see Kreyder 1998.

says, than three (in reference to the *triumvirate*). In both *Porcie* and a decade later in *Antigone*, Garnier marshals a vocabulary of internecine warfare, replete with numerous reflexive verbs that emphasize the horror of civil war (*s'entre-égorger* [to cut each other's throats]; *s'entre-ouvrir l'estomach* [to cut open each other's stomachs], etc.). In both, a chorus laments civil warfare and regrets that soldiers are not instead fighting foreign enemies.

Garnier's next two tragedies (again Roman, thus forming a trilogy) pursue similar concerns: *Cornélie* (1574) begins with a monologue that details Rome's misfortunes; and in *Marc Antoine* (1578), the last of the three Roman plays, Garnier takes up the story of Mark Anthony and Cleopatra (already celebrated by Jodelle in his *Cléopâtre captive*), arguing that unchecked passion can bring down a leader and his country. Notable, too, are the comments made about how the populace suffers from war. For example, Caesar is reminded in Act IV that as leaders fight for power ". . .le peuple en porte seul la peine" (the population alone carries the weight) (1493). Although it interrupts the trilogy of Roman plays, *Hippolyte* (1573), which tells the story of Phaedra and Hippolytus, and which seems to focus on the private sphere, also arguably engages with the problem of war and expresses a desire for peace (see Usher 2012). The tragedy that immediately precedes *Antigone*, *La Troade*, published in 1579 but perhaps written as early as 1574–75, depicts the pain of the Trojans following the fall of their city, with particular emphasis on Hecuba, whose husband Priam was murdered, and Andromache, whose husband Hector is also dead. *La Troade* reads differently to Garnier's earlier tragedies. There is decidedly more action and a variety of different literary techniques, for example, dialogued lamentation in Act I in which Hecuba and the choir sing of their pain, emphasizing its physicality (tear-stained hair dragged through black dust, nudity, etc.).

Antigone's main themes—horror at civil war, praise of justice and clemency—thus thread through all of Garnier's plays published up until this point. *Antigone* goes even further than *La Troade* in terms of the amount of action and the variety and quality of dramatic techniques—there are more exchanges between characters and somewhat fewer monologues.[19] Many lines in *Antigone*

[19] As one critic phrased it, in *Antigone*, "[la] préparation dramatique est meilleure que dans les pièces précédentes et le dialogue vivant progresse au détriment des monologues" (the dramatic preparation is better that in the earlier plays and lively dialogue takes somewhat over from monologues) (Rohou 1996: 72). More recently, Jean-Dominique Beaudin has noted that in *Antigone* Garnier worked hard to alternate "la crainte et l'espoir" (fear and hope), such that "le spectateur peut espérer que la chaîne des erreurs et des malheurs va se briser" (the spectator can hope that the chain of errors and misfortunes will be broken) (Beaudin: 41). Until *Antigone*, continues Beaudin, Garnier "n'avait pas montré autant de sens dramatique" (had not demonstrated such an understanding of drama) (48). That Garnier progressed is a widely held opinion. Over a fifteen year period, writes one scholar, Garnier "a perfectionné la structure dramatique et creusé la peinture

indicate the staging or movement of characters, for example when Antigone calls out to her mother: "Go on no further, but stop here in this place. Remain here. Where do you flee?" (lines 986–87). The choir, too, seems to invite us to imagine characters as embodied presences: "Here is poor Haemon [. . .] who darkens with sorrow the appearance of his bright face" (lines 1944–45); "I think I glimpse Eurydice emerging. Did she hear some news of [Antigone's] death?" (lines 2458–59); "But is this not unlucky Creon?" (line 2618). *Antigone* also emphasizes the very physical, corporeal, actions of the actors. Jocasta, for example, calls out to her son: "Why do you shoot your burning gaze again and again upon your twin brother?" (lines 693–94); and the chorus describes Ismene: "She is coming. Her face is drowned by waves of tears, which wash the color from her cheeks" (lines 1887–89). In other words, the play, though still heavily rhetorical and driven primarily by language, focuses more than Garnier's earlier ones on the embodied nature of suffering.[20] It is arguably easier in *Antigone* than in Garnier's earlier plays for the reader to picture specific actions and gestures, to imagine an actual performance.

After *Antigone*, Garnier published two more major works: *Bradamante* (1582) and *Les Juives* (1583). The first is a tragicomedy based on an episode of Ariosto's *Orlando Furioso* (1516–32), which had first been translated into French in 1543. Garnier probably wrote the play with the hope that it would be performed at court, where tragicomedy had become popular under Henri III and Catherine de Médicis. *Bradamante*—Garnier's most nationalistic play—evokes the battle between Christians and Muslims, the latter likely meant to stand in for France's Huguenots.[21] The second work, Garnier's final tragedy, is reputed as the author's *chef-d'œuvre*. Of all Garnier's tragedies, *Les Juives* was certainly the most popular in its time.[22]

---

des caractères" (perfected dramatic structure and explored character development) (Lazard 1980: 111). The formal changes, as Raymond Lebègue noted many years ago, meant that the themes Garnier had been developing since the beginning of his career ring out clearer than ever in *Antigone*: "Peu de pièces de Garnier révèlent aussi clairement ses idées morales et religieuses" (Few of Garnier's plays reveal as clearly his moral and religious ideas) (Lebègue: 270).

[20] More than his earlier tragedies, *Antigone* seems to come to life with "le mouvement nécessaire à une représentation animée et contribue à produire un climat tragique angoissant" (the movement necessary for a lively production and contributes to generating a tragic climate that is harrowing) (Beaudin: 51).

[21] The nationalistic tone is evident from the beginning, when Charlemagne talks of "Ma courageuse France" (my brave France) which is "pleine de guerriers" (full of warriors) (line 15). It is just as evident when Bradamante speaks of "ma nation, / L'incomparable France" (my nation, / Incomparable France) (lines 572–73).

[22] The dedicatory letter betrays the author's frustration—he wrote the play "sur le poinct de prendre congé" (when about to take his leave). The themes are those first explored in *Porcie*: tyranny, the pain of those who live under it, and civil war. Garnier fol-

3. Garnier's Sources: Seneca, Statius, and Sophocles

How is Garnier's *Antigone* related to, and different from, the *Antigone* of Sophocles, written in fifth-century (BCE) Athens? What did Garnier *do* to his source text(s) in order to create a new play? Garnier's *Antigone* can be divided into three main parts: Acts 1 and 2 draw primarily on Seneca's *Phoenician Women*;[23] Act 3 on Statius's *Thebaid*; and Acts 4 and 5 on Sophocles's *Antigone.*[24] Garnier's *Antigone* is thus much larger in scope than Sophocles's. The first three acts draw on Seneca and Statius in order to foreground what we might call the back story to most versions of Antigone. Eugène Rigal noted long ago that Garnier's *Antigone* and *La Troade* were "moins des drames que des collections de drames" (less dramas than collections of dramas) (Rigal 1889: 249).[25] Many critics have criticized Garnier's use of sources; others have praised it.[26]

lows the example of the Catholic and Protestant dramaturges (Chantelouve, Théodore de Bèze, Riveaudeau, Jean de la Taille) in selecting a biblical, rather than classical, subject. Yet the language and characters are strikingly similar to those of Garnier's earlier plays.

[23] The tragedies of Seneca are, of course, of central importance for the birth and evolution of French Renaissance tragedy. It is a topic too large to discuss in any detail here. See Braden 1985 and, most recently, the seminal study and nearly exhaustive study of Caigny 2011.

[24] The influence of other classical sources on *Antigone*—for example Aeschylus's *Seven Against Thebes*—is minimal. In addition to the notes to the present edition, for details and interpretation of Garnier's use of sources, see Moufflard 3:108–25 and Gras 1965: 45–50.

[25] Of *Antigone*, Bernage offered a similar summary: "C'est moins une tragédie qu'une suite de paraphrases libres des pièces, des ouvrages divers" (It is less a tragedy than a collection of free paraphrases of other plays, of various works) (Bernage 1970: 92). Similarly, Pinvert said of *Antigone* that it is "une mosaïque" (a mosaic) in which "l'excès des emprunts et l'habilité même de leur agencement nuit à cette unité dramatique sans laquelle l'intérêt languit et l'admiration hésite" (the excessive amount of borrowings and the very astuteness of their ordering harms this dramatic unity without which interest languishes and admiration becomes hesitant) (Pinvert: 1.xviii).

[26] Rigal wrote that "La tentative était manquée" (the attempt failed) (Rigal 1889: 249); Bernage castigated "l'inexpérience qu'atteste une accumulation d'éléments aussi disparates" (the inexperience to which this accumulation of such disparate elements attests) (Bernage 1970: 94). Garnier is not without his defenders, however. Raymond Lebègue wrote as follows: "Si, dans *Antigone* et dans *La Troade*, Garnier contamine plusieurs sources, c'est précisément pour nourrir ses tragédies du plus grand nombre possible d'infortunes cruelles qui doivent bouleverser les spectateurs" (If, in *Antigone* and *La Troade*, Garnier contaminates several sources, it is precisely to fill his tragedies with the greatest possible number of cruel misfortunes that must overwhelm the spectators) (Lebègue 1990: 73).

The first two acts of *Antigone* draw almost exclusively on Seneca's *Phoenician Women* (*Phoenissae*),[27] which tells the tells the story of Oedipus after he has abdicated the throne of Thebes to wander upon Mount Cithaeron, accompanied by his daughter Antigone. Polynices, who has been ousted from the throne by his brother Eteocles, plans to return from exile, along with the soldiers who make up the "Seven Against Thebes." Jocasta is still alive—while she has already committed suicide at this point in the story in Sophocles's *Oedipus the King* and in Seneca's *Oedipus*, both Seneca's *Phoenician Women* and Garnier's *Antigone* resuscitate her for the important task of pleading for peace with her warring sons.[28] Seneca's play, however, lacks a chorus—Garnier thus seeks out other models for the choral odes of the first two acts. As noted in the Appendix, he draws on choruses from Seneca's *Oedipus* and Sophocles's *Antigone* for Act 1; and on Seneca's *Oedipus* for Act 2. It must also be noted that Garnier's use of the term Piety (Fr. *Piété*) in the title and throughout the play—the value attributed to Antigone—has strong resonance with the opposition between *pietas* and *impietas* that undergirds Seneca's *Phoenician Women*. As the play's modern editor noted, "*Pietas* denotes right and natural relationships between family members, particularly parents and children, and a corresponding right relationship of humans to gods. Jocasta's love for her sons, then, embodies *pietas* in contrast to Oedipus's involuntary *impietas* against his parents and deliberate rejection of a father's duty towards his sons; Oedipus's attitude in turn is set against Antigone's *pietas*, as her brothers' *impietas* towards each other is set against Jocasta's love for them" (SenPhW: 276).[29]

The third act of Garnier's *Antigone* draws mainly on the *Thebaid*, a Latin epic of 9,741 hexameters by the Roman poet Publius Papinius Statius, a poem

---

[27] Seneca's *Phoenician Women* is likely unfinished, either because it was abandoned *en route* or because it was Seneca's last play, thus unfinished when he died in 65 CE. Some scholars believe that the play is indeed finished and that, if it stands out, it is because Seneca was intentionally aiming to invent a new dramatic form. See for example Tarrant 1978: 251–53. The natural models of Seneca's *Phoenician Women* are, of course, Sophocles's *Oedipus at Colonnus* and Euripides's *Phoenician Women*.

[28] Jocasta first pleads, "If they have any goodness in them, my imploring tears should move them to put down their weapons" (lines 566–67), then "Cast your club far off into the land. Take off this great shield that protects your chest" (lines 686–88). Garnier's depiction of Jocasta indeed draws on Seneca's play, but Seneca was not the first to represent Jocasta occupying such a position. Second-century BCE Estruscan vase paintings show Jocasta and Antigone attempting to hold back their brothers (See LIMC 4.1: 29, #13, #14). Propertius, too, makes brief mention of Jocasta's striving for peace: ". . .the Theban chieftains [fought] and fall to win a throne, while in their midst their mother strove to part them" (Propertius 2.9.50).

[29] For further perspectives on Seneca's *Phoenician Women*, on points that pertain to topics of central importance also to Garnier, see *inter alia* Tarrant 1978, Barchiesi 1988, Fantham 1983.

that influenced many poets in the Middle Ages and the Renaissance, including Dante and Chaucer,[30] and whose topic is clear from its very incipit: "Pierian fire falls upon my soul: to unfold fraternal warfare [*fraternas acies*], and alternate reigns fought for in unnatural hate, and guilty Thebes [*sontes... Thebas*]" (StTheb 1:1–3), verses even more forceful in the Latin, where the first words are indeed "fraternas acies." As its title suggests, the *Thebaid* is "an aggregate of the myths of Thebes, especially those concerned with the sons of Oedipus" (Statius 2008: xiii), with particular focus on the matter treated by Aeschylus in his *Seven Against Thebes*. Statius thus takes up the story of the battle fought by brothers Polynices and Eteocles, for control of Thebes, including the deadly duel between the brothers and the ensuing tyranny of Creon. As Burgess phrased it, the *Thebaid* is an epic of "unmitigated despair" (Burgess 1971–72: 59); Jane Wilson Joyce called it "a meditation on autocratic rule" (Statius 2008: xi). As the notes to the present edition show, Garnier's reworking of Statius differs from his close line-by-line imitation of Seneca in the first two acts. Garnier here more frequently borrows an idea in order to rewrite it completely (e.g., Polynices's speech to Adrastus). In addition to Statius, Garnier also borrows in this act from Euripides's *Phoenician Women* (Mouflard: 3.113). As was the case for the first two acts, Garnier again draws on Seneca's *Oedipus* for the choral portions (see Appendix).

Acts 4 and 5 draw mainly on Sophocles's *Antigone*, the earliest printed editions of which appeared, in the original Greek, in 1502 (in Italy) and in 1528 (in France). Garnier's play is not the first adaptation of Sophocles—in 1542, Gentien Hervet translated it into Latin and Luigi Alamanni rendered it into Italian.[31] A French prose translation of *Antigone* might have existed—it is mentioned by Calvy de la Fontaine, but no copy of it survives (Lebègue 1944: 17). In 1573, Jean-Antoine de Baïf published his French translation of *Antigone*—following in his father's (Lazare de Baïf's) footsteps, for the latter had already published translations of *Electra* (1537) and *Hecuba* (1550).[32] Baïf's translation of *Antigone* cuts quite a different figure to Garnier's adaptation in Acts 4 and 5. As the play's most recent editor, Simone Maser, points out, Baïf's translation, which is dedicated to Charles IX on the occasion of his marriage to Elisabeth of Austria, makes a certain number of changes to Sophocles's text so that the play would *not* resonate too strongly vis-à-vis current political and historical circumstances: Baïf frequently silences direct mentions of the State, reducing the conflict between Antigone (and the unwritten laws) and Creon (the State) to a conflict between

[30] For details, see the references listed by Joyce (Statius 2008: xi, n. 3).

[31] See Alamanni 1997, complete with an introduction and notes by Francesco Spera.

[32] In his *Art Poétique* (1555), Jacques Peletier sung the praises of Lazare de Baïf, writing that with the latter's death "la France a perdu en plusieurs sortes: Mais la principale perte, est qu'il a si peu écrit" (France suffered a huge loss in various ways, but the principal loss was that he wrote so little) (Goyet 1999: 280).

two individuals.[33] In a word, Baïf sidesteps a question that *Antigone* would seem to raise, namely that of the *raison d'Etat*, i.e., whether the state's law is supreme, a question particularly pertinent in the context of the atrocities committed during the Saint Bartholomew's Day Massacre, which occurred on August 24, 1572.[34] Based on these differences, it is most likely that Garnier had access to various other editions of Sophocles while writing Acts 4 and 5. Garnier had a basic reading knowledge of Ancient Greek, as did his contemporaries Pibrac and Renaud de Beaune, and it would seem that, in writing *Antigone*, he consulted his Greek sources in Greek.[35] It is likely that he also consulted Latin and French translations.[36]

4. Antigone in the Arms of a Lawyer

Just as Garnier's first tragedy, *Porcie*, invites its readers to see in the play's representation of Roman civil wars an allegorical depiction of France's own calamities, *Antigone* can and should be read in a similar way. Such, for example, is the position of George Steiner: "[the] desolate Argos lamented by Jocasta is France" and "[the] House of Laius [i.e., Oedipus, Antigone, etc.] intimately parallels that of the Valois or the Guises" (Steiner 1996: 139). The most recent editor of a French edition of *Antigone* argues for the same kind of allegorical relationship between text and context.[37] But as Steiner's uncertainty suggests ("the Valois *or* the Guises"), it can be difficult to fix the exact parameters and limits of such

33 As Maser puts it, "par modération ou par prudence, il n'encourage pas à la rébellion contre le roi et va même jusqu'à louer les hommes d'avoir eu la sagesse et de se donner des lois et de se ranger sous le sceptre des rois pour le bien commun" (out of moderation or prudency, he does not encourage rebellion against the king and even goes so far as to praise men for having the wisdom to give themselves laws and to take up a position under the scepters of kings for the public good) (Baïf 1993: 5).

34 For a fuller study of Baïf's translation, see especially Augé-Chiquet 1909: 174–84.

35 Scholars think that Garnier consulted the Greek text because he sometimes makes small mistakes not to be found in contemporary translations (Mouflard: 3.84).

36 Perhaps Garnier had access to Henri Estienne's edition of the *Tragoediae selectae* (1567), which included *inter alia* a Latin version of Sophocles's *Antigone*. See Sophocles, *Tragoediae selectae Aeschyli, Sophoclis, Euripidis. Cum duplici interpretatione latina, una ad verbum, altera carmine. Ennianae interpretationes locorum aliquot Euripidis*. (S. l.,) : excudebat H. Stephanus, 1567 [BnF RES-YB-934]. He may also have read Sophocle's *Antigone* in the Latin translation of Lalemant, published in 1570.

37 Jean-Dominique Beaudin writes that, in a general fashion, "la légende des Labdacides permet au public de retrouver dans la lutte fratricide entre Etécole et Polynice des situations qui se rapprochent des guerres civiles religieuses et politiques" (the legend of the Labdacids allows the audience to uncover in the fratricidal battle between Eteocles and Polynices situations that resemble the religious and political civil wars) (Beaudin: 8).

allegorical readings.[38] Indeed, allegory can be misleading—if searched for, it can usually be found, but exactly what it means in detail often remains conjectural.[39]

The dedicatory epistle that accompanies *Antigone* goes beyond allegory to set up a very concrete relationship between *Antigone* and its historical context. In that epistle, Garnier offers his play to a certain Barnabé Brisson, supposedly to honor the latter's recent promotion to the rank of *président à mortier* (principal magistrate). Garnier sings Brisson's praises ("What Frenchman has not heard of your celebrated name?") and then dedicates *Antigone* to him. The act of dedication proper occurs at the very end of the epistle and pertains not just to the play, but to its principal female hero. The dedication in fact blurs the boundary between play and non-play by situating the play's characters *as if* they were alive in sixteenth-century France. Garnier offers Brisson his tragedy, he says, in order to tell him about the "misfortunes of this pitiful Antigone" who "lives anew in our France." Distraught, Antigone is said to throw herself "into [Brisson's] arms, so that [he] might offer favorable support, as she was the kind and noble support and guide of her wretched father." Garnier thus offers his *Antigone*, the play, to Brisson by describing Antigone, the character, as leaping into Brisson's arms. The dedication blurs boundaries in several ways. The depiction of a lamenting woman ("this pitiful Antigone") in the arms and requiring the support of a lawyer like Brisson situates the play in relation to the realities of early modern courtrooms. But the fact that Brisson's support is compared to that of Antigone for her father Oedipus also situates Antigone as a Brisson-like figure. The play and its historical moment are weaved tightly together in a fashion that goes beyond the search for more obvious allegorical connections. Given that the Wars of Religion were as much a series of failed attempts to legislate about the conditions for

---

38 The hypothetical nature of allegorical readings of *Antigone* is also clear in Beaudin's reflections: "On ne doit pas non plus écarter la possibilité d'une influence des idées de Jean Bodin [. . .] ainsi que celle des débats qui ont eu lieu [en 1576] aux Etats généraux de Blois" (Neither must we ignore the possibility that the play was influenced by the ideas of Jean Bodin [. . .] as well as by the debates that took place at the Estates General in Blois [in 1576]) (8), in that (and here Beaudin builds on Mouflard) "la rivalité entre Monsieur et Henri III à la mort de Charles IX présente des affinités avec celle d'Etéocle et de Polynice, puisque Monsieur, duc d'Alençon, avait pensé qu'il pourrait alors occuper le trône, avait été arrêté et s'était évadé en 1575" (the rivalry between the Duke of Alençon and Henri III at the death of Charles IX presents affinities with the rivalry between Eteocles and Polynices, since the Duke of Alençon had thought that he might occupy the throne, before being arrested and then escaping in 1575). Beaudin further notes that the actions of Catherine de Médicis "ne sont pas sans faire songer à l'entremise de Jocaste dans la tragédie" (might make us think of Jocasta's intervention in the tragedy) (8). Just as for Steiner the Labdacids are either the Valois or the Guise, for Beaudin the rivalry *might* allude to the Duke of Alençon and Henri III. While the play clearly does relate to the troubled times, the exact allegorical connections remain open to debate.

39 On allegory, see Compagnon 2003.

peace, that they were so much about law courts and micropolitics, as scholars are coming to appreciate more and more, the play's connection to this context via Brisson is essential (see Christin 1997). According to the dedication, Garnier saw Brisson's election as the sign that a new age of justice was to begin, as one of the captains who might steer France towards peace and justice.[40]

Dedicating *Antigone* to such a man was not, then, a small thing. Nor was it a personal *thing*. The dedication brings *Antigone* into the purview of the social and political history of the Wars of Religion in a direct manner. The image in the epistle of Antigone jumping into Brisson's arms conjures up an image of a supplicant vis-à-vis his/her defender that was common in the law courts of Renaissance France. We see this parallel in a trial in which Brisson himself was involved. In a letter, jurist Etienne Pasquier describes a famous trial in which he represented the accused (a certain Arconville) and Brisson represented the accuser (Bobie). Bobie's family had been massacred and, although there was no evidence to support this claim, Bobie accused Arconville of the murders. Bobie's seemingly unfounded accusation satisfied most people and Pasquier's job was thus to overturn this public condemnation. Brisson, as noted, was there to defend Bobie. Pasquier's description of the *avocat*-client relationship strongly resonates with Garnier's dedicatory epistle. Pasquier describes Bobie as being "aux pieds de Monsieur Brisson" (at the feet of Monsieur Brisson) and as having many "larmes à ses yeux" (tears in his eyes).[41] He also describes Arconville, his own client, as well as Arconville's family, as being at *his* feet. The latter's wife, too, had tears in her eyes: "[à mes] pieds estoit le Gentil-homme [Arconville] & avec luy sa femme larmoyante, comme aussi deux petits enfans" (at my feet was the gentleman [Arconville] and with him his weeping wife, like two little children).[42] Garnier's dedication thus betokens a concrete connection to the historical context and situates the play as a kind of "courtroom drama" addressed to a member of

[40] When Brisson created his *code civil* in 1587, its preface resonated strongly with *Antigone:* "Toute parfaite législation doit commencer à la piété et la religion [. . .] car la justice, à laquelle toutes lois, toutes constitutions et bonnes coustumes doivent se referrer, a deux principales parties [. . .] à savoir la piété et la religion envers Dieu, et l'équité [à savoir] l'égalité entre les hommes" (All perfect legislation must begin with piety and religion [. . .] because justice, which all laws, constitutions, and good customs must obey, have two principal parts [. . .] i.e. piety and religion towards God, and equity [which is to say] equality among men) (Quoted by Gambier 1957: 42). It seems as though Brisson listened to the appeals of Antigone, as Garnier called for in his preface seven years earlier.

[41] Pasquier, *Lettres*, col. 312.

[42] For a fuller exploration of the relationship between Garnier's *Antigone* and the historical context, as well as for the following idea of *Antigone* as "courtroom drama," see Usher 2015.

the Paris Parliamant, an official body that indeed played a key mediating role during France's civil strife.[43]

5. Publication and/or Performance

Was Garnier's *Antigone* primarily a play to be seen or a text to be read? On the one hand, we know for sure that Garnier's play had a good number of readers in its early years of existence. It was published twice in 1580, both as part of Garnier's collected works (titled simply *Les Tragédies*) and separately in a smaller and cheaper octavo format.[44] On the other hand, there is no proof that the play was ever performed in the sixteenth century—nor any proof that it was *not* performed either. Critics have hypothesized about the play's performance history since at least the nineteenth and early-twentieth centuries. One group of scholars (especially Adolf Ebert and Eugène Rigal) argues that French Renaissance tragedies like *Antigone* were specifically *not* written for performance.[45] Another group of scholars (Gustave Lanson, Jules Haraszti, and later Raymond Lebègue) disagrees. To prove his point, Lanson famously put together an impressive list of some seventy theatrical representations that took place in France between 1552 and 1600 (Lanson 1903). The historical exactitude of some of these supposed performances has since been put into doubt, but details of other previously unnoticed ones have also emerged (Lebègue 1944; Lebègue 1944–45; Lebègue 1951: 199). As already noted above regarding Jodelle's *Cléopâtre captive*, some tragedies were definitely written for performance in schools—and it is not unlikely that many of the period's tragedies were indeed read out, if not fully performed, in France's different *collèges*.[46] Michel de Montaigne mentions having acted in plays

---

[43] On the Paris Parliament during the Wars of Religion and the overlap between theater and the courtroom, see especially Houllemare 2011.

[44] "En 1580, Garnier réunissait ses tragédies dans un recueil collectif, qui contenait en outre une tragédie nouvelle, *Antigone, ou la Piété*. Pas de poésies liminaires d'amis: Ronsard maintenant se taira, j'ignore pourquoi" (In 1580, Garnier gathered his tragedies together in a volume of Collected Works, which additionally contained one new tragedy, *Antigone, ou la Piété*. There were no preliminary encomiastic poems written by friends: Ronsard, for reasons I do not know, would keep quiet) (Pinvert: 1.xviii). On the octavo-format publication, see Pinvert: 1.lxii. Pinvert notes that this extra publication allowed owners of the earlier tragedies to purchase Garnier's latest play without having to purchase the collected works.

[45] For a summary of this debate, see Lazard 1980: 150–53.

[46] Between 1539 and 1544, for example, the Scottish humanist George Buchanan, invited to teach at Bordeaux's Collège de Guyenne, organized performances of his Latin translations of *Alcestis* and *Medea*, as well as of his own tragedies *Jephtes* and *Baptistes*. Performances of Marc-Antoine Muret's *Jules César* also took place there (Geoffrey 1973: 8; Bernage 1970: 2). Similar performances of tragedies also took place in Paris, at various

by Buchanan, Muret, and their colleague Guérente, a practice that Montaigne sees as integral to the education of a prince.[47] What such performances resembled is largely a matter of guesswork.

Given the partial and sometimes hypothetical nature of many records, the stageability of Garnier's play is uncertain. In 1907, Colbert Searles stated that of all sixteenth-century tragedies in France those of Garnier in particular "perhaps seem to us moderns so little adapted to stage representation" (Searles 1907: 225). He nevertheless concluded that both *Les Juives* and "to a greater or less[er] extent [. . .] all of the tragedies of Garnier" are, or were, "playable" with, he adds, "the probable exception of *Hippolyte* and *Cornélie*" (229).[48] About two decades later, Raymond Lebègue argued that *Antigone* both *is* and *was intended to be* performable (Lebègue 1924), underscoring notably that the very last words of every original edition of the play are "La représentation en est hors les portes de la ville de Thebes" (Events are staged outside the gates to the City of Thebes), a phrase overlooked, suggests Lebègue, by his predecessors.[49] Despite apparent requests,

---

institutions and especially at the Collège de Boncourt where Muret transferred after his time in Bordeaux. The Collège de Boncourt was, with the Collège de Coqueret, at the epicenter of France's literary renewal, counting Belleau, La Péruse, Grévin, Jean de la Taille, and Etienne Jodelle amongst its students (Geoffrey 1973: 8).

[47] "J'ai soustenu les premiers personnages és tragedies latines de Bucanan, de Guerente et de Muret, qui se representerent en nostre college de Guienne avec dignité" (I acted the main roles in the Latin tragedies of Buchanan, Guerente and Muret, which were performed with dignity in our Collège of Guyenne), moreover adding that acting in tragedy was to be recommended, both to young students and to princes who might thus see and learn from "l'exemple d'aucuns des anciens, honnestement et louablement" (the example of some of the Ancients, honestly and in a manner worthy of praise) (Montaigne 1965: 176).

[48] Eugène Rigal affirmed that Garnier's tragedies were not written for production—but (interestingly) that *Antigone* might just perhaps be the exception: "Si [. . .] on voulait mettre en scène *Antigone* (1580) [. . .] on y arriverait sans difficulté sérieuse" (if [. . .] one wanted to stage *Antigone*, it could be done without great difficulty), further adding that the action "se transporterait dans cinq *mansions*, autrement dit dans cinq compartiments différents" (would take place in five different villas—in other words, in five different stage sets) (Rigal 1911: 90). Yet, because of the five different spaces that he identifies, Rigal ends on a note of uncertainty: "Conclurons-nous de toutes ces constatations que Garnier a vraiment conçu Antigone en vue d'une scène à la décoration multiple? Nous ne croyons pas en avoir le droit" (Will we conclude from all these affirmations that Garnier really conceived of Antigone with an eye to its performance with these multiple stage sets? I do not believe that I can say that) (Rigal 1911: 93).

[49] Lebègue concludes in this respect: "[Selon Rigal], Garnier n'avait pas en vue la représentation, mais l'impression de ses pièces [et s'il] décrit avec tant de précision le lieu où erre le roi aveugle, c'est pour imiter les beaux vers descriptifs de Sénèque" ([According to Rigal], Garnier did not have performance in mind, but rather that his plays would be printed. [And if] he describes with such precision the place where the blind king wan-

Garnier managed not to have his tragedies staged at court (Lebègue 1956: 85), but that does not rule out other venues. Lebègue as argues specifically that Garnier wrote *for the stage*, given that Garnier both privileges the spectacular (supplications, hallucinations, etc.) and concerns himself with the question of *bienséance* (Lebègue 1951: 201). Lebègue also underscores that Garnier's characters frequently name each other, as if to help the audience recognize who is arriving on stage (Lebègue 1951: 203). More recently still, Jean-Dominique Beaudin, in his recent French edition of *Antigone*, makes efforts to underscore when certain verses can be interpreted as serving the role of stage directions.

Whether or not *Antigone* was staged in the sixteenth century, it has been staged more recently.[50] In 1944, Thierry Maulnier staged a version of *Antigone* at the Théâtre Charles de Rochefort (renamed since 1973 the Théâtre Tristan-Bernard), situated 64, rue du Rocher in Paris's eighth *arrondissement.*[51] It was one of a number of *Antigone*s performed during the Second World War, the most famous of which was Jean Anouilh's (1944) about which critics still disagree: was it pro-Resistance? or collaborationist? For George Steiner, it was the latter; for Leo Weinstein, the former.[52] As a Genevan journalist phrased it, there was a

---

ders, it is in imitation of Seneca's beautiful and descriptive verses). To Rigal's emphasis on the indeterminate nature of the places in Acts 2 and 3, Lebègue responds as follows: "pourquoi, alors, [Garnier] a-t-il écrit la phrase finale de l'Argument? [La représentation en est hors les portes de la ville de Thebes] Pourquoi indique-t-il ce lieu, qu'aucun de ses prédécesseurs n'avait choisi, sinon parce qu'il voulait situer sa pièce en vue d'une représentation" (Why, then, did [Garnier] write that final sentence in his summary? [Events take place outside the gates to the City of Thebes] Why does he indicate this place other than because he wanted to situate his play in preparation for a theatrical production?) (Lebègue 1924: 248). Lebègue's study of the play, comparing the places selected for scenes in Seneca, Euripides, and Sophocles, establishes unity of place, a rule recently advanced by Jean de la Taille—all five of Garnier's Acts would seemingly take place in the countryside outside the gates of Thebes, in conformity with the final sentence at the end of the play (Lebègue 1924: 248). In Lebègue's opinion, Garnier had probably heard of the performances of other tragedies—Jodelle's *Cléopâtre captive*, the *Sophonisbe*, etc.—and thus hoped for something similar for his own tragedy.

[50] Other plays staged more recently include *Les Juives* in 1922, 1936, 1937, 1946 and in 2001 at the Théâtre du Marais, thanks to E. Génovèse. *Hippolyte* was staged in 1982 by Vitez at the Théâtre national de Chaillot.

[51] Three photographs, by Louis Silvestre, can be viewed of this production at Richelieu under the call number 4-ICO-THE-721. The three images show: (1) Monsieur Lucien Delong, Mademoiselle Tassencourt (Creon et Antigone); (2) Mademoiselle Tassencourt, Mademoiselle Sylvie Deniau (Antigone et Ismene); and (3) Monsieur Lucien Delon and another male actor (Creon and Haemon). Because of rights issues, none of these could be reproduced here.

[52] See Steiner 1986: 193; Weinstein 1989: 2.126; Witt 2001: 218. The most extensive textual study of Anouilh's *Antigone*, which demonstrates why it is so difficult to assign the play to one category or the other, is Meyers 2011.

veritable *bataille d'Antigone*, somewhat akin to the *bataille d'Hernani*.[53] Maulnier (1909–88), in any case, was a journalist whose opinions were on the extreme right of the political spectrum—he graduated from the Ecole Normale Supérieure the same year as, and knew, Robert Brasillach. Maulnier wrote regularly for *Action française*[54] and, as Debbie Lackerstein has noted, he believed in a kind of *ideal fascism* that even Nazi Germany could not deliver—he believed that "France could tap its own reserve of energy to achieve a similar rejuvenation" (Lackerstein 2012: 121). During the war, he was "pro-Vichy and in favor of the National Revolution, but he was not an enthusiastic collaborator, [a fact for which he was] often attacked in the collaborationist press" (121). Maulnier's production attempted to allegorize Garnier's play, using it to represent the "tragic" fascist who struggles between purity and *grandeur*.[55]

Quite different was Jean-Marie Villégier's intention when he staged Garnier's *Antigone* in 1997 at the Louvre Auditorium. His *Illustre-Théâtre* has, since its founding in 1985, done much to bring Garnier back to life in France, producing not just *Antigone* but also *Les Juives*, *La Troade*, and *Bradamante*. Villégier's decision to stage Garnier had to do with a radical position that aimed "raconter autrement l'histoire du théâtre" (to tell the history of theater in a different manner) and to "repérer les contradictions derrière l'unité de façade" (seek out the contradictions that exist behind surface unity), to advocate for "une mémoire de découverte" (a memory open to discovery) in place of "une mémoire trop docile" (too docile a memory). The company has thus exhumed "bon nombre d'ouvrages trop vite expédiés dans les fosses communes du 'mineur'" (many works which had been too quickly thrown into the communal grave of 'minor' literature). The director and the company's choices are not motivated simply by the idea of *digging up* forgotten works, but of rethinking certain long-held views about French theater that tend to foreground seventeenth-century classical theater to the detriment of earlier, less *harmonious* works: "Il faut visiter le théâtre français dans ses impuretés, dans ses racines, qui, comme toutes les racines, se jouent des murs de clôture" (We must explore French theater in its impurities, its roots, which, like all roots, push at the surrounding walls).[56]

---

53 See Witt 2001: 218. For an introduction to the *bataille d'Hernani*, see Usher 2010.

54 Later in life, Maulnier would write for *Le Figaro* newspaper and be elected to the Académie française (in 1964, taking over the *fauteuil* of Henry Bordeaux). It has been suggested that such a post-occupation career was possible because Maulnier kept (compared to individuals like Brasillach) a relatively "low profile" (Lackerstein 2012: 121, n. 44).

55 On this, see Witt 2001.

56 I here quote the company's website: http://www.illustretheatre-jmvillegier.fr/historique.php See also Dobby-Poirson 2006: 7. Villégier's *Antigone* was staged from May 22 to May 24, 1997 at the Louvre Auditorium (Figure 1), with Agnès Proust in the role

Figure 1: Jean-Marie Villégier's production of *Antigone* at the Louvre Auditorium in 1997. Photograph © Marie-Noëlle Robert.

6. Critical Opinions on *Antigone*

Garnier's reputation in general, and that of *Antigone* in particular, has risen and fallen over the centuries. Many of Garnier's contemporaries sang his praises. La Croix du Maine (1552–1592) wrote that Garnier had "ce rare et excellent don d'orateur qui est une chose fort peu commune" (this rare and excellent gift of being an orator, which is a most unusual thing) and that one rarely saw "un excellent poète et fort bon orateur tout ensemble" (an excellent poet and a very good orator all in one person) (Quoted Mouflard: 3.143). Equally laudatory was Pierre de Ronsard, who announced in a poem included in the first edition of *Porcie* that thanks to Garnier "La Scene des Frâçois / Se Change en or qui n'estoit que de bois" (The French stage / Formerly made of wood has been turned into gold). Garnier's early reputation did not however survive the centuries. By the twentieth century, Garnier had become little more than a largely forgotten precursor to Corneille and Racine.[57] When Antoine Vitez staged Garnier's *Hippolyte* in 1982 at the Théâtre national de Chaillot, almost all reviews described Garnier

of Antigone, Marc Zammit playing Creon, Richard Lukas as Oedipus, and Geneviève Esménard as Jocasta.

[57] By 1925, one scholar called Garnier a "précurseur méconnu de notre théâtre classique" (a little-known predecessor of our classical theater) (Bever 1925). In 1952, another scholar called him "notre plus grand tragique avant Corneille" (our greatest tragedian

in terms of his anteriority vis-à-vis his more illustrious descendants: the *Figaro* explained that "Un siècle avant Racine, Robert Garnier a puisé la trame de sa tragédie dans l'œuvre de Sénèque et d'Euripide" (a century before Racine, Robert Garnier had sought out the main outline for his tragedy in the works of Seneca and Euripides), adding rather unflatteringly that the result was an "alliance de barbarie antique et de préciosité baroque" (an alliance of antique barbary and baroque preciosity).[58] Other journalists published similar summaries of the 1982 production.[59]

Comparing Garnier to Corneille and Racine is certainly justified,[60] especially because anyone even vaguely familiar with seventeenth-century French theater will experience some uncanny moments in reading or watching a tragedy by Garnier. Corneille's Sabine in *Horace* (I, 1) finds herself split between brother and husband, a situation not dissimilar from that of Jocasta, who is split between two sons in Garnier's play. And as Corneille's Cinna draws his "peinture effroyable" (awful painting) (I, 3), he utters a line already pronounced by Garnier's Antigone: "Encore degoutant du meurtre de son pere" (Still dripping with the blood of his father's murder) (line 667); in the same play, Auguste's famous line—"Je suis maître de moi comme de l'univers" (I am my own master—and master of the universe)—is an extension of a line pronounced by Garnier's Oedipus in *Antigone*: "Je suis maistre de moy" (I am my own master) (line 119). Similar moments occur in Racine. When Racine's Phèdre says "Misérable, je vis!" (Wretched me, I live!) (IV, 6), she is indeed repeating the exact words of Garnier's Antigone (line 1352). More globally, Racine's *Phèdre* is indeed a descendant, via Rotrou's *Thébaïde*, of Garnier's *Antigone* (Mesnard 1:379). The problem, so to speak, is that it is all too easy, after establishing such filiations, to dismiss

before Corneille) (Saulnier 1952: 88), a complement that simultaneously excluded Garnier from serious consideration.

58 Anon, "Hippolyte à Chaillot," *Le Figaro*, le 11 février 1982.

59 The popular magazine *Le Nouvel Observateur* called *Hippolyte* simply "Une version de 'Phèdre'" (A version of *Phèdre*), as if it came *after* Racine! (*Nouvel Observateur*, March 1, 1982). *Le Monde* titled its article "Une autre Phèdre" (Another Phèdre) (*Le Monde*, March 6, 1982) and in *24 heures*, a huge headline read "Phèdre cent ans avant Racine. . ." (Phèdre, a hundred years before Racine. . .) as if Garnier had just been discovered for the first time (*"Paris: Antoine Vitez ressusscite 'Hippolyte': Phèdre cent ans avant Racine. . .", 24 heures*, April 8–9, 1982). Even the popular television magazine *Télérama* made the connection: "Cent quatre ans avant la *Phèdre* de Racine, Garnier déjà mettait en alexandrins l'amour incestueux de la femme de Thésée" (A hundred and four years before Racine's *Phèdre*, Garnier was already busy putting into alexandrines the incestuous love of the wife of Theseus) ("Hippolyte à Chaillot," *Télérama*, March 10, 1982) as did the Anglophone review *Passion: The Magazine of Paris*, which called the play "the sixteenth century predecessor of Corneille and Racine." (Hippolyte, *Passion: The Magazine of Paris*, May 12, 1982).

60 I made a similar *rapprochement* in the title of my article on *Hippolyte* (Usher 2012).

Garnier because he is not Corneille or Racine.[61] Thierry Maulnier—whose politics we have already encountered—invited readers and theater-goers in 1944 to appreciate rather than excoriate the difference: "J'invite le lecteur à découvrir dans les tragédies de Garnier ce qu'il ne trouvera ni dans le *Cid* ni dans *Andromaque*, la jeunesse de la tragédie française" (I invite the reader to discover in Garnier's tragedies that which will not be found in the *Cid* or *Andromaque*—the youth of French tragedy) (Maulnier 1944: 7). While Maulnier's point is most likely motivated by a reactionary, perhaps fascist, nostalgia for Frenchness (in the face of "foreign" invaders), his comment might productively be reinstrumentalized to different, more politically satisfying, ends.

The twentieth century's scorn for Garnier—or at best, its timid acceptance that he was in some way a precursor to Corneille and Racine—originated in the nineteenth century. Sainte-Beuve did not much care for the theater of Jodelle and Garnier—just as he did not much care for Ronsard's *Franciade* and many other works that did not satisfy his aesthetic prejudices.[62] Sainte-Beuve wrote Garnier off, in the kind of peremptory judgment for which he is famous, as belonging to "l'école artificielle et savante" (the artificial and erudite school [of theater]) (Sainte-Beuve 1828: 1.392).[63] Slightly later, Louis Petit de Julleville, something of an éloge paradoxal to Garnier, called him first "un vrai poète" (a true poet), whose poetry "abonde en belles narrations" (is abundant in fine narrations), but also stated that Garnier was not however a dramatist: "Pourquoi faut-il que la science du théâtre et l'art de construire une pièce animée, intéressante, de développer une situation dramatique par la lutte des caractères opposés ou des passions contraires, lui fasse complètement défaut?" (Why is it that the science of theater and the art of constructing a lively and interesting play, of developing a dramatic situation via a struggle between opposed characters or contrary passions, were qualities he simply lacked?) (Julleville 1892: 79).[64] In 1883, Emile

[61] One of his editors in the early twentieth century could not resist the temptation, writing of Garnier's plays that "Il y a trop de maximes, parce qu'il y a trop de Sénèque" (There are too many maxims because there is too much Seneca) (Pinvert: 1.xxvi).

[62] On Sainte-Beuve's rejection of the *Franciade*, see Usher 2010: lix-lxiii.

[63] Sainte-Beuve here is specifically referring to the theater of Etienne Jodelle and Robert Garnier.

[64] Indeed, Julleville describes Garnier as writing tragedies that are characterized by "l'absence presque complète d'action dramatique" (the almost complete absence of dramatic action) and "une sorte d'immobilité sur la scène" (a kind of immobility on the stage) (Julleville 1892: 82). Garnier's understanding of theater is described as follows: "Il conçoit la tragédie comme l'exposition, l'étalage [. . .] d'une situation pathétique, à peu près sans nœud et sans dénouement" (He conceives of tragedy as the exposition, the displaying [. . .] of a situation full of pathos, almost completely without a main crux or any denouement) (82). Julleville does acknowledge *Antigone* as being of the plays where "l'action est plus nourrie" (the action is more fully developed)—"Garnier s'efforce visiblement d'étendre son procédé dramatique et de lui donner plus d'intérêt avec plus de mou-

Faguet produced a hefty tome about sixteenth-century French tragedy whose judgment of *Antigone* was just as severe. Faguet begins his discussion by noting—with detectable frustration—that "Il est impossible de ramener cette tragédie à une unité quelle qu'elle soit" (it is impossible to find any unity whatsoever in this tragedy) (Faguet 1912: 220).[65] Like Faguet, Lanson and others in the nineteenth and early twentieth-century found Garnier hard to read and difficult to classify.[66] Such opinions continue into the 1970s. One critic wrote again

vement" (Garnier is visibly striving to extend his dramatic method and to make it more interesting by giving it more movement) (82). Still the judgment remains largely negative.

[65] Faguet chastises Garnier in no uncertain terms: "Si Garnier, comme il paraît au titre qu'il a choisi, veut que sa pièce soit une *Antigone*, il faut qu'il confesse que c'est une *Antigone* en deux actes précédée de trois actes de prologues" (If Garnier, as it would appear from the title he has chosen, wants his play to be an *Antigone*, then he must confess that it is a two-act *Antigone* preceeded by a three-act prologue) (220). Garnier's main crime, for Faguet, is indeed disunity: "Il ne se peut rien de plus mal ordonné, ni qui tire plus en sens contraires l'esprit du spectateur" (Nothing could be more badly arranged, nor which stretches as much the spectator's mind in opposing directions) (221). That is the main prong of his attack—but not the only one: "Passe encore pour le manque de personnage central unique" (I will not even mention the lack of any one central character) (221); "Il n'y a même pas d'idée maîtresse qui ramène à un point unique l'esprit du spectateur" (There is not even one main idea to bring the spectator's mind back to one specific point) (221). The lack of unity is a "défaut sans compensation possible" (fault without any possible compensation) (221). The appraisal is unambiguous and categorical—and (like most appraisals) tells us more about its author's taste than about the work under investigation.

[66] In his *Esquisse d'une histoire de la tragédie française* (1920), Lanson barely makes any mention of Garnier's *Antigone*—he cites it, for example, as one example of Renaissance "unité d'action" (unity of action): "on admet *l'unité* d'une misère faite de plusieurs catastrophes frappant sur la même victime [. . .], conception opposée au sens classique ultérieur" (a kind of *unity* of misery is allowed, made up of several catastrophies besieging the same victim [. . .], a conception that stands in opposition to the later classical sense) (Lanson 1966: 18). About thirty years later, in 1948, an extract of *Antigone*, alongside extracts from *Bradamante* and *Les Juives*, is included by Jean Boullé in his short anthology of French Renaissance Tragedy published by Larousse—the kind of publication that often has a significant impact on the literary taste of several generations of high-school students. Boullé's appreciation is a curious one. On the one hand, he quotes and agrees with Faguet's negative assessment, noting that "[Le] manque d'unité nuit à l'œuvre, qui emprunte trop ouvertement à Sophocle, Sénèque et Stace" (The lack of unity damages this work, which borrows too openly from Sophocles, Seneca and Statius) (Boullé 1948: 79). On the other hand, Boullé seems able to overlook the lack of unity and to appreciate the complementarity of the plays supposed two halves, for if the second of the two extracts is somewhat predictable (Antigone talking with Ismene about her desire to bury her brother), the first is—if we try to imagine Boullé's horror at the play's disunity—less so, for he selects the exchange between Jocasta and Polynices from Act II (lines 656–911). In other words, while clearly upset by the play's lack of unity, he also seemingly appreciates the importance of Jocasta's pleas for an end to war.

a kind of éloge paradoxal: "Son style offre des vers dont ses successeurs, plus expérimentés sous le rapport de la méthode et de la langue, n'ont point dépassé l'énergie et la grâce" (His style offers verses which his successors, more experienced in terms of method and language, will not surpass in terms of energy and grace) (Bernage 1970: 106).

More recently, Madeleine Lazard has attempted to restore to Garnier some of his original reputation, acknowledging that the unity and literary merits of his works "le mettent très vite au rang de premier poète dramatique français» (situate him in the position of being France's first dramatic poet) and adding that "[a]ucun n'a été plus souvent joué au XVIe siècle, aucun avant Corneille n'a eu un tel succès de librairie, aucun n'a vu ses pièces aussi fréquemment réimprimées" (no other [author] was more performed in the sixteenth century, no other before Corneille was such a best-seller, no other saw his plays as frequently reprinted) (Lazard 1980: 105). Charles Mazouer, in his recent study, is less laudatory: for him, both *La Troade* and *Antigone* "procèdent par juxtaposition et accumulation" (proceed by juxtaposition and accumulation), thus weaving together representations of suffering "dans une dramaturgie qui se contente d'enfiler les épreuves, le plus grand nombre d'infortunes possibles" (in a dramaturgy that contents itself with stringing together the greatest possible number of misfortunes) (Mazouer 2002: 284).[67] Old opinions clearly linger. More recently still, in a book aimed at the general reader, Christian Delmas has spoken of Garnier largely in terms of his shortcomings compared to, and his lack of influence on, Corneille: "la tragédie de Garnier lèguera à Corneille *du moins* son inspiration et sa thématique, ainsi que sa coloration fortement oratoire" (Garnier's tragedy *at least* bequeaths to Corneille its inspiration and themes, as well as its highly oratory nature) (Delmas 1994: 125; emphasis mine). Literary history, as written in France, clearly still keeps the author of *Antigone* in the role of the predecessor. Rendered into English, *Antigone* might perhaps be read both on its own terms and within a wider and more global history of *Antigone*s. Such, in any case, is this translator's hope.

7. Conclusions

Antigone was once called "une incitation à la sagesse" (an incitement to wisdom) (Morel 1964: 18). Teaching this "Englished" Antigone in Morningside Heights, I was struck by how true this judgment proved to be. The play guided students to ask questions about the meanings, costs, and necessities of more contemporary wars, just as it aided its first readers to reflect on their own difficult times. But discussion overflowed analogy: Garnier, in the particular ways his characters debate their situation, in his very foreignness compared to other versions

[67] See Mazouer's summary of Garnier's *Antigone* (Mazouer 2002: 285).

of Antigone's story, also helped understand other performances and adaptations of tragedy in more subtle and nuanced ways. If Garnier's *Antigone* is to become part of a dialogue about the history of theater and the history of war, it must be read wholly as a production of its specific context; and yet also in a consciously de-contextualized fashion. Classroom discussion also touched on the *Theater of War* project, which organizes readings of Sophocles's *Ajax* and *Philoctetes* for "military and civilian communities across the United States and Europe," with the goal of forging "a common vocabulary for openly discussing the impact of war on individuals, families, and communities."[68] It is not hard to imagine that Garnier's play may have served a similar purpose in the 1580s, nor is it difficult to think that it might again be enrolled into such a program today. In any case, the present translation wrestles Antigone from Brisson's arms and seeks out new ones—yours, dear reader—that might usher her into new discursive settings, new dialogues, new debates.

68 http://www.outsidethewirellc.com/projects/theater-of-war/overview

The Tragedy of Pious Antigone (1580)

Notes on the Translation

While most of Garnier's *Antigone* is written in alexandrines, most of the choral parts are in octosyllables. To capture something of this distinction, I have rendered the alexandrines into prose and the choral parts into free verse.

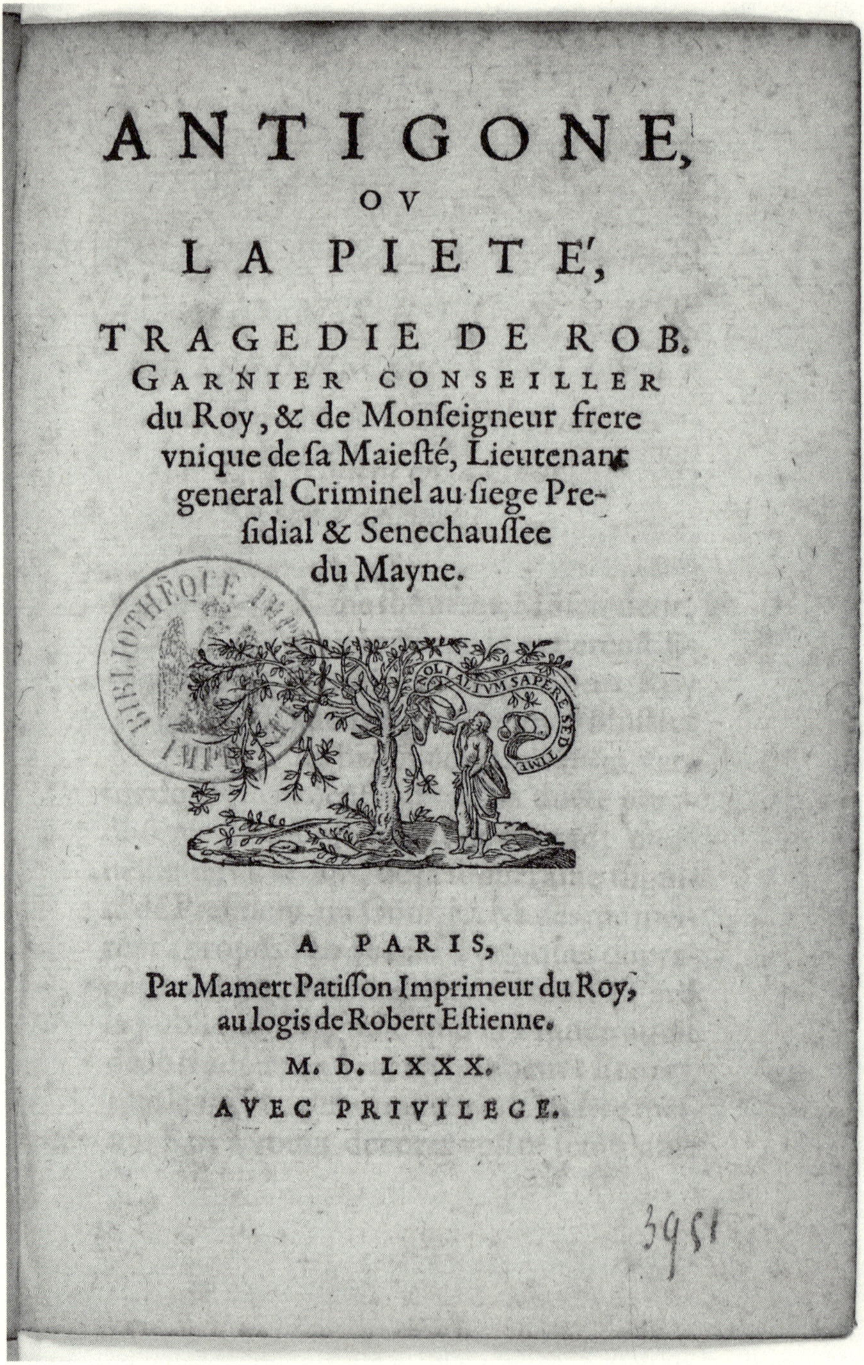

ANTIGONE,
OV
LA PIETE',

TRAGEDIE DE ROB. GARNIER CONSEILLER du Roy, & de Monſeigneur frere vnique de ſa Maieſté, Lieutenant general Criminel au ſiege Preſidial & Senechauſſee du Mayne.

A PARIS,
Par Mamert Patiſſon Imprimeur du Roy, au logis de Robert Eſtienne.
M. D. LXXX.
AVEC PRIVILEGE.

Figure 2. Title Page of Garnier, *Antigone* (1580). © Bibliothèque nationale de France.

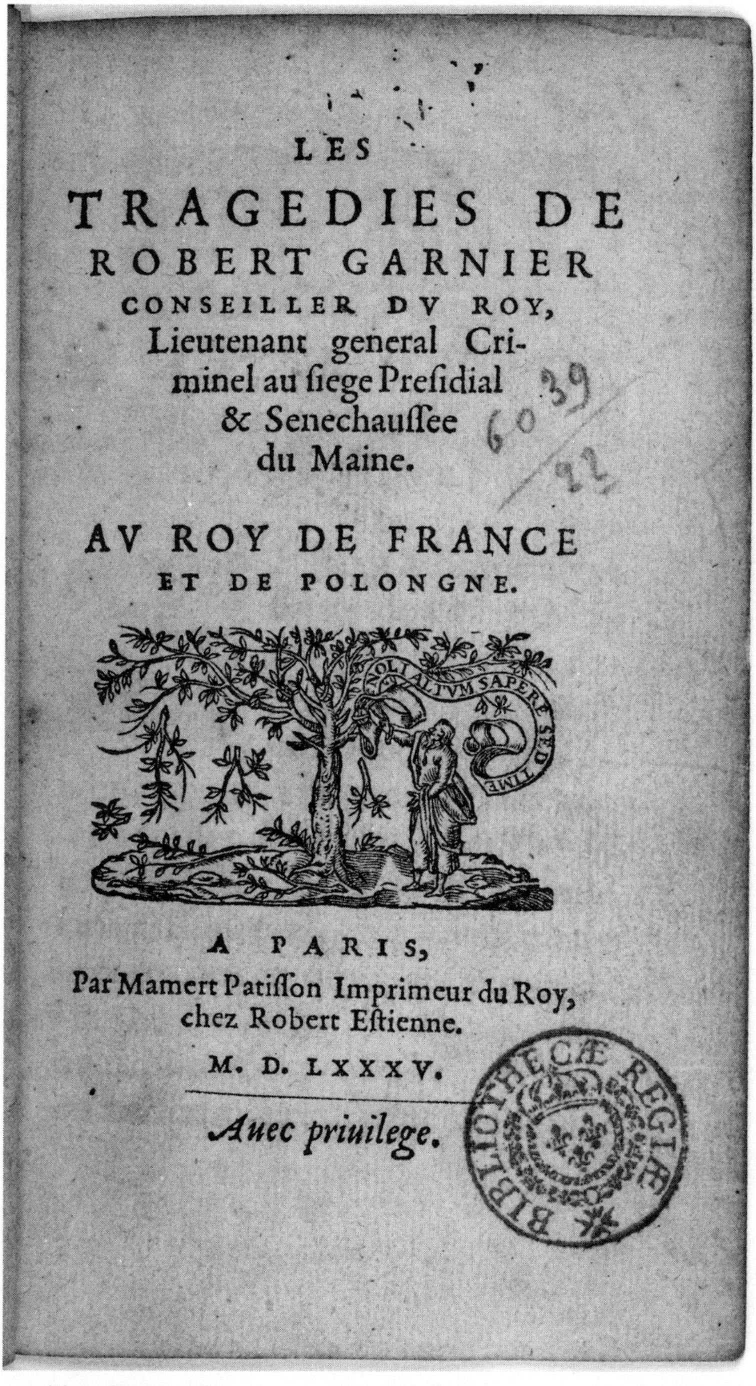

LES

TRAGEDIES DE
ROBERT GARNIER
CONSEILLER DV ROY,
Lieutenant general Cri-
minel au ſiege Preſidial
& Senechauſſee
du Maine.

AV ROY DE FRANCE
ET DE POLONGNE.

NOLI ALTVM SAPERE SED TIME

A PARIS,
Par Mamert Patiſſon Imprimeur du Roy,
chez Robert Eſtienne.

M. D. LXXXV.

Auec priuilege.

Figure 3. Title Page of Garnier, *Les Tragedies de Robert Garnier* (1585). © Bibliothèque nationale de France.

TO MONSEIGNEUR BRISSON
Counselor to the King in his private Counsel,
And President in his Court of Parliament.[1]

I recall, Monseigneur, that when the noble liberality of our good king (whose thirst for celebrating the fine and admirable virtues of his subjects is never slaked) honored the learned wisdom of Monseigneur de Pibrac[2] with that sovereign honor of becoming President of the Court, the muses fed my hand one of my tragic works, so that I might testify in my own manner to the public happiness felt by France regarding his promotion. And now that the same goodness of our same king has chosen to adorn your own virtues with the same honor, in this same court, those same tragic muses again come to extract from my hands this work in the same style and fashion, in order, as I present it to you, to show that I do not want to be the only one not joining in the universal excitement of the kingdom regarding this new decoration of your merits. For what Frenchman has not heard of your celebrated name? Whose ear is not nourished by and crossed through with the sounds of your praises? Indeed, who is not taken over by marvelous admiration on seeing the stars and men plotting the embellishment of such a worthy subject? I cannot say that our century (although wretched) is an iron age[3] when I see virtue thus bursting with the purple of senators, on the throne of supreme justice in this kingdom, such as we see it shining in the right equity of these six venerable fathers, who occupy in this sacred areopagus the first rank in authority. The virtuous ages of our ancestors cannot boast of having produced anything similar.[4] At least, we must hope from our good prince, as from a second Augustus, the return of a golden age, whilst under the attendant good fortune, such pilots remain at justice's helm. But I digress, Monseigneur, and, without thinking about it, goaded by my impetuous desire, I have set sail

[1] Barnabé Brisson (1530–91), a magistrate and, as of 1580, *président à mortier*. For more about this person, see Introduction.

[2] Guy du Faur de Pibrac, a magistrate and, as of 1577, president of the Parliament of Paris. Garnier had dedicated his "Hymne de la Monarchie," discussed in the introduction, to Pibrac.

[3] Iron age: reference to the most corrupt of the four ages, according to Ovid (golden, silver, bronze, iron). See Ovid, *Metamorphoses*, 1:89–150.

[4] Areopagus: a rock situated to the nort-west of the Acropolis in Athens, the place where the Council of Elders met in Ancient Athens (akin to the Roman Senate).

on the sea of your praise and instead of offering you a tragedy, I seem to want to enter into panegyrics. I return to my subject, then, to tell you about the misfortunes of this pitiful Antigone, who living anew in our country of France, as if greatly troubled, throws herself into your arms, so that you might offer favorable support, as she was the kind and noble support and guide of her wretched father.

Your most affectionate servant,
R. Garnier.

The Argument of *Antigone*[5]

Everybody knows how Oedipus, son of Laius, King of Thebes, and of Jocasta, his wife, was exposed to death upon Mount Cithaeron as soon as he was born, for it had been predicted to the king that one day his son would kill him. And how Porbas, the shepherd of Polybus, King of Corinth, who chanced to pass by and who, seeing the child abandoned in a tree, his two legs bound by wicker, and considering him to be a fine child and pleasing, carried him to the queen, his mistress, who had no children. And how she nurtured and raised him as her own. And how, grown up, having consulted Apollo's oracle about the truth of his origins, it was said to this child that he would find his father near Thebes. Having made his way there, he chanced to meet the king (whom he did not recognize) and to quarrel with the king's men. The king ran to help his men and was killed in the tussle. And how, after returning to Thebes and liberating it from the troublesome sphinx, he married Queen Jocasta, his mother, and had four children with her, Eteocles, Polynices, Antigone, and Ismene. How a little while later, the city being polluted by a deadly, long, and incurable plague, he heard from the oracle that the contagion would not stop until the death of the late king had been avenged. This led to the uncovering of the time, place, and circumstances of the murder; he discovered that he himself was the murderer and, further, that he had committed incest with his mother. And how, horrified by such abominations, he plucked his eyes out with his own hands, left the city, and performed penitence on Cithaeron's rocky heights, spending his wretched days in lamentation and grief, alongside Antigone, who did not want to abandon him. Now, meanwhile, his sons Eteocles and Polynices, disagreeing over rights to the kingdom, finally agreed to govern each in turn, a year at a time. Following this agreement, Eteocles, as the elder, took up his position, but delighting in it so much when his time came to an end he did not want to let it go, nor step down from governing to make way for his successor. Rightly indignant, Polynices fled, to seek Greek princes and to ask for their help in recovering his kingdom. Amongst others, he sought out Adrastus, king of the Argians who, after making Polynices his son-in-law, assembled a strong army in order to chase out the intruder and to get Polynices back to his lands. They set up camp near the walls of Thebes, where Eteocles remained and who stationed all of his

[5] This summary is by Garnier. It was quite common to include such summaries at the start of plays in the sixteenth century.

troops in the battlefields. Right away, a cruel and bloody battle took place, in which most of the two armies perished, even the generals and captains. Polynices—extremely displeased by the deaths of Tydeus, his brother-in-law, and by the deaths of Capaneus, Hippomedon, Amphiareus, and Pathenopeus, all courageous fighters and noble lords—summoned his brother Eteocles to combat. The two brothers entered into such furious battle, with the two armies looking on, that they both died on the spot. When Jocasta learned of this, she stabbed herself in the breast and died. The Argians, moreover, seeing Polynices dead, for whom they had taken up arms, and feeling amazingly weakened by the loss they had suffered, lifted the siege and departed in haste. Creon, Jocasta's brother, having made himself king, buried his dead while outlawing—on pain of death—the burial of enemy corpses, especially Polynices's, which is the cause of such a fatal war. To ensure respect of his ordinance, he has guards sit and keep watch for anyone breaking it.[6] Despite this, Antigone resolves to bury her brother and not to let him be eaten by beasts and birds, but as she went about this pitiful rite, she is taken and led to Creon, who sentences her to death. She descended and was shut in a cave, so as to die there from hunger; but, without waiting for such a long death, she hangs herself with a noose made of her own hair. Creon had pledged to marry her to his son Haemon. After finding her dead in this cave where he had gone to rescue her, vanquished by love and by sorrow, Haemon plunges his sword into his body and falls dead atop the one he loved. The news of this pitiful occurrence reached the ears of the queen, his mother, seizing her with such intolerable torment that she immediately killed herself. Creon, overwhelmed by the sadness of such disasters, so many and so sudden, laments and grieves, thus concluding the calamities of which this play tells.

This subject has been treated differently by Aeschylus in the tragedy called the *Seven Against Thebes*, by Sophocles in his *Antigone*, in Euripides's *Phoenician Women*, and in Seneca and Statius in their *Thebaids*. Events take place outside the gates to the City of Thebes.

---

[6] Here and throughout the rest of this *argument*, the changes in tense, between past to present, are Garnier's.

Act I

Oedipus, Antigone.

OEDIPUS

[1] You who escort with such constancy your father, blind and buckled by old age,[1] my aide, my guide, Antigone my daughter, alas I must ask this: please leave.[2] Leave alone this man of sorrows that I am,[3] so that I might sigh out my worries as I wander through these deserts.[4] Leave me, I pray you. [5] Do not let

---

[1] Line 1: The play begins after the events described in Sophocles's *Oedipus the King*. Oedipus has abdicated and left Thebes and now wanders in the wilderness. The Seven Against Thebes army is poised to attack the city, with Oedipus's son Polynices at its head. Polynices and Eteocles had agreed to rule Thebes in turn, but Eteocles, who ruled first, refused to surrender the throne to his brother. Unlike Garnier's other tragedies (and indeed perhaps a majority of French Renaissance tragedies), this one begins not with a monologue, but with a dialogue.

[2] Line 3: The play opens by closely imitating Seneca's *Phoenician Women*, which begins: "Guidance for your blind parent [*caeci parentis regimen*], only solace for your weary father [*fessi. . . patris*], my daughter [*nata*]: to me it is worth the cost to have produced you, even as it happened; but abandon your ill-fated father [*infaustum patrem*]" (SenPhW: 1–3). Note that *regimen* is "more commonly used of the management or control of public or private affairs" (Frank: 76). On use of *nata*, see Frank: 77. Garnier insists more than Seneca on Oedipus's old age—the only mention in Seneca is at SenPhW: 350. See also Frank: 87, who notes that in Seneca "Oedipus does not seem to be particularly old and frail." See also note to line 2429.

[3] Line 4: Eng. *wretched* < Fr. *malheureux* renders Lat. *Infaustus* (SenPhW: 3), a word that "has a semantic range which extends form 'unlucky' [. . .] through 'ill-omened' in a general sense [. . .] to the very specific 'cursed by the gods'" (Frank: 79).

[4] Line 5: Seneca does not offer any description of the place where Oedipus wanders at this point, although it is clear that he wanders in the wilderness. It has been noted that "Oedipus [. . .] is as wild as the countryside through which he roams, like King Lear on the heath" (John G. Fitch, "Introduction," SenPhW: 276). Reading Garnier and Seneca side-by-side leads to the intriguing point that Garnier's "Vaguant par ces *deserts*" (line 5) connects etymologically with Oedipus's cry in Seneca: "*desere* infaustum patrem" (abandon your ill-fated father) (SenPhW: 3), as if to underline the continuity of person and place.

my sad life sadden yours.[5] Do not waste your years guiding my steps. Do not use up your blossoming youth at my side. Leave, my daughter. What good is your faithful guidance to me?—I choose to be lost. I wish for no guide along the path[6] I follow, for I seek a path that will lead me away from worry,[7] that will tear me away from this world and unyoke the earth and the heavens from my body which deserves their thunder.

To flee the sight of the heavens, I have blinded myself, but that is not enough, for the heavens see me.[8] The all-seeing heavens bear witness to my crime but, alas, they do not cast me down into the infernal abyss. They make abominable me suffer on to swallow still the flavors of the earth and the freshness of the air. Remove your hand that holds me tenderly[9] and allow that I wander these mountains alone. I will head to Mount Cithaeron's high and wooded hills[10] where, as soon as I was born, as soon as I came into this world, my mother abandoned me in a tree, so that crows could feed on my barely born flesh. Cithaeron calls after me still and to *that* place I must retire.[11] It is Cithaeron that

---

[5] Line 6: In French, Garnier uses three etymologically related words in lines 4–6 (*malheureux* [misfortunate, miserable], *malheurer* [to make misfortunate/miserable], *malheur* [misfortune, misery]), which has the effect of accentuating the *pathétique* nature of the opening (Beaudin: 177). These terms have been rendered by Eng. *man of sorrows/be sorrowed/sorrow.*

[6] Line 11: Eng. *path* < Fr. *chemin* renders Lat. *via* (road, way, etc.). On the importance of this image see Henry 1985: 148. It has been suggested that we might see here an indication that Oedipus is moving on stage (Beaudin: 177).

[7] Line 12: Direct alteration of SenPhW: 6: ". . .the path that can draw me from this life [*ab hac vita*]."

[8] Line 16: Garnier's parallel structure ("ne voir plus le ciel" [flee the sight of the heavens] / "du ciel je suis veu" [the heavens see me]) emphasizes the importance of the sky and perhaps of heaven or of Christ—much more than in Seneca, where we read "non video . . . diem / sed videor" (I cannot see the daylight . . . / but I am seen) (SenPhW: 9–10).

[9] Line 21: Hands are a key image throughout the play, as in Seneca. See Frank: 94.

[10] Line 23: It has been suggested that certains verses, like this one, can be read almost as stage directions (Beaudin: 178).

[11] Line 28: Garnier's description of Mount Cithaeron (a mountain in Central Greece where Oedipus was abandoned as a child by his parents Jocasta and Laius) is centered on its relevance for the story of Oedipus, differing from Seneca who also connected it to other celebrated stories (SenPhW: 13–26), including that of Agave's tearing apart of her son Pentheus. Seneca's enumeration "suggests that violence is woven into the fabric of the house of Thebes" (Frank: 81). On Oedipus's desire to return to Mount Cithaeron, see also Frank 86. For Beaudin, Cithaeron "devient comme l'incarnation géographique du destin du personnage" (becomes the geographic embodiment of the character's destiny) (Beaudin: 178). The choice to leave aside the proliferation of mythological references is indicative of Garnier's style—and is surely different from the kind of mythological additive schemes we find, notably, in Ronsard. See also note to line 35.

I must desire, my first land, my first abode—[30] for this reason, it must also be my final refuge. As an old man, I want to die in the place where, as a small child I was destined to die as soon as I was born. Give me my death, make my death a cruel and bloody one,[12] give me the death that has pursued me since I was stolen away from the breast. [35] Oh murderous Cithaeron, you are still cruel to me, stretching out my days, cutting them short.[13] Take this body, which is your due, this carcass of mine, and submit it to the ancient decree.[14]

Oh, but why do you still hold on to me, my daughter? Do you not see that [40] my father calls to me and draws me towards death? How he appears before me, horrible and frightful? How he follows me still, how he will not leave me alone? He shows me his wound and the blood that spurts out over my proud murderous hand?[15]

---

[12] Line 35: The meaning of MFr. *cruel* here implies the bloodiness of Lat. *cruor*. Garnier, moreover, particularizes, saying "tu *m*'es cruel" (line 35), whereas Seneca makes a more general statement: "Always bloody, always savage, cruel, ferocious, when you kill and when you spare! [*cum occidis et cum parcis*]" (SenPhW: 35), a choice in accordance with the one made above (see note to line 28). (Here, Fr. *cruel* has thus been rendered by Eng. *cruel and bloody*.)

[13] Line 36: As in Seneca, Oedipus's prayer is somewhat of an "inversion of the usual kind of prayer, in which a deity is asked either to grant something positive or to avert an evil" (Frank: 86–87). As in Seneca, Garnier's text here exhibits certain prayer characteristics: invocation, a list of requests, occasional alliterations—even more present in the French text (Fr. *moy, mort, moy, mort, mort, mamelle, meurtier*, etc.).

[14] Line 38: The "ordonnance ancienne" (ancient decree) referenced here is, of course, the original curse (and prophecy thereof) regarding Oedipus's destiny (to kill Laius and sleep with Jocasta). The choice of term is significant. Cotgrave defines *Ordonnance* as "An Ordinance; Edict, Order, Decree, Statute, Institution, Constitution; a Precept, Appointment, Commaundement (sic)." The connotation, with a seeming political resonance, reworks a quite different tone in Seneca: "animus gestit antiqua exequi / supplicia" (My spirit is eager to execute the punishment of old) (SenPhW: 37–38). It is thus the term *antiqua supplicia* that has been morphed into Fr. *ordonnance*, Eng. *decree*. (In Seneca, the *supplicia* is taken up again by the term *poenae* [punishments] at SenPhW: 46).

[15] Line 44: According to Robert Garapon, Garnier's Oedipus more consistently condemns himself, and is condemned for, killing his father than for sleeping with his mother (Garapon 1989: 32–36), a trend established by the present lines (39–44) and taken up elsewhere (97–101, 161–66, 179–86, 232–33). The exceptional mention of incest is at lines 87–88. Garapon's explanation underscores that Fr. *parricide* referred, in the sixteenth century, to both the murder of one's father and the murder of the king (Garapon 1989: 36). Cotgrave defines Fr. *parricide* as follows: "A Parricide; a murtherer (sic) of his owne father; also, any heinous murtherer (sic)." Garapon suggests comparison with Du Bellay's *Regrets*, sonnet 134. For Garapon, then, this emphasis has to do with Garnier's decision to specifically condemn murder of kings, in opposition to certain contemporary French protestants who "s'interrogent sur la légitimité du tyrannicide, et arrivent à la conclusion qu'il est licite de tuer le roi qui ne respecte pas les devoirs que le lient à ses

ANTIGONE

Tame, my father, tame and temper this bitter pain.

OEDIPUS

But who could tame such misery? Of what further use is my soul in this guilty body? My soul, why do you not leave? Alas! Why do you not leave such a wicked house? Are you waiting for further parricide? For further incest? How I fear that, how I fear just that. My daughter, leave me. My crime against my mother makes me fear for you.[16]

ANTIGONE

Order not that I abandon you. For fear of no one shall I leave you. Nothing, nothing save death could separate us.[17] I will be your companion in good fate and bad.

May my twin brothers invade the kingdom and take possession, as they see fit, of the paternal domain. *I* will have my father—I want nothing more. I leave them everything else and ask for nothing. My father alone do I want, he is my share, I hold on only to him, he is my only inheritance. No one will take him from me. Not he whose hand unjustly holds on to the fine Theban scepter; nor he who captains the Argolid forces.[18] And not even Jupiter, were he to destroy the lands with deadly thunderbolts and, steaming with anger, now to descend to

---

peuples" (wonder about the legitimacy of tyrannicide and reach the conclusion that it is justified to kill a king who does not respect the duties that connect him to his populations) (Garapon 1989: 36).

[16] Line 52: As might be expected (see note to line 44), here emphasis is placed first on father killing, then on incest. Still, the fear expressed is nevertheless primarily directed at Antigone as a possible object of her father's incestuous desire, based on Seneca: "Am I capable now of committing a crime? I *am* capable, wretched man [*miser*], I give warning [*praedico*]: leave your father, leave while a virgin [*virgo*]. After my father, I fear everything [*timeo post patrem omnia*]" (SenPhW: 48–50). On the different way Seneca's verses have been interpreted, see Frank: 93. Note, too, that Garnier, unlike Seneca, does not mention Antigone's virginity: although Lat. *virgo* can refer simply, like Gk. παρθένος, to an "unmarried girl," in the present context it might refer specifically (and likely does) to her virginity (Frank: 93). See also Statius, where it is said of Antigone that "her chaste virginity [*casta. . . virginitas*] does not delay her" (StTheb 11:355–56). See notes to lines 2169 and 2214.

[17] Line 54: Seneca's Antigone begins by addressing her father personally as *genitor* (SenPhW: 51). There are many times, in Seneca, when Oedipus identifies himself as a father (SenPhW: 3, 49, 93, 95, 98, 121, 135, 230, 295, 301, 333, 336), an "obsessive insistence on his paternity [which] suggests unresolved guilt concerning his incest" (Frank: 76).

[18] Line 65: I.e. neither Eteocles, who currently rules Thebes, nor Polynices, who was exiled to Argos, can steal Oedipus from Antigone.

be among us, could make my hand let go of you. I will be your guide even though this angers you. Do not push me away. Do you want to deprive me of the greatest happiness that I might ever know?

Should you wish to climb up to the wooded top of a shady hill, I am ready. Should you wish for a valley, for a dark cave, for a forest's horror, I am ready, too, for that. Should you wish for death, if only a sudden death can extinguish your incurable torment, then I will die with you and the ferryman Charon will lead us both across the waves of the Acheron.[19]

But soften, I pray, this obstinate heart. Overcome your ill, overcome your rage. What of your courageous heart?[20] Do you wish to give in to disaster?[21]

OEDIPUS

Oh such virtue! Good gods, is it possible that *I* fathered such a good daughter? Is it possible that, alas, an incestuous bed could have produced such a virtuous child?[22] Henceforth I will believe that a criminal she-wolf can breed in its womb a god-fearing sheep. That from a timid pigeon can issue forth an eagle.

---

[19] Line 80: Acheron is a river in the underworld that souls have to cross to reach the empire of the dead. Charon is the ferryman who carries the souls across.

[20] Line 83: Garnier's Antigone calls Oedipus to summon up courage and, from his heart, MFr. *generosité*, a term Cotgrave renders as "Generositie; gentilitie, gentrie; generousnesse, noblenesse, great worthinesse; brauerie of disposition, gallantnesse of humor; courage, valour, stoutness." The inflection is somewhat different from the correlated call in Seneca, where Antigone asks Oedipus to vanquish his troubles "magno robore" (with sturdy resolve) (SenPhW: 78), the term *robor*, whose first meaning is "a kind of hard oak," implying "hardness" and "strength" (LS). This term (*generosité*) forms part of the particular conceptual abstract vocabulary that Garnier deploys throughout. MFr. *genereux* has been transposed here via Eng. *courageous*.

[21] Line 84: The end of Antigone's plea in Garnier might be considered less strong than in Seneca. Whereas Garnier ends with a question, Seneca ends with a bold call for action: "Fight back [*resiste*]; amid such evils, to die is a defeat" (SenPhW: 79).

[22] Line 88: The term *vertueux* (Eng. virtuous), describing Antigone, stands in pointed (and, in the French, rhymed) opposition to *incestueux* (Eng. incestuous), describing her parents' relationship. See also note to line 44. The choice of the adjective *vertueux* is striking when compared with Seneca's text, where Oedipus's question is formulated as follows: "aliquis est ex me pius?" (Is some child of mine *pious*?) (SenPhW: 82), harnessing one of the many meanings of Lat. *pius*, which can mean "who acts according to duty," sacred, holy, or upright, but also (here) natural or uncorrupted. The word comes back, in Seneca, several verses later (*pii quoque erimus*, SenPhW: 89). As has been noted, Oedipus and Jocasta can be distinguished in terms of *pietas*: "*Pietas* denotes right and natural relationships between family members, particularly parents and children, and a corresponding right relationship of humans to gods. Jocasta's love for her sons, then, embodies *pietas* in contrast to Oedipus's involuntary *impietas* [. . .]; Oedipus's attitude in turn is set against Antigone's *pietas*, as her brother's *impietas* towards each other is set again Jocasta's love for them [etc.]" (Fitch: 276). On *pius* in Seneca, see Frank: 103. Despite the subtitle

That from a cowardly deer might be born a roaring lion. That shady nighttime begets light and that from dusky evening emerges the dawn. For from a polluted marriage, forbidden by nature, from a mother and a son, such a child can be born.

Leave me, my love. Do you want me to abide my father's death without avenging his injury? Why do you hold on, with your virgin's hand, to my parricidal hand? To my inhuman arm, stained by the same blood that gave birth to me?[23] What wicked, abominable, and pestiferous breeding!

All I do is extend the course of my ills. I live not; rather, I experience the funereal sufferings of one who sinks into his grave. My soul is a prisoner of this body, like a body shut up in its coffin. You think you do me good by extending my life, but nothing is so dear to me as quickening my destined end.[24] You delay the death I wish to hasten and while you think you save me, your hand puts me to death. For life is my death[25] and my devouring ill can only be cured by death. *One offends just as greatly in forcing life upon someone who does not desire it as in taking the life of another.*[26] Thus, leave me. I have, with my desire, abandoned the ancient dignity of the kingdom of Thebes; but in renouncing this royal crown I did not also abandon the power I have over myself. I am my own master.[27] No one must defend me or give me orders—I alone have this right.

---

of Garnier's play (*ou la Pieté* [Or Piety]), Garnier has here chosen specifically *not* to echo Seneca's use of *pius*. See also notes to lines 114, 308, 329, 525, 569, 687, 2174.

[23] Line 101: See note to line 44.

[24] Line 108: The central theme of the first act is obviously Oedipus's suicide, a particularly Senecan and Stoic topic according to which "the decision to end one's life should be based on *ratio* and not on *affectus*" (Frank: 99). Based on Seneca's other writings on the topic, "Oedipus would thus appear to be an undoubted candidate for suicide, since there are few discernible advantages to weigh against his disadvantages—his agonizing guilt, his isolation, his blindness, the behavior of his sons" (Frank: 100). See also Tadic-Gilloteaux 1963 and Griffin 1986. On suicide in Garnier, see Lebègue 1975: 287.

[25] Line 111: An antithesis widely used by Garnier's contemporaries (Lebègue: 275).

[26] Line 114: Such truths, here secured as a general truth (here by Italics, by quotation marks in the 1580 text) are already in Seneca. Different, though, is how Seneca finds an occasion to talk of Antigone's conception of *pietas*: "You do wrong, though with honorable intention; you call it loyalty/piety [*pietatem vocas*] to drag about your unburied father [*patrem insepultum*]" (SenPhW: 96–97). See also note to line 88.

[27] Line 119: "Je suis maistre de moy" (I am my own master) renders Seneca's "I keep kingship over myself [*regnum mei retineo*]" (SenPhW: 105) and anticipates Auguste's celebrated line in Corneille's *Cinna*: "Je suis maître de moi comme de l'univers" (I am my own master and master, too, of the universe) (Act 5, Scene 3). This verse of Corneille is, of course, one of his most famous and imprinted with the particular Cornelian tone. Pocock, for example, lists it as one particularly emblematic of Corneille's verse and style: "these somewhat harsh attitudes and their embodiment in ringing but inhuman lines are typical of Corneille" (Pocock 1973: 78). Also noted by Lebègue: 275.

ANTIGONE

Do you have no pity for my bitter pain?[28]

OEDIPUS

Do you have no pity for your father's sorrow?

ANTIGONE

Your sorrow is great, but a courageous heart can overcome any sorrow, indeed knows not what sorrow is.

OEDIPUS

My sorrow knows no cure.

ANTIGONE

You are not guilty for the sorrow that torments you.

OEDIPUS

Not after I polluted myself with my father's blood?

ANTIGONE

No, for you did not want to commit that crime against him.

OEDIPUS

I married my mother and I slaughtered my father.

ANTIGONE

But you knew nothing of this. You did not think you were doing it.

OEDIPUS

It is a crime, inconceivable and horrific.

ANTIGONE

No. An accident, born of chance and error.

OEDIPUS

An error that makes my blood freeze when I think about it.

---

[28] Line 121: This stichomythic exchange (lines 121–36) is a moment of rupture vis-à-vis Seneca's *Phoenician Women*, which Garnier has been imitating quite closely up to this point. Garnier highlights the importance of Oedipus's ignorance at the moment he committed his crimes. See notes to lines 134 and 136.

ANTIGONE

Really, it is but an error, it is but an imprudence.[29]

OEDIPUS

What monster ever committed such malice?

ANTIGONE

No one is evil if such was not his will.[30]

OEDIPUS

These are wasted words[31]—you cannot defeat my stubborn heart with your convincing arguments. I want to die. I want to bury my suffering with my slavish soul in the infernal abyss. And if dead souls can sink even deeper, then I wish to plunge even lower than hell's vault.

Is it your plan, by stealing the sword from my hand, by taking away the cord destined to strangle me, by steering my steps away from the steep cliffs, by keeping me away from poisonous herbs, to keep me from dying? You strive in vain to shut off from me the hell that gapes wide open. *Death is always there—and whereas life (anyone's life) can be stolen away at any given moment, death cannot be, death cannot be removed. Whoever wants to die finds death quite ready. A thousand and a thousand pathways stretch towards the deep Acheron and all mortal men, at the moment they wish, there descend.*[32] Oh death! Oh sweet death! Come stifle my senses and pierce my heart through with your deadly darts. Tear apart my breast, capable of so many horrors. Rip away my pitiful life and quash it under this hard rock in eternal rest. May Phoebus never again shine down on me. Leave behind the Styx, my father, and forever accompany that executioner Alecto, my soul's companion.[33] See her sulfurous brands, her whips, her snakes swelled by

[29] Line 134: The opposition between crime and cognizance of wrongdoing can already be found: in Seneca's *Hercules furens*, where Amphitryon asks "Whoever gave mistaken action [*errori*] the name of crime [*nomen. . . sceleris*]?" (SenHerc: 1237); and in Seneca's *Hercules on Oeta* (lines 885–86). Oedipus himself, in Sophocles's *Oedipus at Colonus*, makes the distinction. See Beaudin: 181 and Lebègue: 275.

[30] Line 136: Antigone ends this exchange by emphasizing the necessity of free will (*volonté*) in establishment of responsibility and guilt. Beaudin has commented: "Antigone rejette toute idée de prédestination" (Antigone rejects totally the idea of predestination) and that "Il n'est pas interdit de voir là le refus d'un concept essentiel de la théologie calviniste" (It is not impossible to see here a rejection of an essential concept of Calvinist theology) (Beaudin: 181–82). See also line 188.

[31] Line 137: Following the stichomythic exchange, Garnier returns to following Seneca's text. Lines 137–86 closely imitate SenPhW: 140–81.

[32] Line 154: Verses (lines 153–54) re-cast by Hardy in his *Panthée* (v. 1079). See Lebègue: 275.

[33] Line 161: Styx, a river of the underworld. Alecto, one of the Furies.

black poison that crawl over my lungs, my eternal suffering. Take her as vengeance to console the pain inflicted by my horrific crime.[34] If this is still not enough for you, for it is true that no horror could be like or equal to my crime, if you suffer still from how slight my suffering is, if you prefer that I find myself amongst the sad shades on the muddy swamps of hell's groaning hollows, then order that the earth be cleaved open and push me deep inside. Have me carry the rock that forever falls down. Have me suffer the thirst and hunger of Tantalus. Have me share in the suffering of wily Prometheus, of thundering Salmoneus and treacherous Ixion.[35] All their sufferings combined will not suffice for punishing me who was damned before I was born.

Come on, Oedipus, come on, no half measures: punish yourself. It is not enough to be an enemy in your own eyes—your eyes on their own committed no crime. You are wholly guilty and no part of you is exempt from punishment. Open up your stomach and tear apart your breast, rip out your heart with your bloody hand, your parricidal hand, and may it itself pay the price of your father's deadly wound.[36]

ANTIGONE

For God's sake, my father, calm your torment, for it is not the result of a crime but of your fatal sorrow.[37] Listen to this poor girl and may your gentle ear not turn away in disdain[38] my supplicant's voice. I do not ask that once again you

---

[34] Line 166: See note to line 44.

[35] Line 176: Prometheus: for giving fire to mortals, Zeus punished him by binding him to a rock with steel chains and by having an eagle peck constantly at his liver, which would constantly renew itself. Salmoneus: tried to imitate Zeus's thunderbolts by riding a chariot with copper and iron wheels along a bronze road, for which Zeus punished him by striking him down with a real thunderbolt. Ixion: Zeus punished him by attaching him to a flaming wheel that turned without end.

[36] Line 186: See note to line 44. On these lines, it has been noted: "Le thème de la main criminelle, qui constitue le *leitmotiv* des répliques de l'Oedipe sénéquien, est répété aussi dans Garnier. Cette image avait déjà fait son apparition dans les tragédies du cycle romain, mais toujours à l'état d'ébauche. Ici la main qu'Oedipe tourne contre lui-même et qui devient l'exécutrice de l'auto-vengeance garde beaucoup de la violence et de la volupté sadique du modèle latin" (The theme of the criminal hand, which constitutes one of the leitmotivs of Seneca's Oedipus, is also repeated in Garnier. His image had already appeared in the Roman cycle [of Garnier's plays], but only in draft form. Here, Oedipus turns his hand against himself and the hand becomes the author of revenge directed at the self, keeping much of the violence and sadistic pleasure of the Latin model) (Federici 1975: 61).

[37] Line 188: See note to line 136.

[38] Line 189: Seneca uses a parallel structure (*parens/natae*) to emphasize family ties between father and daughter (SenPhW: 182–83), whereas Garnier has Antigone refer to herself as "pauvrette" (poor girl).

take up Agenor's scepter in your hand.[39] I do not ask that with sound laws you govern your free subjects, nor that you restore to your family, buried in sorrow, its ancient honor.[40] I do not request that you rip from your beaten soul the grief that kills you.[41] *It is so that great hearted men* *must be victorious in their battle with fortune; they must not succumb to that pain that tries to master us; rather, such men must crush under foot that gnawing sadness as it crawls through the soul, like an incurable poison unless it is tempered by reason.*[42]

Why, for a cure, do you resort to death? Unless it is that your strength surrenders to Fortune, that you are not strong enough in your struggle against its assault and that you cannot stand up to its advances. But ah! What more could Fortune do to you? Could Fortune possibly be more hostile to you? Jupiter, who can do anything, could not increase that overwhelming sorrow that causes you to lament.[43]

What good do you hope to find on the dark shores, oh eternal companion of sorrowful souls, that you do not already have here? Do you not suffer as much here as you would ever on Acheron's shore? What irritates you so? What furor goads you to sink down into Pluto's marshes? Is it so that you will no longer see the light of day—now invisible to blind you? Your eyes no longer see

[39] Line 192: Agenor: son of Poseidon and Libya, father of Cadmus, who built the Cadmeia (citadel of Thebes).

[40] Line 196: Garnier uses three negative structures: Antigone does not ask Oedipus (1) to govern with "loix salutiares" (sound laws) (line 193); (2) to restore the ancient family in new glory; (3) to put an end to his pain. While Seneca *does* make these three points, his mention of (2) above is briefer—we read only: "I do not seek to lead you back to [. . .] your royal state [*regni*], flourishing in power and glory" (SenPhW: 184–86). Garnier adds the notion of *loix salutaires* and of reigning over *peuples volontaires* (free subjects). See line 1812. The addition is of key importance for several reasons. Firstly, Garnier here uses a term (*loix salutaires*) which will later refer to the unwritten laws by which Antigone will defend her stand against Creon, thus translating Sophocles's reference to laws that are "ἄγϱαπτα" (SophAnt: 451–52). Secondly, and even though in a negated sentence, Garnier here puts into circulation certain ideas about good governance and sound politics (i.e. that there are certain kinds of desired laws and that the people, in such a situation, is *volontaire*). Already indirectly, Antigone hints at her opposition to tyranny. See line 1812.

[41] Line 198: Of these lines (191–98), Jondorf notes: "The 'marks of sovereignty' here are three: the outward symbol of kingship ('le sceptre d'Agenor'); the function of law-giver; and the fact that the office of king is vested in one family" (Jondorf 1969: 63).

[42] Line 204: Lines 199–204 rework SenPhW: 288–92.

[43] Line 212: Garnier leaves aside Seneca's discussion of Oedipus's innocence at this point. In Seneca, Antigone states: ". . .no blame [*culpa*] attaches to this heart of yours. And you have all the more reason to call yourself guiltless [*insontem*], father, in that you are innocent [*innocens*] even despite the gods' intentions" (SenPhW: 203–05). Note that, in Seneca, "Antigone's insistence on Oedipus's innocence contrasts sharply with Oedipus's strong sense of guilt" (Frank: 136). See Pack 1940. See also notes to lines 236 and 677.

the daylight's friendly brightness. Is it to deprive yourself of the royal crown? To abandon your palaces? You deprive yourself of them. Is it to banish yourself far from your land, far from your wife and children? You leave them hated— from that your inhuman fate delivers you. You should thus not lament the fact you live—life steals from you as much as death normally steals from those who die. What good can this desired-for death give you? What more will you have as an Acherontic soul?

OEDIPUS

I want to separate myself from my body.[44] I will flee myself on Pluto's shores, I will flee these two hands, these two parricidal hands,[45] this heart, this stomach, these dripping entrails made horrific by crime.[46] I will escape the heavens, the air, the sea, and the earth, these edifices of the gods.[47]

Might I once again stride through the fertile countryside that Ceres makes beautiful with fields of golden hair?[48] Might I breathe the air? Drink the water that runs in abundance? And feed on the goods produced by the Earth?[49] Might I once again, polluted by Jocasta's kisses, reach out to touch your chaste hand?[50] Might I hear the sound that again cleaves my heart open with the sacred names 'father,' 'mother,' and 'child'?

---

[44] Line 231: Here, Oedipus responds more directly to the question asked in Seneca ("Whom, father, do you flee?" [*quem, genitor, fuges?*], SenPhW: 215), than to the questions that Antigone asks in Garnier (lines 228–29). On the climactic nature of that question in Seneca, see Frank: 136.

[45] Line 233: See note to line 44.

[46] Pluto: a ritual title of Hades, the god of the dead.

[47] Line 236: Federici comments: "Comme chez la plupart des personnages stoïciens, la volonté de passer de l'état de victime à celui de bourreau est proclamée à haute voix, avec un orgueil furieux, et acquiert des tonalités macabres" (As is the case for most Stoic characters, the will to go from victim to executioner is proclaimed out loud, with furious pride, such that it acquires macabre tonalities) (Federici 1975: 62). Note also that, once again, Garnier does not render Seneca's mention of Oedipus's innocence—"I flee the terrible crimes that I did in innocence [*quae feci innocens*]" (SenPhW: 218). See note to line 212.

[48] Line 238: Ceres: the goddess of agriculture.

[49] Line 240: These lines (231–40) are among those quoted in 1946 by Thierry Maulnier, a year after he produced an adaptation of Garnier's play, noting that "Je ne suis pas sûr que le goût du public ait encore placé à leur véritable niveau [ces] terribles plaintes" (I am not sure that the public's taste has yet place [these] terrible complaints at their true level) (Maulnier 1946: 67). See also notes to line 1308 and 2183.

[50] Line 244: Garnier has Oedipus say that he is MFr. *polu* (polluted), whereas Seneca offers three adjectives to describe Oedipus's evil-doing hand, "nefandus incestificus execrabilis" (evil, incestuous, accursed) (SenPhW: 223), three adjectives in asyndeton

Ah! What good has it done me, now in this eternal night, to extinguish light in both eyes, given that all of my other senses, equally marked by my crimes, are not closed like them?

My whole body must rot underground and my sad soul must wander on the dark shores, Pluto's victim. What do I accomplish here other than infecting both the air and the earth with my body?

I could not yet see the wandering light of day,[51] I had yet to enter into this world, I was still contained within my mother's soft flanks, and yet already I terrified, already I was feared. Some are devoured by the severe Fates as soon as they issue forth from their mother's womb, but I, alas, I had hardly come into the world, barely indeed had my mother conceived me, than already death was brandishing its spear, eager to kill me—as it now delays.[52] My death—the death of pitiful me—was decided upon before I received the spark of life, before I was alive.

Oh the strange occurrence: a father wants to unmake his little child even before he makes him, before he begets him; he orders the death of he who should survive him. Ah! He fears something different and his timorous soul thinks that this child will be his murderer.

Thus, before my birth, indeed before my making, I was already a criminal guilty of a horrible crime,[53] I was already a parricide and my new life, by hostile fate, was both guilty and innocent. I was given over to torture as soon as I could taste this world's air, as soon as I was filled with it. My feet were pierced through with a flaming skewer and high up was I hung in the moving forest of craggy Cithaeron, atop a rock, to feed the crows with my tender young flesh.[54] But alas, destiny, mischievously set on my future sorrow, tore me away from torture, preserving me—for the meantime, so that with a dagger I might

---

(Frank: 142). Such groupings of adjectives is typical of Latin tragic style. See Coffey and Mayer 1990 on *Phaedra* 416.

[51] Line 253: Oedipus here (lines 253–300) evokes his past, drawing on SenPhW: 243–74 and (to a much lesser extent) on EurPhW: 1595–1614. One notable absence from Garnier's play is Oedipus's earlier mention, in Seneca, of his fate. There, Oedipus imagines himself as if a new Sphinx's riddle: "'He was son-in-law to his grandfather, rival to his father, brother to his own children and parent to his brothers, the grandmother in one labor bore children for her man, but for herself grandchildren as well.' Who could unravel such a monstrosity?" prompting Oedipus's own response: "Even I, who triumphed over the Sphinx, would be slow and stumbling in interpreting my fate [*haerebo fati tardus interpres mei*]" (SenPhW: 134–39).

[52] Fates (or Parcae): the three Roman goddesses of Destiny.

[53] Line 272: Seneca describes the crime as "unheard-of [*ignotum*], brutish [*efferum*], unprecedented [*invisitatum*]" (SenPhW: 264–65).

[54] Line 280: Oedipus's father, Laius, had his son's ankles pierced, so that they could be joined together with a strap. The swollen wound gave Oedipus his name: Oedipus means 'Swollen Foot.'

one day open up my aged father's breast, he whom I was told to kill by the prophetic voice—too true alas!—of the Delphic oracle. At present, I have slaughtered him with this hard-hitting hand, truly hard and cruel. At present, I have conquered the Theban Empire through his death, and the hand that stole away his soul carries the honor of his scepter.

That, however, was not even all, for heaven, wanting to overload me with crimes and piling them up in great heaps, made me (oh great infamy!) the incestuous husband of my mother, his wife. What Scythian, what Sarmatian or what cruel Getan, devoid of all reason, ever committed anything of the sort?[55] I washed my hand in the blood of my father, I polluted with incest my mother's bed, I fathered children in her fertile womb—they are to me both siblings and children.

Now, I have left everything except you, my Antigone. I have left wife, children, and the throne of Thebes—this is the cost of my crime, alas! But today, here my offspring battle for the Theban throne. One brother seeks out the other brother's property—and his life. So much each brother burns with the desire to rule, so much that desire torments them, so much this longing for power forces them to violate all that piety commands.[56]

This misfortune is bound to Agenor's scepter, which must always be won through parricide.[57] Thus my two children rush fiercely like determined strong-clawed lions. Polynices complains that his brother steals his rights and, tricking him, violates his promise. He invokes the support of the great and angry gods against those who broke pacts with them. From exile, he armed for his dispute the Greek cities, the youth of Argos.[58] He wants to defeat his twin who will not return to him the stolen kingdom he desires to possess.[59]

---

[55] Line 295: Scythian, Sarmatian, Getan: inhabitants of Scythia, Sarmatia, and Thrace. In the Renaissance, "Scythian" was a common insult, meaning roughly "Barbarian" or "uneducated foreigner."

[56] Line 308: These lines are central to the play and to its historical and political relationship to the Wars of Religion, in that they introduce the fraternal battle between Eteocles and Polynices. It can be noted that whereas Seneca speaks of broken pledges—"spernitur pacti fides" (the pledges of the pact are disregarded) (SenPhW: 280)—Garnier instead writes of piety (v. 308). Oedipus's presentiment of civil war and what it means for Thebes is a key characteristic of his character in Seneca—it "has no parallel among the human characters in Senecan drama" although might be compared with "the prophecy of Agamemnon's murder (*Agamemnon* 37–52) by the Ghost of Thyestes" even if their function is different (Frank: 152–53). See also notes to line 88, 114, and 338.

[57] Line 310: Garnier translates after Seneca: "No one will bear that scepter without accursed blood [*sine . . . cruore*]" (SenPhW: 277–78).

[58] Line 318: Argos: Greek city in the north-east Peloponnese, the term also refers to the whole of the Peloponnese in opposition to Hellas.

[59] Line 320: Garnier emphasizes the fact that the conflict is between brothers, with references to "mes deux enfans" (my two children) (line 3101), to Polynices who com-

The land of Cadmus is overrun with men-at-arms. Everywhere there are horses, darts, fire, tears, lament, and cries.[60] The laborer takes flight. This whole shore resounds with chaos and noise.[61]

ANTIGONE

Even if, father, you have no other reason to live than to defend Thebes and to deliver it from fratricidal combat, you should not die. Instead, you should extend your life in order to lend Thebes your help. You can calm this fiery war.[62] You alone have power over both armies. From your children's hands you can wrestle the swords that they have drawn to hack each other apart.[63] You can put an end to the furor that burns like poison in their hot breasts. You can chase danger away from your homeland now threatened by foreign soldiers. You can bring peace and, as if binding all of our hearts together with a divine rope, you can bring sacred concord.[64] Live, I pray you, live for us if you no longer wish to live for yourself. Your life is our life. Whoever kills you also kills us.

---

plains of "son frere" (his brother) (line 313), and who now leads an army against "son germain" (his twin) (line 319), whereas Seneca opposes the two brothers with reference to *hic* and *ille* (SenPhW: 281–82). N.B. "Nowhere in [Seneca's *Phoenician Women*] are Eteocles and Polynices identified by name," probably because the audience would have known which was which (Frank: 154).

[60] Line 321: The land of Cadmus: Thebes.

[61] Line 324: Compare this description (lines 321–24) with Ronsard, *RL* 11:41, lines 99–126. See also Balibé 1975: 271. The description of war here can also be compared with Seneca: "No light destruction is coming upon weary Thebes [*fessis. . . Thebis*]: weapons, flames, wounds are imminent, and any evil worse than these" (SenPhW: 285–87). As Frank notes, "the weariness of Thebes is the result of all the trials she has endured: the Sphinx, the plague, the horrifying discovery of Oedipus's true identity, and now, the conflict of Eteocles and Polynices" (Frank: 155). See also Wurnig 1982: 102–03.

[62] Line 329: Garnier speaks of "une guerre enflamee" (a fiery war) (line 329), compared to Seneca who talks of the threat of "impii belli" (unnatural, or impious war) (SenPhW: 290). Again, Garnier sidesteps this opportunity to make connections with the idea of piety. See note to line 88.

[63] Line 332: Garnier multiplies usage of pronominal and reflexive verbs, most frequently (as here) to underscore the fratricidal warfare. See Lebègue 1949. See also lines 355, 543, 555, 577, 1005, 1141, 1204. Compare with note to line 999.

[64] Line 338: Compare Garnier's mention of "une corde" (a rope) (line 337) and of "une sainte concorde" (a holy concord) (line 338) with Seneca's allusion to giving "good faith to the broken treaty [*foederi laeso fidem*]" (SenPhW: 293). See also note to line 308.

OEDIPUS

These damned children respect me?[65] Could they really disarm their hands and keep the faith? Traitors, evil-doers, hungry for carnage, so gifted for cruelty, deceit, and outrage, covetous of empire, they would not know how to do anything worthy of me, their father, nor worthy of my bloodline. They are drowning in evil, their minds offer up nothing save the plotting and planning of awful things. Their minds are animated by fury alone. Fear of the great gods causes no terror in them, they are in awe of nothing. Neither respect for their father, nor love of their country is natural to them.[66] They will murder each other if the gods' goodness does not hold back their furious swords. This is why it is fitting that I wish to die. I remain too long in this world. As I put off my death, I am about to endure worse passions than I suffer already.

ANTIGONE

By your graying hair, that ornament of old age,[67] by your gentle hand that trembles from weakness, by these dear knees that I hold close and kiss, I pray you: wipe out this deadly thought from your afflicted soul and leave behind this desire for death, where too cruel destiny beckons you. Live here as long as Nature will allow, then welcome death when it offers itself to you.[68] It arrives early enough and never brings with it a second life into the human breast.

OEDIPUS

My daughter, stand up, you benumb my heart. Your noble wish wins out over mine. Calm your pain, you my dear life, calm your sadness and distress that my sorrow causes you. These crying moans that you send into the air race through my bones and drive me out of my mind. I will live, my sweet dear, in order to please you and I will drag my body across this solitary mount for as long as you please. Nothing can torment me if it is you who wish it—I have no other will. I will cross the waves of the Aegean Sea, I will bury my head in Mount Etna's flames, if this you so desire. And from atop a cliff, touching the sky with my hands, I will without fright throw myself down into the depths. Should you so desire, I will make myself the food of a ravishing lion, of a gluttonous she-wolf. I will live, I will die, in accordance with what you want. Your will alone will direct me.[69]

---

[65] Line 343: Garnier follows Seneca, SenPhW: 295 et seq.

[66] Line 355: Seneca's Oedipus does not place any hope in the gods (Lebègue: 276). See also note to line 332.

[67] Line 361: These verses (lines 361–70) are of Garnier's own invention, inserted between SenPhW: 307 and 308.

[68] Line 367: Antigone will also counsel her mother against suicide (see line 1300).

[69] Line 388: Oedipus's reference to following Antigone's *volonté* (will) is key to the play's Christianization of the classical sources, rendering Seneca's triple mention of

ANTIGONE

Live, then, and in peace. [390] Allow not past sorrows to trouble your thoughts.

OEDIPUS

I want to remain in this hollow cave,[70] in these sad, remote, and horrifying mountains, surrounded by bushes and where the fine crystal water of a wave-busy stream wanders in its eternal path.[71] Here, [395] sat in an outcrop, supporting myself on my elbow, I will entertain my afflicted spirit with the hope that friendly death will shortly come to take me and lead my soul down towards Erebus.[72] And you, my consolation, [400] will bring me what I need.[73] Now, return

Oedipus acting "iubente te" (at your [i.e. Antigone's] bidding) (SenPhW: 314, 318, 319), Lat. *iubens* referring to "commanding" and "ordering." On Oedipus's sudden change of heart, a common feature in Senecan drama, see Frank: 159. More generally, on Garnier's changes to Seneca's text, see Lebègue: 275, note to lines 1–388: Lebègue emphasizes how the changes "ont un caractère moral et religieux: il met en lumière l'amour réciproque d'Oedipe et d'Antigone [. . .] et place la culpabilité non dans le fait, mais dans la volonté de mal faire" (have a moral and religious quality: Garnier underscores the reciprocal nature of the love between Oedipus and Antigone [. . .] and places guilt not in what occurs, but in the will to do wrong).

[70] Line 391: Garnier departs somewhat from Seneca, with no mention of a messanger (*nuntius*) and Oedipus's many lines (SenPhW: 328–47; 350–62) condensed (lines 391–402). The changes mean that Garnier's first act ends in a somewhat different way to the first part of Seneca's play. Whereas Garnier's Oedipus calls out for Antigone to visit Jocasta, such that the latter might put an end to war, Seneca's Oedipus is seemingly much more angry, even if he makes a similar call: "Do you see an old man [*senem*] given to temperate thoughts? Is it a lover of peace and calm [*placidaeque amantem pacis*] you call to take your side? My spirit is swelling with anger, my pain is burning beyond measure, and I want some outcome greater than the random efforts of young men's madness. A war that is just a civil war is insufficient [*non satis est adhuc / civile bellum*]: let brother rush upon brother [*frater in fratrem ruat*]. Nor is that enough. As must happen so there can be an outrage after my style, one appropriate to my marriage bed, let your mother have your weapons! [*date arma matri*!]" (SenPhW: 350–58). The expression "frater in fratrem ruat" is the clause "described as the curse of Oedipus upon his sons by almost all commentators," although "Oedipus's 'curse' is no more than an exhortation for his sons to commit what is, in his eyes, the most impious crime imaginable" (Frank: 173). As Frank also notes, the clause is "the conclusion of Oedipus's twisted desire for his sons to act in accordance with their impious birth" (Frank: 174).

[71] Line 394: Lebègue finds "ce décor [. . .] moins romantique que celui qu'avait brossé l'Antigone de Sénèque" (a scene [. . .] less romantic than the one sketched by Seneca's Antigone) (Lebègue: 276).

[72] Line 398: Erebus: personification of the infernal Shades.

[73] Line 400: Oedipus's resignation here contrasts with his frenetic wishes in SenPhW: 328–47 (Lebègue: 276).

to your mother and if you are able to, have her calm the damned quarrel of her sons.[74]

THE THEBAN CHORUS

Oh Father whom by various names[75]
Are invoked throughout the universe[76]—
The Nomian one, Evoe, Hagnos,
Bassareus, the Thessalian—you who are
Always decorated with green vines;[77]

You who were born of thunder
And who lived in the thigh
Of Jupiter, who carried you
Until you were born in Nysa,[78]
Which, afterwards, you conquered;

---

[74] Line 402: These verses announce and justify Antigone's presence in the second act (Lebègue: 276).

[75] Line 403: There are no choral odes in Seneca's *Phoenician Women*. Indeed, this absence is an exceptional characteristic, especially given that the tragedy's title seemingly refers to a chorus, whose function would likely be similar to that in other Senecan tragedies (see SenTBL: 117). As Beaudin has noted (187–88), Garnier's ode has several sources, in choral odes from Seneca's *Oedipus* (lines 403–508) and in Sophocles's *Antigone* (lines 1115–52), as well as in Horace's *Odes* (2:19), the third book of Ovid's *Metamorphoses*, Ronsard's *Hymn de Bacchus*, etc.

[76] Line 404: In MFr. this choral ode consists of thirteen five-lined stanzas of octosyllabic verse—which stands out against the alexandrines used in the main body of the play. To appreciate what the octosyllable might have evoked to Renaissance readers, it can be recalled: (1) that this line form was first employed in France in the tenth-century hagiographic *Vie de Saint Léger* (Life of Saint Leodegarius); and (2) that, while it would later suggest light verse, in the sixteenth century the octosyllable was generally the meter of the ode, largely thanks to Ronsard and others (See PEP: 970). *Les Quatre Premiers Livres des Odes* (*First Four Books of Odes*) (1550) was indeed Ronsard's first major publication. On Ronsard's odes and for an introduction to the genre in Renaissance France in general, see RP 1:1472–77.

[77] Line 405: These epithets all relate to Bacchus-Dionysos. A similar listing of names is used by Ronsard in *Franciade* (3:1472) and in his "Hymne de Bacchus" (RP: 2:596, line 83).

[78] Line 412: Dionysos was raised in the mountains of Nysa, the home of the Hyades (rain nymphs). This is also evoked by Ronsard in his "Hymne de Bacchus:" "ton pere marry / A Nyse t'envoya pour y estre nourry" (Your saddened father / Sent you to Nysa so that you could be raised there) (RP: 2:595, lines 23–24).

You who cause to ring out
With the sound of your Maenads[79]
The shady hilltops of double-faced
Mount Parnassus, of Mount Cithaeron,
And surrounding peaks

When with naked satyrs—who have
Goats' feet and heads with horns, who
Dance in many lustful leaps—
You celebrate to the sound of drums
Your great unknown mysteries.

When the rebellious Giants[80]
Climbed up to the Phlegrean Fields,[81]
To challenge the heavens, with great violence
You killed Gyges and Mimas, using
The furnaces of Mount Etna;[82]

[79] Lines 414: Maenads: the female followers of Dionysos.

[80] Line 423: Lines 423–47 are imitated after Horace's *Odes* (2:19) (Lebègue: 276), an "Ode to Bacchus." In particular, Garnier draws on Horace's account of the revolt of the giants against the Olympian gods, described as follows: "When an impious cohort of giants attacked / your father's palace on high, you assumed the fangs and horrible jaws / of a lion and Rhoetus retreated" (lines 21–24) (HO: 2.19). The episode is also evoked by Ronsard in his "Hymne de Bacchus": ". . .quand tu vis la race / Des Geans qui gaignoyent par armes au Ciel place, / Les Dieux tournant le dos, valeureux tu t'armas / Des dents d'un grand Lion, en qui tu te formas, / Et d'un coup de machoire au milieu de la guerre / Tu culbutas du ciel Mime et Gyge par terre, / Et sur le haut d'Olympe en trofée tu mis / Les corselets sanglans de ces deux ennemis" (when you saw that race / Of the giants warring with weapons to enter the heavens, / Turning their backs to the gods, you courageously armed yourself / With the teeth of a great lion, whose form you took on, / And with a bite of the jaw in the midst of the war / You threw Mimas and Gyges from heaven, to the earth, / And upon the Olympian heights you raised as a triumph / The bloody bodies of your two enemies) (PR: 2.598, lines 157–64). Cotgrave translates MFr. *corselet* as Eng. "A verie little bodie." On Horace's rehabilitation of Dionysos, see Baltinski 1991.

[81] Line 424: The Phelegrean Fields (or Campi Flegreia), meaning the "Burning Fields," are an area near Naples, Italy, where volcanic activity gave rise to a caldera (a collapse of land following an eruption).

[82] Line 426: Gyges: one of the Hecatoncheires, he took part in the revolt against the Olympians. Mimas: another giant who fought against the gods. The punishment alluded to here is how Hephaistos killed Mimas by Hephaistos who launched molten iron at him. (Mimas is also evoked in Seneca's *Hercules Furens*, 976 et seq.).

You took vengeance, courageous one,
On the raging King of Thrace.[83]
Agave and the Edonian chorus[84]
Punished Pentheus,[85] that mocking one,
Who insulted your great name.[86]

Fearless, you descend to Hell,
The tigers fawn upon you,
The noisy rivers bend to your will,
You cross over the barbarous seas—
Their waves obey you.

Your famous name has spread
To the Ganges and the churning River Aras,[87]
And your vine-clad army[88]
Penetrated victoriously as far as
Those nations that possess fine jewels.

Listen,[89] father, oh good Denys,[90]
Bring together the disunited hearts

[83] Line 429: Allusion to Dionysos's vengeance against King Lycurgus (king of the Edonians of Thrace): when the latter expelled Dionysos from his kingdom, the god responded by making him insane—in that insanity, he killed his wife and sons. According to Homer (*Iliad* 6:136–37), "against Lycurgus, the gods that live at ease wax wroth, and the son of Cronos made him blind; and he lived not for long, seeing that he was hated by all of the immortal gods." The story was also told in a lost play by Aeschylus, called the *Edonians*, known by fragments.

[84] Line 430: Agave: daughter of Cadmus and Harmonia. Edonian: of the Edoni, a Thracian people in southern Thrace.

[85] Line 431: Pentheus: the son of Agave, daughter of Cadmus.

[86] Line 432: In spite of the warnings of Tiresias, Pentheus refuses the worship of Dionysos and locks him up, but Dionysos frees himself and tricks Pentheus, who ends up being killed by his mother Agave. See Euripides's *The Bacchae*.

[87] Line 439: River Aras: one of the longest rivers of the Caucasus.

[88] Line 440: Eng. *army* renders MFr. *exercite*, a Latinism (from Lat. *exercitus*).

[89] Line 443: At this point, the chorus switches from praising Dionysos and his past exploits to calling upon him to rescue Thebes, a movement modeled on Sophocles's chorus in *Antigone*. There, Thebes and its inhabitants are there said to be struck by a plague (Gk. *νόσος*): "Thou see'est with what a plague our townsfolk sicken" (SophAnt: 1041), "the city, with all its folks, / is gripped by a violent plague" (SophAntDG: 1140–41).

[90] Line 443: Garnier uses MFr. *Denys* to refer to Dionysos—it is a French form of the Gk. name also used by Ronsard in his "Hymne de Bacchus", in particular in the part of the hymn that deals with Dionysos's presence in France: "lors que tu courois vagabond

Of these brothers in discord.
Banish all calamities from
Our Boeotian shores.

Guard the City of Thebes[91]
From civil strife.
Your mother conceived you in Thebes
And your father, too,
First received you there.[92]

Here, the Thyiades,[93] crying out,
Walk in the evening through the grass,
Their Nysean thyrses dressed up
In curls of vine branches,
Leaping about with disheveled hair.

Come, come, Evach,[94] Agyeu,[95]
Come oh god that protects us,
We call on you, we pray you,
We who are afflicted, we call out to you:
Chase off all sorrow from this place.

---

par le monde / Tu vins camper ton ost au bord gauche de l'onde / De mon Loir, qui pour lors de ses coutaux voisins / Ne voyoit remirer en ses eaux les raisins" (as you were wandering through the world / You install your army on the left bank of the waters / Of my River Loir, which at that time, of the neighboring hills / It did not see the grapes reflected in its waters) (PR: 2.598, lines 169–72).

[91] Line 448: The specific call (MFr. "*Garde* la Thebaine cité," Eng. "*Guard* the City of Thebes," italics mine) echoes the one in Sophocles. There, the chorus calls out: "*μολεῖν καθαϱσίῳ ποδὶ*"—a line that Llyod-Jones does not render very literally; David Greene renders it (accurately) as "Come with healing foot" (SophAntDG: 1142). The key word here is, of course, Gk. *καθαϱσίῳ*, which means "cleansing, from guilt, purifying" (LSJ).

[92] Line 452: Allusion to Dionysos's birth. He was born to a mortal woman, Semele, and to Zeus. Taunted by Zeus's wife Hera, Semele wanted Zeus to prove his godhood—when he descended (blazing because of bolts of lightening), this killed Semele, for no mortal could behold an undisguished god. Zeus saved the unborn Dionysos and sewed him into his thigh.

[93] Line 453: Thyiades: women who celebrated the orgies of Dionysos.

[94] Line 458: Eng. *Evach* renders MFr. *Evach*

[95] Line 458: Eng./MFr. *Agyeu* is borrowed from the Gk. *ἀγυιεύς*, meaning "guardian of the streets and highways" (LSJ). In Euripides's *Phoenician Women*, Polynices uses the term to refer to Apollo (SophPhW: 631).

If we receive, oh lord,
From you this desired happiness,
As the sky turns about and
As the sea ebbs and flows,
We will sing in your honor.[96]

[96] Line 467: This choral ode, as a whole, thus announces a certain hope that Dionysos will return to Thebes and restore order by bringing an end to civil strife, in particular to the conflict between Polynices and Eteocles.

Act II

Jocasta, Messenger, Antigone.

JOCASTA

Sun, you who shine your light on the earth and the vaulted heavens as you gallop around the wide sphere of the sky[1], cast down your sights in pity and, observing this great expanse, observe the disastrous plight of our poor race. See how, after so many troubles, one after the other, we are threatened now by the gravest of dangers: Thebes is falling into ruin and furious Greek troops now arrive to beat down our seven gates. My children, fired up by a raging and cruel desire to occupy the ambushed kingdom of their old father, strive in opposing camps to steal from each other the hereditary scepter.[2]

Bassarid Agave, with her sacred thyrsus, mortally attacked impious Pentheus, Pentheus her child.[3] With his wet blood, cruel Agave bathed the Edonian chorus—but the bloody crime of her heart, maddened by the Bacchic fury, went no further.[4] As for me, not only have I been wicked, but I gave birth to

---

[1] Line 468: Garnier begins the second act by imitating not Seneca's, but Euripides's *Phoenician Women*. Compare with EurPhW: 1–6.

[2] Line 479: Garnier uses the pronominal verb *s'entredespouiller* (literally: *to despoil one another*). See note to line 332.

[3] Line 480: Garnier, here, returns to Seneca: "Lucky Agave! [*Felix Agave!*] She carried that horrific deed in the hand that had committed it, a bloodstained maenad bearing spoils of her dismembered son. . ." (SenPhW: 364 et seq.). Of these lines, Frank notes: "The exclamation [. . .] instantly establishes Jocasta's misery, since any woman who could describe as 'fortunate' a mother who unknowingly dismembered her own son must be truly wretched. The reference to the crime of Agave creates a link between Jocasta and Oedipus [. . .] since not only do they both mention it in their respective opening speeches, but, more strikingly, they both envy the crime: Oedipus wishes that his mother had killed him as Agave killed her son, and Jocasta envies Agave, whose guilt she considers to be light by comparison with her own" (Frank: 177).

[4] Line 481: Bassarid: name of the Thracian Bacchants. The name means "those who wear fox skins." Edonian: here, also refers to the Thracian Bacchants.

these wicked ones about whom I lament.[5] I gave birth to them so that they would be the bright light of this great city that is about to die.

MESSENGER

Oh race of agèd Creon, bring help, I pray you. Bring prompt help to this, our shared land. Hurry, hasten, fight back the firebrands that are ready to be launched at the roofs of our houses. The enemy arrives and this long plain is brimming with soldiers led by Polynices who makes this vehement demand: that the agreement about the Theban scepter be respected. He has thrown all of Greece into battle. Seven different squadrons surround the walls ready for battle. Help! Defend our walls from your children at arms, each against the other.

ANTIGONE

Come on, Mother, come on[6]—surely your maternal tears will cause the weapons to fall from their warring hands. You can reconcile them in solid love and have them rule the kingdom each in turn.[7]

JOCASTA

Alas, I do not know what to do! Polynices rightly complains that Eteocles chased him away to wield alone the ancient scepter even though he himself has equal claim to it. Still, banished from his native land, he has already for three harvests wandered from town to town, wretched and sorrowful, before Adrastus made him his son-in-law.[8] He appealed to the armies of neighboring kings with which he now engulfs the Cadmean countryside, in order to recover from the hands of Eteocles the honor of being the legitimate lord of our cities.[9] He is

---

[5] Line 487: Jocasta will play a central role in the play, being a strong (maternal) voice for peace. Here, she asserts her maternity—she is mother to Polynices and Eteocles, but also to the war that they fight. Compare with Seneca: "That I am guilty [*quod sum nocens*] is a trivial thing: I have made others guilty [*feci nocentes*]" (SenPhW: 367–68). She continues: "Even this too is trivial: I have born sons who are guilty [*peperi nocentes*]" (SenPhW: 368–69). On this expression (*peperi nocentes*) in Seneca, see Frank: 179.

[6] Line 502: Here, Eng. *Mother* renders Fr. *Madame*. See other examples of this, e.g. line 1242.

[7] Line 505: Antigone's statement that motherly lamentation will bring peace is not translated directly from Seneca, although it is close in sentiment to SenPhW: 403–06.

[8] Line 513: Adrastus: A Greek king, the leader of the Seven against Thebes. When Polynices arrived in Argos, he bickered with Tydeus, awakening Adrastus who was reminded of the oracle according to which he was to marry his daughters to a lion and a wild boar. Polynices thus married Adrastrus's daughter Argia and Tydeus married his other daughter Deipyle.

[9] Line 515: Cadmus: legendary founder of Thebes, chased after his sister Europa who had been abducted by a white bull.

right to want what the law justly grants him and he should indeed strive to obtain it—but he must do it the correct way.[10]

To whom do I offer my support? Alas. . . To which of the two do I lend my favor, being the mother of both? I cannot please one without displeasing the other; I cannot do well by one without undoing the other, nor can I wish success on one without wishing failure for the other.[11]

Both of them are my children, but even though I love them with equal affection, like my very soul, I nevertheless feel more inclined towards the one whose cause is best and who has the most troubles. *We tend to pity the wretched and are thus won over to their cause.*[12]

MESSENGER

As you spend your time lamenting, a flurry of flags approaches the city. And dense battalions bristle on the plain like wavering ears of wheat, which grow golden yellow in the fields.[13] The soldiers glisten because of their ironclad backs; their brows, which grow pale underneath the armor, are wrinkled by anger; their eyes shine like lightening produced by the quarrels of stars.

Already the trumpet sounds out an awful burst. Already the proud squadrons encourage each other as they march in formation through the dusty plain, ready to clash against each other in angry ardor.[14] See how the captains, long spear in hand, advance first, far ahead of their battalions, maddened

---

[10] Line 519: The previous lines recapitulate SenPhW: 370–79.

[11] Line 525: These verses (lines 520–25) find their model in Seneca: "I do not know what I should hope for or decide. [. . .] As a parent, what prayers should I make? On each side I see a son. I can do nothing loyally [*pie*] without destroying my loyalty [*pietate*]; any hopes I have for one son will harm the other if realized" (SenPhW: 380–82). See note to line 88.

[12] Line 531: Here, Jocasta expresses love for both sons, but nevertheless has more support for Polynices who has been wronged (line 529), a support grounded in a general principle according to which one feels more pity (Fr. *pitié*) for those who are in a difficult situation (lines 530–31). Compare to Seneca: "thought I love each [son] with equal affection, my spirit inclines where it is pulled by the better cause [*causa melior*] and the worse situation [*deterior sors*], for it always favors the weak [*semper infirmo favens*]; misfortune brings the wretched closer to their loved ones" (SenPhW: 383–86). Note that Seneca "presents Jocasta's predicament as a mini-*suasoria*: a mother is torn between her two sons, one of whom has been wronged by his brother and is now preparing to commit the impiety of attacking his own city, and the other of whom stands as the defender of his city but is responsible for the violence which threatens it" (Frank: 177). On the idea of the *causa melior*, a "common expression in the context of civil war," see Frank: 183.

[13] Line 535: Possible reminiscence of Du Bellay's *Antiquitez*: "Les ondoyans cheveux du sillon blondissant" (s. 30). (Lebègue: 277).

[14] Line 543: Garnier uses the pronominal verb *s'entrechoquer* (literally: *to knock into/ shock each other*). See note to line 332.

and ready to fight and to win glory by risking their blood in dangerous battle, for a chance at victory.[15] Onwards! Move on! It is time! Hurry up! You will soon see them locked together in battle.

ANTIGONE

Go on, Mother, and with no fear for their weapons, approach them before they reach each other. Make their shields and lances fall from their hands. Knock from their sides their murderous daggers that thirst for their blood. And if a gluttonous thirst to murder each other[16] hounds them so strongly that respect gives in to disdain, their obstinate hearts overwhelmed by anger too great, then let us plant ourselves in the midst of the opposed armies, let our breasts take on their bloody lances,[17] let us pacify this war wherever the first blows of these angry brothers fall amongst us.[18]

JOCASTA

I am off, quickly I go, and ready to confront their knives and to offer up my head, to offer up my breast, so that whichever of them murders his brother can murder another, too.[19]

If they have any goodness in them, my imploring tears should move them to put down their weapons. But if they lack goodness, they will have to begin their slaughter with me, to rush at me.[20]

---

[15] Line 547: Garnier's messenger speaks the words of Seneca's *setelles* (attendant), SenPhW: 387–400. (See Frank: 183). Garnier focuses more attention on the fratricidal nature of the conflict, whereas Seneca mentions the "seven kings [*septena reges*]" (SenPhW: 391). Garnier does not reproduce the attendant's final lines: "Go, restore love to the brothers and peace to all: check this unnatural warfare [*impia arma*] by interposing as a mother [*matris*]" (SenPhW: 402).

[16] Line 555: Garnier uses the pronominal verb *s'entre-homicider*. See note to line 332.

[17] Line 559: As Lebègue notes, "L'Antigone de Sénèque invite sa mère à recevoir les premiers coups, mais ne s'offre pas au danger" (Seneca's Antigone invites her mother to receive the first blows, but does not offer herself up to danger) (Lebègue: 277). Federici notes: "On la dirait dévorée par une frénésie de martyre qui la conduira au suicide" (She is as if devored by a frenzy for martyrdom that will lead her to suicide) (Federici 1975: 69).

[18] Line 561: Antigone's words are briefer in Garnier than in Seneca (SenPhW: 403–06). Another key difference is that whereas Garnier's Antigone speaks in the first person plural—"Appaisons cette guerre. . ." (let us pacify this war) (line 560)—Seneca's only ever encourages her mother: "Either break up the fighting [*solve bellum*], mother [*mater*], or be first to suffer it" (SenPhW: 406). See also notes to lines 991 and 1087.

[19] Line 565: Compare Garnier's line ". . .que celuy d'eux / Qui meurtrira son frère, en puisse meurtrir deux" (lines 564–65) and Seneca's: "The one who wants to attack his brother [*fratrem*] must attack his mother [*matrem*] first" (SenPhW: 408–09).

[20] Line 569: Seneca again marshals a vocabulary focused on piety: "He who must be loyal [*qui fuerit pius*] must lay down arms at his arms at his mother's request; he who

ANTIGONE

The flags are raised in the wind above the troops, the enemy squadrons rush at our own, the curved vault of the air resonates from the shaking of so many legions fired up for combat.[21] Call upon your gentle prayers to soften the violence of their warring hands. They march heavily—you will have reached them before they confront each other and begin to fight.[22]

JOCASTA

The troops advance slowly, but the two captains rush to meet each other.[23]

What whirlwind will carry me through the air? What Stymphalian bird will carry my body in flight?[24] What Sphinx or what hungry-throated Harpie will plummet down amidst the two armies,[25] carrying me upon its back, so that I might arrive there in time and beseech my proud children with prayers?[26]

MESSENGER

She rushes off, crazed, as a Maenad rushes about on Mount Cithaeron, her mind sickened[27]—or like an arrow shot by a Scythian, or like a boat chased along by the North wind's fancy, or like one sees a shining star gliding, rushing through the evening sky.

May the gods forbid that our princes, moved by her powerful voice, soil their impetuous blades that plot for brotherly death. Instead may they embrace each other and break up this quarrel.[28]

---

is disloyal [*qui non est pius*] must begin with me" (SenPhW: 409–11). Garnier, instead, speaks of *bonté* (goodness). See note to line 88.

[21] Line 570: In these verses, Garnier follows Seneca (SenPhW: 414–18), but he suppresses the word *mater* (SenPhW: 416).

[22] Line 577: Garnier here uses the verb Fr. *entre-affrontez*, to the same effect as his numerous pronominal verbs. See note to line 332.

[23] Line 579: These two lines (578–79), spoken by Jocasta, are spoken by the *satelles* in Seneca (SenPhW: 419).

[24] Line 581: Stymphalus: a district in Arcadia haunted by odious birds of prey. It was Hercules's sixth labor to destroy them.

[25] Line 582: Sphinx: a monster in Thebes, with the head of a woman and the winged body of a lion. Oedipus solved its riddle. Harpies: winged demons whose name in Greek means "The Snatchers" and who carry off children and souls in their claws.

[26] Line 585: Jocasta's words correspond to SenPhW: 420–26.

[27] Line 586: Seneca says that Jocasta heads off "like a madwoman [*furenti similis*]" (SenPhW: 427), such that Garnier's direct reference to her acting "ainsi qu'une Menade" (as a Maenad) (line 586) is striking, perhaps linking back to the earlier mention of Agave. See line 480.

[28] Line 595: Whereas Garnier has the messenger express a prayer ("Permettent les bons dieux. . ." [May the gods allow. . .]), Seneca already describes Jocasta's success in bringing about peace: "Conquered by a mother's prayer [*victa maternal prece*], the warfare

CHORUS

Burning ambition causes
Us so much suffering![29]
How much misfortune it brings us!
If nurturing peace does not descend
Upon our dying people,
We will see Thebes reduced to ashes.

This misfortune hounds us still;[30]
Bound to us, its oppression
Of the Labdacids has never stopped
Since our ancestors,
Leaving the Tyrian fields,
Drank of the Castalian waters;[31]

Nor since Cadmus chased
The counterfeit bull that carried off
On its sweet back
Lovely Europa, his sister;
Nor since that deceitful abductor
Took her to Europe. [32]

---

was halted. [. . .] Peace wins the day [*paci favetur*]. The mother [*mater*] displays and tears her white hair, begs as they shake their heads, drenches her cheeks with tears" (SenPhW: 434–41).

[29] Line 596: This choral ode is not in Seneca. As Beaudin notes, it is based primarily on Seneca's *Oedipus* (lines 715–43)—although it differs from it significantly. Unlike the previous choral ode, the verses here are heptasyllabic. The heptasyllable, one form of French *vers impair* (odd-numbered meter), was used by Ronsard in some of his odes, in imitation of Pindar. See PEP: 618 and Nello 1968.

[30] Line 602: In *Oedipus*, Seneca has the chorus talk of how "the ancient wrath [*veteres irae*] of the gods [. . .] follows us [*secuntur*]" (SenOed: 711–12). See also SophAnt: 594–97: "Of the Labdacides I see descending / Woe upon woe; from days of old some god / Laid on the race a malison, and his rod / Scourges each age with sorrows never ending."

[31] Line 607: Compare with Seneca's *Oedipus*: "Castala's grove lent its shade to the Sidonian wanderer [*Sidonio. . . hospiti*] [Oedipus]" (SenOed: 712–13).

[32] Line 613: Labdacids: descendents of Labdacus, the son of Polydorus and a king of Thebes. Among his descendants was Laius, father of Oedipus. Castalia: the spring on Mount Parnassus. Cadmus: son of Agenor, chased after his sister Europa, whom Zeus had abducted by disguising himself as a white bull. He carried her to Gortyna. At a certain point, Cadmus realized his pursuit was in vain and fled to Thrace. Seneca evokes this story as follows: ". . .great Agenor's son [Cadmus], weary with tracking Joyce's thefts [i.e. Europa] over all the world, in fear halted beneath our trees, worshipping his sister's ravisher; and, by the advice of Phoebus, bidden to follow a straying heifer which had

Nor since, tired from having crossed
As far as watery Dirce[33]
(Having neither recovered the virgin
Not caught her bellowing abductor[34])
He made his new residence
At the foot of Mount Cithaeron.

He built our city and gave
Frontiers to the land, in
Boeotia, named after the Ox.[35]
Ever since that time,
Misfortune has been rife there
And now it fills the land.

Ever since, cruel monsters
Are born there continuously.
On Cephissus's glistening[36]
Banks a proud snake
With a thousand coils crawls along
And poisons the land. [37]

Higher than the old oaks
The serpent raised in anger
Its long and hissing head,
The rest of his body remaining

---

never bent beneath the plough or the slow wain's curving yoke, he gave over his quest and named a nation [Boetia] from that ill-omened [*inauspicata*] heifer" (SenOed: 715–24).

[33] Line 615: Dirce: a spring in Boeotia, situated at the place where Dirce died. Dirce's story is recounted in Euripides's *Antiope*. On reconstructing the *Antiope* (dated circa 408), see Schaal 1914, Kambitsis 1972, as well as Wecklein 1923.

[34] Line 618: The "bellowing abductor" (Fr. "mugissant larron") is the bull. Cotgrave renders MFr. *mugir* as "To low, or bellow, like an Ox, &c."

[35] Line 622: Cadmus founded Thebes in Boeotia, at the site to which the cow led him. Garnier here alludes to the (probably spurious) etymology according to which Boeotia (Gk. *Βοιωτία*) derives from Gk. *βοῦς*, meaning "ox." On this and other etymologies for Boeotia, see Buck 1979: 75.

[36] Line 629: Cephissus: a river that flows through the Athenian plain.

[37] Line 631: Compare with Seneca's *Oedipus*: "From that time on, our land has e'er produced strange monsters [*nova monstra*]: either a serpent, rising from the valley's depths, hisses on high above the ancient oaks and overtops the pines; ever higher, above the Chaonian trees he lifts his dark-blue head, although his greater part still lies upon the ground" (SenOed: 725–30).

Twisted up in many and many a knot
On the withering grass.

In the fields, sown with its teeth,[38]
Then sprung up crops of men.
As soon as they were born,
Already men at arms
And organized into battalions,
They killed each other with their weapons.[39]

They lasted but one day
Alive upon the earth.
The morning was their youth,
Midday their maturity, and
The evening's brown darkness
Was their last old age.[40]

From his disaster,
Actaeon grew horns.[41]
We saw in the monstrous form
Of the Sphinx our misfortune:

---

[38] Line 626: Allusion to the dragon killed by Cadmus and whose teeth, on the advice of Athena, he sewed in the earth. These teeth grew and gave birth to men who, as armies, immediately fought each other. (Cadmus killed the dragon, guardian of the well of Ares, because the dragon had slain men sent by Cadmus to fetch water for a sacrifice). As Beaudin also notes, the similarity between the story of civil strife and the present story of Eteocles and Polynices is obvious.

[39] Line 637: Compare with Seneca's *Oedipus*: ". . .the earth, teeming with impious birth [*impio partu*], brings forth armed men [*arma*]: loud resounded the battle-call from the curving horn, and the brazen trumpet sent forth its piercing notes. Their tongues and lips, ne'er nimble before, were first employed in the battle-cry of their unfamiliar voice" (SenOed: 731–37).

[40] Line 649: Compare with Seneca's *Oedipus*: "The kindred bands [*agmina. . . cognata*] filled the plains, and this offspring, worthy the seed that had been sown, measured their life by a single day; born after the passing of the Morning Star, they perished ere Herperus arose" (SenOed: 738–42).

[41] Line 650: Actaeon: a famous Theban, remembered as a hunter transformed into a hunted deer by Diana upon whom he stumbled during her bathing. See Callimachus, *Hymn* 5.

Oedipus's brutal incest
And that atrocious parricide.[42]

Jocasta, Polynices.

JOCASTA

Turn your eyes towards me, noble warriors.[43] Point your spears and your murderous swords at me, thrust them into my breast—into this guilty chest that carried the mutinous seed of these damned battles.[44] Unleash the violent assault of your strong hands on this mortal body.

Either you who arrive from the shores of Argos, or else you who come down from Agenor's fort, foreigners, citizens, whoever: strike me down who gave birth to these divided brothers,[45] who conceived them with my own son, their brother, who still dripped with the blood of his father's murder.[46] Rip my body apart, tear off my limbs, and with my warm blood quench your thirst.

Do you hesitate? Do you delay? Why, my progeny, do you wish to half-violate nature? Why do you not plunge your weapons into me,[47] if you are not horrified at sullying them in the blood of another drawn from that same womb, in the blood of my entrails, which you do as you massacre each other at the foot of these walls? Put your weapons down, abandon them—or else without fear dip them in your mother's blood.[48] May your hand not be held back by

---

[42] Line 655: Lebègue suggests that this choral ode serves the purpose of allowing Jocasta to cross, without being seen by the audience, from one side of the stage to the other, i.e. to situate herself between her battling sons (Lebègue: 277).

[43] Line 656: Eteocles is not mentioned here, but it is possbile that he is supposed to be present as a non-speaking actor at this point. (See Pinvert: 2.445).

[44] Line 660: Compare SenPhW: 449–50.

[45] Line 665: Compare with what Sabine says in Corneille's *Horace* (I,1)—Sabine is split between her husband and her brother, just as here Jocasta is seemingly split between her two sons. (See Pinvert: 2.445)

[46] Line 667: Corneille will take up this line ("Encore degoutant du meurtre de son pere" [still dripping from the murder of my father]) in *Cinna* (I, 3).

[47] Line 672: Eng. *me* here renders MFr. *flanc*, which here (and further on) connotes the maternal womb. See line 778.

[48] Line 677: Again, Seneca speaks in terms of piety—"Give your mother [*matri*] your right hands, give them while they are loyal [*piae*]" (SenPhW: 450–51); "Your choice is in your hands: if you decide on sacrosanct loyalty [*sancta si pietas placet*]" (SenPhW: 455). See note to line 88. Note also that, again, Garnier removes any suggestion in these lines of Oedipus's legal innocence: "Previously it was an error that made us guilty without our intent, the blame was entirely that of Fortune transgressing against us" (SenPhW: 451–54). See note to line 212.

respect, I offer up my throat and my naked breast.[49] [680] I stand between the both of you. Whom must I first call towards peace with my crying voice? To which of you should I call out? Whom shall I, a shared mother, welcome with a sacred accolade? I answer: to you who have wandered for so long, [685] separated from the embrace of your family.[50] Approach, my child, may your tensed hand re-house that odious sword in its sheath.[51] Cast your club far off into the land. Take off this great shield that protects your chest.[52] [690] Unstrap this helmet, which, with its tall crest that terrifies me, weighs down on your head. Reveal your face. And, why do you hesitate? Why do you shoot your burning gaze again and again upon your twin brother? Do you fear he will move and that, [695] as he embraces you, he will treacherously kill you? No, no. Fear not. Do not be afraid of him. I will protect you from his deceitful sword by making a shield with my body—he will first have to puncture that before that inhuman man can pierce and reach your own.

[700] What else do you fear? Do you doubt my faith? Do you, alas, not trust me? Me, I who am your mother.[53]

POLYNICES

After such faith-breaking as my brother's, I am no longer sure of anything.

---

[49] Line 679: Federici notes: "la Jocaste de Garnier amplifie l'horreur de la situation par tous les moyens que la rhétorique lui offre, brodant sur le thème du matricide qu'elle répète à un rythme accéléré jusqu'à la fin" (Garnier's Jocasta amplifies the horror of the situation by all available rhetorical means, elaborating on the theme of matricide that she repeats, at an accelerated rhythm until the play's end) (Federici 1975: 70).

[50] Line 684: Jocasta, then, first addresses Polynices.

[51] Line 687: The sword that Garnier calls "odieuse" (odious) (line 687) Seneca calls "impium / ensem" (SenPhW: 467–68)—again, Seneca continues to weave together ideas of that which is *pius* and that which is *impius*. See note to line 88.

[52] Line 689: In Seneca, Jocasta calls for the shield to be put down so that mother and son can embrace—"Your shield prevents your mother's breast from uniting with your breast; set it aside too" (SenPhW: 469–70). The emphasis in Garnier is quite different—there is still a call for the shield to be put down, but no mention of the fact that this would allow a mother-son embrace.

[53] Line 703: Seneca is more severe than Garnier, saying outright his distrust of his mother: ". . .the laws of nature [*iura natura*] have no power any longer. After this example of brothers, I must not trust even my mother" (SenPhW: 478–80). Lebègue also notes this difference, stating that "Garnier atténue la dureté de la réponse de Polynice" (Garnier softens the harshness of Polynices's response) (Lebègue: 278).

JOCASTA

Take the broad cutlass from its sheath,[54] put the rondache[55] back on your arm, buckle your helmet, do not stand there defenseless against your armed brother, do not let yourself be surprised.

It is you who must put down your weapons first, you who are the only cause of mistrust. Put them down, I pray you[56] and allow me a little space so that I can embrace Polynices in peace after his long exile—it is my first chance to welcome him and, alas, I fear also my last.

Disarm, children. Is it fitting to remain armed before your mother here present? To offend her eyes with glistening steal and to frighten her in her old age with so many soldiers? You wage a war wherein the greater glory is in being vanquished, not in securing victory.[57] *Do you fear that you are being tricked? Ah! It is much better to be tricked than to deceive one's own kind, to be the victim of some grave crime than to commit it oneself, to lose a royal crown than to steal one.*[58]

Yet, do not be afraid, my children. Your mother will ensure that the deceitful son does not trick the other.[59] I do not—I did not—come here to burden my white-haired old age with sorrow, nor to fuel your impieties; I came, rather, to break down your rock-hard and angry hearts.

Eteocles has thrown his club to the ground, he has cast off his shield.[60] So now, let me hug you with my maternal arms—I see you, Polynices, and kiss you, and I cannot get enough.

Oh my dear Polynices, a foreign land has for a long time kept captive your traveling soul! You have wandered through the deserts for a long time, along quiet shores, through wave-rumbling seas, a fugitive, an exile, chased down by Fortune, helpless, with no guide, and with no place to go.

Ah, I was not, your own mother, at your wedding. I did not lead the bride to the ceremony. I did not, to celebrate the wedding, arrange flowers around the royal house, I did not make the marriage bed fragrant with Sabean incense, nor did I decorate the bedstead with elaborate gold.

Chased off by your own kind, you gave yourself to an enemy prince who made you his son-in-law.[61] And now, after having stayed distant from my eyes for

---

[54] Line 704: A *cutlass* is a short, broad sword, often with a basket-shaped handguard.

[55] Line 705: A *rondache* (MFr. *rudache*) is a circular shield.

[56] Line 708: Jocasta now addresses Eteocles.

[57] Line 719: Garnier reworks SenPhW: 491–92: "you both want to wage a war in which the best outcome [*optimum*] is defeat [*vinci*]."

[58] Line 724: Garnier takes up and generalizes SenPhW: 493–94.

[59] Line 725: In Seneca, too, Jocasta's role is as peace-bringer: "your mother [*mater*] will ward off treachery [*insidias*]" (SenPhW: 496–97).

[60] Line 730: Jocasta addresses Polynices, following SenPhW: 500 et seq.

[61] Line 747: In Argos, Polynices married Argea, daughter of King Adrastus.

so long, finally you return. Not, as I had hoped, because your brother willed it, but rather to ransack our land like some enemy prince.

Oh my son, my dear son, my fear and my hope, my son whom I have wished so much, longed so much to see again, you deprive me of the great joys I had been awaiting, for you come to attack us, not to defend us. Alas, my son, my dear son,[62] must I, upon your most desired return from lengthy exile, drown myself in tears at the shared sorrow instead, as I had thought I would, of crying for joy? My son, was the choice this: never to see you again, or else, upon seeing you, to banish sweet peace from the heart of our land and to plunge our people and our fine city into murderous civil madness? Without you, we would see no war here; and without war, we would not see you. War holds onto you with such a tight grip that we cannot have you without also having the war.

But even though your travels have been hard on me, as you come to ransack the Amphionic walls[63] and our plentiful fields, I shake with joy at seeing you, I embrace you and kiss you, I am buoyant with joy—so long as your quarrels continue no more and you cease your battles.[64]

How close was I to seeing carnage and catastrophe descend upon you both, my two children! I shake and I shiver with icy fear that your bright armor poured into my heart. For the sake of my womb,[65] where you spent nine whole moons, where before your birth you were born; for the sake of my graying hair; for the sake of the trials that your father and I suffered; in the name of piety and for the noble heart of poor Antigone, she who supports your father,[66] get rid of this army and chase far from our crenels, far from our fine towers, these flaming torches. Have your warring troops march off elsewhere, order all these

[62] Line 756: Garnier does not reproduce Seneca, who has Jocasta mocked by a god at this point (Lebègue: 278).

[63] Line 767: Amphionic walls: the walls of Thebes, named after Amphion, the son of Zeus and Antiope, who, with his twin brother Zethus, built Thebes.

[64] Line 773: Compare Garnier (vv. 772–73) with Seneca: "Grim is the price of seeing you and harsh, but your mother accepts it [*sed madri placet*]" (SenPhW: 524–25).

[65] Line 778: Eng. *womb* here renders MFr. *flanc*. See line 672. Jocasta's political and peace-bringing role is tied throughout to her status as mother, hence the insistence here on her womb that hatched warring sons. Garnier's reference to "les flancs" (her side/belly) wherein "neuf Lunes vous fustes" (you were for nine months) translates Seneca: "By my womb's heavy pangs through those ten months [*per decem mensum graves / uteri labores*]. . ." (SenPhW: 535–36). Garnier's realism (talking of a nine—and not a ten—month pregnancy) is noteworthy.

[66] Line 783: In both Garnier and Seneca, Antigone is said to possess piety, to which Garnier adds a "cœur debonnaire" (noble heart). On piety, see note to line 88. The tone, however, is slightly different: Garnier writes of "la pauvre Antigone" (poor Antigone); Seneca writes instead of "the loyalty [*pietatem*] of your renowned sister [*inclitae. . . sororis*]" (SenPhW: 536), the Lat. adjective *inclitus* (famous, illustrious) pointing in a rather different direction to Fr. *pauvre*. See notes to line 88 and 841.

foreigners to retreat, carry off your flags to other regions, stop terrorizing us with so many army legions.

Enough attacks on your dear homeland,[67] which prays to you with joined hands and teary eyes; enough punishment of your birthplace—you have made it endure enough. Your homeland has seen its fertile plains overrun with horses, armor, and soldiers. It has seen its hills flash like lightening from the dazzling helmets, from the shields and bucklers[68]; it has seen its fields bristle with menacing spears rather than planted with the fine stalks of golden crops; it sees its tilled lands churned by horses, its shepherds chased off and their flocks slaughtered[69]; captains with proud brows raised up for display upon triumphant chariots, giving rewards to their troops; burning villages; shepherds' huts turned into lodgings for foreign soldiers. And the worst, it sees the two brothers raging at each other in bloody wrath, each after the other's life, and like frenzied bears, attempting to rip each other apart with injurious blows.[70]

This is the city, my son, where God ordered you be born and where you wish to be the only lord. What boiling rage and what madness compels you to want the immediate destruction of your own kingdom and, in wishing to conquer it, have it sacked by soldiers?[71]

How can this be? Would you want to bring down[72] these heaps of stones,[73]

---

[67] Line 790: Compare this description (lines 790–98) with Ronsard, *RL* 11:41, vv. 99–126. See also Balibé 1975: 271.

[68] Line 797: Eng. *buckler* is a kind of small shield.

[69] Line 800: In the middle of this enumeration of what Thebes observes of its own ruin, Garnier here changes tense (from past: *your homeland saw*, to present: *it sees*), underscoring how destruction has happened and still occurs.

[70] Line 809: The description of the war-torn polis is based on, but different from, SenPhW: 543 et seq.

[71] Line 815: Of these lines (810–15), Jondorf notes: "[they] contain nothing to tie the passage down to Thebes, and a sixteenth-century reader or playgoer would therefore be free to make his own analogies" (Jondorf 1969: 41).

[72] Line 816: Garnier writes "voudrez-vous jetter pié contre-mont / Ces grands monceaux pierreux," literally "will you want to throw upside down / these great stony mounds."

[73] Line 817: Garnier's "ces grands monceaux pierreux" (these great rocky mounds), which likely refer to the walls of Thebes, takes up Du Bellay's sonnet in the *Antiquitez de Rome*, which begins "Ces grands monceaux pierreux, ces vieux murs que tu vois / Furent premièrement le clos d'un lieu champêtre: / Et ces braves palais, dont le temps s'est fait maître, / Cassines de pasteurs ont été quelquefois," which Edmund Spenser (in his *Ruines of Rome*) translated as follows: "These heaps of Stones, these old Walls which ye see, / Were first enclosures but of salvage Soil; / And these brave Palaces, which maistred be / Of Time, were Shepherds Cottages somewhile."

which now shudder,[74] the work of Amphion?[75] Or the rich buildings that make up so many fine and richly decorated palaces? [820] Will your heart, Polynices, will your heart allow you to plunder there if you are victorious?[76] And will you, will you have the courage to watch them be ravaged?[77] To see them pillaged? To watch aging fathers dragged off by their gray hair, [825] their wives snatched by force from their homes, their daughters raped while in their mothers' arms?[78] And to watch young children led off like convicts, their necks in collar shackles, their arms tied up so that they can serve the unbridled pleasures of new masters? Will you still be able to look on at the city troubled by unrest, by shouts, overwhelmed by carnage?[79]

[830] Could you stand once again seeing the city clutched in catastrophe, by civil strife, by cries, and overwhelmed by carnage? Its streets littered with citizens' corpses, piled up upon each other, this way, that way, mixed up without order (a wretched spectacle!) [835] dripping blood out onto the red marshes? Do you want to see houses burn, and those who dwell still within them burn cruelly under the flaming rafters? Do you want to turn Thebes into a tomb, into a funeral pyre, for this to be your inheritance? [840] I pray you, I pray you, get rid of this rancor and fill your heart instead with humble piety.[80]

---

[74] Line 817: Eng. "which now shudder" < Fr. "sourcillent le front." Garnier uses the same expression in *Hippolyte*: ". . .que les rocs, qui sont / Au bord Thriasien, en sourcillent le front" (. . .which the rocks, which are / on the Thratian shore, raise their eyebrows [because of it]) (lines 236–37). In his edition of *Antigone*, Beaudin annotates this word as "élever" (to raise); in his edition of *Hippolyte*, Beaudin defines it as "froncer les sourcils" (to raise one's eyebrows), its more common meaning. The precise meaning of the expression in the present content is not immediately obvious.

[75] Line 818: Amphion is the son of Zeus and Antiope. He and his twin brother Zethus built Thebes. (It can be noted, in passing, that like Oedipus, Amphion and Zethus were exposed on Mount Cithaeron.)

[76] Line 820: See line 1070.

[77] Line 823: Just above the reader was told of what Thebes saw happening to it. Here, it is Polynices who is asked to imagine seeing the city.

[78] Line 826: Montchrestien will imitate lines 822–26 and 835 in his *Reine d'Ecosse* (lines 87–92). (Lebègue: 278).

[79] Line 829: In Garnier, Jocasta does not refer to herself as she does in Seneca: "Shall I, your very mother, ride with my hands tied behind my back, as booty in your parade of triumph over your brother?" (SenPhW: 577–78).

[80] Line 841: As above (line 783), both Garnier and Seneca refer to piety: "Put aside the feverish madness of your spirit, I pray you; bring yourself back to love and duty [*pietati*]" (SenPhW: 584–85).

POLYNICES

Shall I thus always be a wanderer through this world? Shall I spend my whole life roaming? As an exiled man forevermore beg for food at palace after palace, landless and without means? What punishment would I have received if I had broken the faith like that criminal imposter?[81] Must I suffer the penalty that should be reserved for his disloyal heart? Should he really profit from his spite and evil?

To where will afflicted Polynices retire? Where do you want him to go? Eteocles has taken all our shared inheritance—he leaves me nothing.

May he take it all, may he keep the whole kingdom for himself, but may I be left at least with a little thatched cottage[82]—that will be my palace and I will be able to boast of having a place to live, I will not need to go elsewhere.[83] But I have nothing at all and it suits me to live out my life as a slave, living with Adrastus and following him. *Oh, it is tough and tormenting to see oneself become a slave, having been a master; to become nothing, when one was a king!*[84]

JOCASTA

If your desire is to be a sovereign prince,[85] to keep a kingdom in the grip of your hand, and if you cannot live deprived of royal status, then leave your brother and his disloyalty behind. Seek out a different land—this mass of land[86] will furnish your hand with a hundred most fine scepters.

Drive on your proud legions of soldiers into the Lydian fields,[87] those fertile regions where the famous waters of the opulent Pactolus[88] run in a hundred

---

[81] Line 847: Where Garnier writes of Fr. *parjure* (here rendered as Eng. *criminal imposter*), Seneca wrote of breaking faith (*fidem*) (SenPhW: 589).

[82] Line 855: Eng. *cottage* here renders Fr. *maison de chaume* (literally "house of thatch"). As the following lines make clear, the point is obviously that Polynices will be satisfied with a simple dwelling if he cannot have Thebes—but the fact that it is specifically a thatched cottage suggests that here, as at many other places in Garnier's tragedies, we find traces of a fantasy of simple, bucolic life, far away from civil strife, the latter of which is generally associated with urban settings.

[83] Line 857: Although Garnier's Polynices listens to his mother's advice and (seemingly) accepts leaving Thebes to his brother, he does not explicitly state that his mother has changed his mind, unlike in Seneca: "You bid me to leave. I submit to my mother's command [*matris imperio obsequor*]" (SenPhW: 591).

[84] Line 861: These two lines (lines 860–61), presented in *guillemets* as a general truth, stem from Seneca: "It is painful to fall into servitude from kingship [*in servitutem cadere de regno grave est*]" (SenPhW: 598).

[85] Line 862: Garnier follows SenPhW: 599 et seq.

[86] Line 866: Eng. *mass of land* < Fr. *cette masse terrestre* most likely refers to the Earth as a planet, and more specifically to its inhabitable regions or *oikoumene*.

[87] Line 869: Lydia: a territory in west Asia Minor.

[88] Line 870: Pactolus: a river in Asia Minor.

turns from the rocks of Mount Tmolos.[89] Display your army's flags to the twisting banks of the sleepy Meander,[90] to the shores of the deep Eurymedon, and to the clear waters of the Xanthus,[91] whose course is born at Mount Ida. Head to Lycia and to the fields of Syria whence issued our Tyrian fathers.[92] Make the iron of your Argive lances ring out. Make your armor clank on the far-off banks of the Armenian Tigris, where the beautiful blond Sun, before it belongs to us, shows its golden face.[93]

That is where Adrastus must lead his eager forces, that is where he must undertake his conquests.[94] Much better to employ your strength there to win a new scepter, than to wage war on us. There you will be able, without crime, to win a crown. There you will have Thebes and your very brother as he follows your banners, and we who are old, for the success of your armies will invoke the gods.

Consider, also, the doubtful outcomes of the battles often unexpectedly lost; how unstable Mars is and how human destiny is always—and especially in battle—uncertain. Even though Achaeans and non-Achaeans gather together in support of your cause, nevertheless Fortune will have a role to play and the outcome will depend on chance.[95]

Abandon this war, then, in which all is full of doubt, in which victory is no surer than the road[96] that destroys the country, ransacks the precious temples of the gods who protect us.[97]

POLYNICES

So, as salary for his impudent crime he receives the kingdom and I must take my leave? Never, Mother, never. He must be punished for having treacherously banished me from my own land.

---

[89] Line 871: Mount Tmolos: a mountain in Lydia.

[90] Line 873: Meander and Eurymedon: rivers (now in modern-day Turkey).

[91] Line 874: Xanthus: great river of Troy.

[92] Line 876: Lycia: region of Anatolia (now Turkey). Tyrian: originating from Tyre, an ancient city in Phoenicia.

[93] Argive: Greek. Tigris: one of the two great rivers of Mesopotamia.

[94] Line 883: Compare lines 882–83 with Ronsard, *RL* 9:17, line 35. See also Balibé 1975: 272.

[95] Achaean: a native of Achaea, a region in the northern Peloponnese.

[96] Line 899: As Lebègue notes, "Jocaste fait appel au patriotisme et à la piété, et non, comme dans Sénèque [SenPhW: 638–41] au sentiment fraternel" (Jocasta makes an appeal to patriotism and piety and not, as in Seneca [SenPhW: 638–41] to fraternal sentiment) (Lebègue: 278).

[97] Line 989: Compare Jocasta's words (lines 989–990) with Ronsard, *RL* 9:23, lines 163–65. See also Balibé 1975: 272.

JOCASTA

He is well punished who rules over Thebes, for no one has ever governed in that city without there being great calamity. List all the leaders since Cadmus—you will not find one who was not defeated by this collective misfortune.[98]

POLYNICES

There is no greater misfortune than losing one's empire.[99]

JOCASTA

Making war on one's brother is a worse one.[100]

POLYNICES

Do you call it misfortune to pursue a breaker of faith?

JOCASTA

He is your brother.

POLYNICES

But he is but a thief, a kingdom robber.

JOCASTA

He is better liked by the citizens than you.[101]

---

[98] Line 909: This reference to a shared and tragic fate—all rulers of Thebes must suffer—exists in dialogue with the theme of reconciliation and peace: Jocasta who wants to bring her warring sons together, etc. On the intersection of the two themes, see Lebègue 1990: 75.

[99] Line 910: MFr. *empire* has a range of meanings. Cotgrave translates as: "An Empire, or Emperie; also, empire; Imperiall dominion, Seignorie, Soueraigntie; preheminence; iurisdiction, rule, gouernment; the highest dignities, the greatest sway, the most supreme power, most absolute authoritie." The influence of Lat. *Imperium* is also felt, a term that refers both to an individual's power to command, and to the lands and peoples over which that power is wielded.

[100] Line 911: There is no equivalent to these verses (lines 910–11) in Seneca.

[101] Line 914: Jocasta's address to Polynices here changes in tone. No longer is she arguing for Polynices's departure in the hope that it will help restore peace; now, she argues that Eteocles is a better and more rightful ruler of Thebes. This change is essential, given the story that follows between Antigone and Creon, and the later exchange between Creon and Haemon. This key moment in French reads "[Etéocle] est plus agreable / Aux citoyens que vous," literally "[Eteocles] is more *agreeable* than you to the citizens." Cotgrave defines the key term, MFr. *agreable*/Eng. *agreable*, as follows: "Agreeable, acceptable, gracefull, gracious, delectable, welcome, well liked." See note to line 1253.

POLYNICES

And I am more feared.[102]

JOCASTA

Do you wish to rule them against their will?

POLYNICES

A rebellious nation is tamed by force.

JOCASTA

I would not wish to live as one hated by my subjects.[103]

POLYNICES

He who wants to be free from hatred should not reign. [920] *For hatred always accompanies kingship;*[104] *hatred will always be seen in royal courts.* I believe that Jupiter does not rule the heavens without being disliked by the celestial troop. I do not mind being hated by my citizens, [925] as long as I am feared and obeyed.

JOCASTA

That is a great charge, an unbearable burden.

POLYNICES

There is nothing so delicious, nothing so delectable. To keep or win a kingdom, I would happily order the deaths of women and children, I would have [930] temples and houses burned, I would strike down and burn each last thing. In a word,

---

[102] Line 916: These final exchanges between Polynices and Jocasta are strikingly different from those that Jocasta, Polynices, and Eteocles exchange at the end of Seneca's play (SenPhW: 654–64). Garnier has Jocasta chide Polynices for being a bad leader—he is less "agreeable" (line 914) than Eteocles, says Jocasta, and he seems to want to rule by fear and violence; Seneca, on the other hand, paints Polynices as critical of Eteocles. "Rule [*regna*], then, but only as one hated by your people," says Polynices, to which his brother responds: "He who fears to be hated has no appetite for ruling [*Regnare non vult, esse qui invisus timet*]. The god who created the world set these things together: hatred and kingship [*odium atque regnum*]. I think it the mark of a great kind, actually to crush hatred. A monarch is much more constrained by his people's love; their anger gives him more freedom. One who wants to be loved rules with a feeble hand [*qui vult amari, languida regnat manu*]" (SenPhW: 653–59). As Beaudin has noted (203), the difference can be explained by the fact that Garnier read Seneca in an edition of the play in which the dialogue between the brothers was replaced by a set of remarks all pronounced by Polynices. See also Mouflard: 3: 67.

[103] Line 918: Jocasta says, literally, "En la haine des miens je ne voudrois pas vivre" (I would not want to live hated by *les miens*, i.e. my own kind *or* my subjects, etc.)

[104] Line 920: Eng. *empire* renders Fr. *royaume*. (See note to line 910.)

nothing is so sacred that I would not wish to destroy it a thousand times and a thousand times more in order to see on my head a crown of gold. *Whatever the price, it is cheap.* *No one ever pays too much when buying a kingdom.*[105]

CHORUS

Fortune, you always cause
Unrest in royal courts.[106]
Your deceitful hand balances
Upon emperors' heads
The too-wavering joy
Of a glorious crown.[107]

All great things you place
Upon a tall rock, surrounded
By chasms; they are poised
To fall at the first wind,
Which brings them down more
Often than lower edifices.[108]

---

[105] Line 935: About the second act, Mouflard comments that it "donne une impression de lassitude de la part de l'auteur" (suggests a certain tiredness/weariness on the part of the author) (3: 67), a judgment that is surely to be taken *cum grano salis*—the second act is, in the present editor's reading, essential to the play as a whole, in that it foregrounds calls for peace and for piety, arguably the tragedy's main themes. On the other hand, the depiction of Polynices as a tyrant—resembling some other of Garnier's tyrants, gives pause for thought.

[106] Line 936: There is no equivalent choral ode in Seneca's *Phoenician Women*. This ode is based on Seneca's *Agamemnon* (lines 56–106), which focuses on the theme of the inconstancy of fortune. For perspective, see Calder 1975 (on the chorus in *Agamemnon*) and Calder 1976 (more generally on *Agamemnon*). As Beaudin notes (204), it is not known who is supposed to be singing this chorus, but it is most likely the inhabitants of Thebes. The general theme (Fortune's power over, especially, kings) is one that Garnier has addressed elsewhere: see *Porcie* lines 151–91, *Cornélie* lines 1285–86, *Marc-Antoine* lines 181–88.

[107] Line 941: Compare with Seneca's *Agamemnon*: "O Fortune, who dost bestow the throne's high boon with mocking hand, in dangerous and doubtful state thou settest the too exalted. Never have sceptres obtained calm peace or certain tenure; care on care weighs them down, and ever do fresh storms vex their souls" (SenAga: 57–63).

[108] Line 947: This particular theme is developed at greater length in Seneca: "Sails swollen with favouring breezes fear blasts too strongly theirs; the tower which rears its head to the very clouds is beaten by rainy Auster; the grove, spreading dense shade around, sees ancient oak-trees riven; 'tis the high hills that the lightnings strike; large bodies are more to disease exposed, and while common herds stray o'er vagrant pastures, the head highest upreared is marked for death. Whatever Fortune has raised on high, she

Kings are constantly beaten
By various misfortunes.
Worry and fear never leave them.
Never do they rest,
For they feel that at any moment
The crown is being stolen away.

The sea and the two quicksands of Syrtis
Are less bothered by waves—
And Scylla barks less
At the passing ships—
Than fear torments kings with the
Suspicions that prey on their minds.[109]

They fear their neighbors,
They are afraid of their mutinous subjects.
Fear is printed upon their very souls.
They want others to be afraid of them,
And yet their hearts tremble
If they see that they inspire terror.[110]

We do not observe our Theban kings
Become friends because they are brothers.
The ambition that drives them
Forbids that in sincere love
They take it in turns to hold the scepter,
Passing it back and forth.

One brother keeps the scepter,
The other struggles to seize it.
Meanwhile, the citizens suffer on—
It is they who carry the burden.

---

lifts but to bring low. Modest estate has longer life [Lat. *Modicis rebus longius aeuum est*]" (SenAg: 90–102).

[109] Line 959: Syrtis: two large quicksands (*Syrtis major* and *minor*) off the northern coast of Africa. Compare with Seneca's *Agamemnon*: "Not so on Libyan quicksands does the sea rage and roll up wave on wave; not so, stirred from their lowest depths, surge Euxine's waters, hard by the icy pole, where, undipped in the azure waves, Boötes follows his shining wain, as does Fortune roll on the headlong fates of kings" (SenAg: 64–72).

[110] Compare with Seneca's *Agamemnon*: "To be feared they long, and to be feared they dread" (Lat. "metui cupiunt / metuique timent") (SenAg: 73–74).

Even though they are powerless,
They always become war's fodder.[111]

But inland, the countryside rumbles,
Our fine land is destroyed.
The wine-grower abandons his vines,
The stooped-over farmer his cattle,
The shepherd his grassy fields,
And the sad fisherman his rod.[112]

[111] Line 977: More literally, Garnier writes that the citizens (Fr. *le peuple*) "leur sert tousjours de pasture" (always serve them [i.e. the warring brothers] as fodder [i.e. for their war]).

[112] Line 983: Garnier thus connects together the devastation of the countryside and the idea that it is the regular citizens who suffer the most. See Jondorf 1969: 86.

Act III

Messenger, Jocasta, Antigone, Haemon.

MESSENGER

Oh wretched Thebes![1] Oh kingdom overwhelmed [985] by such cruel catastrophe, today suddenly twice as cruel! Oh the rancor of brothers!

ANTIGONE

Hey you, friend—for God's sake go on no further, but stop here in this place. Remain here. Where do you flee?

JOCASTA

Ah, I shake with fear.

ANTIGONE

Tell us, I pray, the cause of your complaint.

MESSENGER

[990] All is lost.

ANTIGONE

Good gods!

JOCASTA

Ah, poor woman!

ANTIGONE

Alas!

[1] Line 984: The first lines of the act, with emphasis placed on Thebes and on fratricidal warfare, seem to gesture towards the Act's source, i.e. Statius's *Thebaid*. See Introduction. Yet, the initial exchange between the Messenger, Antigone, and Jocasta, as Beaudin also notes (p. 205), is Garnier's own invention (lines 984–1007).

JOCASTA

Ah, what shall we do?[2]

ANTIGONE

Do not worry, Mother.[3] Moderation for your soul's suffering, moderation for your pain—moderation![4]

JOCASTA

I am fainting. Ah, daughter!

ANTIGONE

Mother![5]

JOCASTA

Ah! Ah! What shall we do?

ANTIGONE

Alas, that matters not to me—I worry only about you. You alone I pity.

JOCASTA

And I, my love, worry only about you.

ANTIGONE

Were it not for you, I would long to be in the somber realms of the Tartarean king.[6]

JOCASTA

That is where I must descend.

ANTIGONE

No. Rather, we must console each other.[7]

---

[2] Line 991: The use of the first person plural ("que ferons-nous!") again underscores the female solidarity between mother and daughter in their attempt to stop the war. See notes to lines 561 and 1087.

[3] Line 993: As earlier, Antigone addresses her mother, in French, as *Madame* (here rendered as Eng. *Mother*). Here, Antigone is somewhat cast in the role of the Senecan Stoic maid.

[4] Line 993: Eng. *moderation* renders the imperative Fr. *moderez*.

[5] Line 994: See note to line 993.

[6] Tartarus: a region situated below even the underworld (Homer, Hesiod).

[7] Line 999: Again, emphasis is placed on the complementarity of Jocasta and Antigone, especially via the use of the verb Fr. *s'entre-consoler*, echoing the many reflexive and

JOCASTA

Eteocles is dead, then?

MESSENGER

As is Polynices.

JOCASTA

Ah, unhappy old age! If only I could see them. . .

ANTIGONE

Did they die in combat, like courageous warriors?[8]

MESSENGER

They died in combat, but they were fighting alone.

JOCASTA

Were they fighting each other?

MESSENGER

With lance and cutlass.

ANTIGONE

And did they kill each other?[9]

MESSENGER

Yes, both, on the spot.

JOCASTA

Oh poor mother! Ah!

ANTIGONE

Soldier, I pray you, tell us the full story of this slaughter.

---

pronominal verbs used to describe the fraternal conflict between Eteocles and Polynices. See note to line 332.

[8] Line 1002: Antigone's question might be more literally translated as "Did they die in combat, as fighting/bellicose men [Fr. *en hommes belliqueux*]?"

[9] Line 1005: Here (lines 1004–5), Garnier again uses verbal constructions to underscore the mutual destruction of brother by brother. See note to line 332.

MESSENGER

Already Mars was relenting and the hollow trumpet had announced the bloody retreat throughout the lands. Everything smelled of massacre and the countryside was buried in the blood that rolled in waves over the piles of corpses, which boiling Mars's stormy thunder had slain upon the dusty ground.

Courageous Tydeus lay dead on the ground.[10] Valiant Hippomedon met the same fate. Brave Capanaeus, Acron, and Menoeceus, Amphiaraus, Actor, courageous Hypseus and so many other warriors from both sides were also there, heaped in piles on the battlefield. Seeing that, Polynices, shaken by the wretched sorrow of seeing himself responsible for so many deaths,[11] seeks out Adrastus and speaks to him as follows:

"I alone am the cause of this slaughter. My father and—for me alone—so many noble souls, now find themselves on the way to those dark shores.[12] I wish to avenge their deaths against myself, upon me, or else on this hypocritical tyrant of a faith-breaker,[13] so that the Argolide women cannot complain about us, their joint murderers.

It would have been much better—I learn this too late—for me to have taken on this dangerous battle myself before battalions of ordered troops, driven by contrary angers, made a harvest of each other before so many brave captains, beaten by blows, were knocked down dead, face on the ground. But since I cannot undo this crime, then at least now I should like to measure myself against my brother[14]—I head off to fight him. Farewell! Look after my tomb's honor and look after my wife.[15]"

These words said, he again took up his weapons, leaving Adrastus there, who then burst into tears—just like one sees Mount Rhodope, cov-

[10] Allusion to the warriors mentioned in Aeschylus's *Seven Against Thebes*.

[11] Tydeus, Hippomedon, Capaneus, Acron, Menoeceus, Amphiaraus, Actor, Hypseus: participants in the battle between Polynices and Eteocles, as recounted in Aeschylus's *Seven Against Thebes*.

[12] Line 1025: i.e. the dark shores of the underworld.

[13] Line 1027: See note to line 1814.

[14] Line 1037: Polynices's call-to-arms here echoes Statius: "my brother to mortal combat [. . .] I challenge [*fratrem suprema in bella. . . voco*]" (StTheb 11:168–69); "I fight my brother [*fratri concurro*]. What more is there? [*quid ultra est?*]" (StTheb 11:185).

[15] Line 1039: Garnier here condenses a similar idea in Statius: ". . .be kind to my ashes and after this battle seize me and protect me from the birds and my brother and bring back my turn—that is all—and make a better marriage for your daughter" (StTheb 11: 190–92). Polynices's final words, reported by the messenger, are obviously of key importance, for they anticipate Antigone's undertaking in the second part of the play (i.e. to give her brother a proper burial). The fact that Polynices mentions looking after both his tomb *and* his wife (i.e. Argia, the daughter of Adrastus) is also perhaps significant given the very close (and some say proto-incestual) relationship between brother and sister in that Antigone, more than Argia, will show Polynices love after his death.

ered with white snow, melt when Spring arrives into a hundred streams.[16] He mounted his horse, which, bit in mouth, beat its hoof on the ground as it waited for the prick of the spurs. He gave a lively jab of his spur and, shot at by pain, his face stained pale, his eyes glistening with a burning rage, he thus heads off to the foot of the Cadmean city.[17] There, he calls out loud to Eteocles and, seeing that no one heads out onto the dusty field, he leans on his lance and with his eyes mesures out a space suitable for their impending battle.

Meanwhile in the temple, Eteocles was praying to his tutelary gods and making a sacrifice to them when Ephitos ran in, out of breath and his lungs pulsing, to tell him with some effort (such did I hear): "Leave aside, sir, these prayers and no longer busy yourself with the entrails of oxen. It is not the time for sacrifices. Indignant Polynices stands before the walls and he summons you to battle—hurry up and leave, he wishes your differences be settled by the sword."

At these words he gets fired up, as one sees in a thicket a proud bull fire up its strength when it hears its enemy bellow throughout the valley. The animal raises its head and, puffing hard in the thick grove, displays itself all courageous before the flock, which is frightened by its rage.

In just such a way Eteocles, his heart enraged,[18] breathes his rage and rancor through his nostrils. Fire comes out of his eyes, his forehead grows pale—the drained-off blood goes down into his breast. They cover his body with glistening steel, his head with a terrifying helmet. His horse they bring, which he mounts without using a block, ready and nimble, and with a bitter smile.[19] He takes up a sharp-bladed steel lance. He is handed his sword and his golden shield, then he heads out to the field. There, close to Polynices, he heads to the tiltyard.[20]

---

16 Mount Rhodope: a mountain in Thrace.

17 Line 1049: See note to line 321.

18 Line 1070: See line 820.

19 The block: (Fr. *un avantage*) was a small step used for mounting one's horse.

20 Line 1081: Garnier, here, uses somewhat technical language to describe the space where the battle of the two brothers will occur. In Fr., line 1081 reads "D'une juste carriere il entre dans la lice." Beaudin defines MFr. *carriere* as "distance, espace"; MFr. *lice* as a "champ clos destiné à un tournoi, à un combat singulier." Cotgrave's definition of the first term is both more precise and wider—the term can refer to, *inter alia*, "An (sic) highway, rode, or street," "any exercise, or place for exercise, on horseback; as a horse-race, or, a place for horses to run in." Among the translations Cotgrave offers for *lice* is "tilt-yard," which indeed refers to "A yard or enclosed space for tilts and tournaments; a (permanent) tilting-ground" (OED).

The Agenorides come running from all around, they climb up the towers and onto the ramparts, everybody laments and flowing tears [1085] wash each person's ashen face.[21]

JOCASTA

Alas, my daughter, alas! What of our tears? Why do we not lament our bitter sorrows?[22]

MESSENGER

The hunched-over old men and the white-haired mothers, tearing at their hair and beating their bare chests, [1090] cried out for having dragged out their days so long—they wished, because of their grief, to leap from the towers.[23]

Twice, full of venom, they ran against each other.[24] And twice, on contact, they recoiled back from each other. Polynices finally stabbed his wooden spear into the flank [1095] of Eteocles's horse, reddening it with blood. The horse stum-

---

[21] Line 1085: The description of the crowd draws on Statius: "The common folk [*vulgus*] stand forth on the rooftops, a piteous sight, floods of tears are everywhere and from every height comes wailing [*ab omni plangitur arce*]" (StTheb 11: 416–17).

[22] Line 1087: In Statius, even before the battle, both Jocasta and Antigone plea with the brothers not to fight, verses that Garnier does not take up here. Jocasta is described there as "distraught and terrified by the first rumor of her calamity" and as going about "with torn hair and face, breasts bare and bleeding, unmindful of sex and seemliness" (StTheb: 11:315–18). She is also compared to Agave (318–19)—see notes to lines 28, 480, 586. She calls out: "Hear me, alas! Your mother [*genetrix te*], cruel man, begs you, not your father" (StTheb: 11:346–47). Antigone, too, laments and calls for peace: "Brother [*frater*], hold your weapons and look for a moment at this tower, [. . .] Do you see enemies? [. . .] Your Antigone [*Antigone. . . tua*] begs, faithful to the ills of her loved ones and suspect to the kind, sister only to you, O hard of heart!" (StTheb: 11: 363–72). To be noted then is both the way Garnier's question gestures to Statius's description of Jocasta and Antigone and also the first person plural ("Que ne larmoyons-nous?")—see notes to lines 561 and 991.

[23] Line 1091: Garnier adapts Statius: "Here old men [*senes*] complain that they have lived too long, there mothers stand bare-breasted and tell their little sons not to look" (StTheb: 11:418–19).

[24] Line 1092: The beginning of the description of the fraternal battle follows Statius: "Twice [*bis*] they rode in vain, twice [*bis*] a kindly error made the horses swerve in collision course and the spears struck aside and fell clean of impious blood" (StTheb: 11:449–51). Garnier's description quickly accelerates, however, focusing very specifically on the (named) brothers and leaving aside other elements, such as the long lament made by Piety, inclusion which might have been expected given Garnier's subtitle and key themes: "Long time had Pity [*Pietas*] been sitting in a secluded part of heaven, offended by earth and the company of the gods [. . .] she wept the fraternal strife [*fraterna. . . bella*] like a hapless sister [*soror felix*] or anguished mother [*anxia mater*] [. . .] I am nothing now among the nations, nowhere is any reverence for me" (StTheb 11:457–67).

bled and fell heavily, as when a fir tree, beaten by the storm, is broken on Mount Parnassus and crashes headfirst noisily to the ground.

The horseman thought that his lance's bloodthirsty blade had plunged into his brother's groin. He drew his sword hastily and, blinded by frenzy, rushed at the man he saw lying on the ground. But as he kicks the palfrey with too much rage, and jolted by his spurring lance, he falls down towards poor Eteocles and onto the hacked-up body of the injured horse. They get up on their feet and, their swords in their right hands and their glistening shields on their left arms, they attack each other with all of their force, determined to inflict or suffer death.

Under the helmets, hatred and anger boil. As the two brothers look at each other, their strength and vigor grow ever greater. They stiffen their bodies with a leg outstretched, then, leaning over their swords and stretching out their arms, they thrust their sword tips now at their visors, now at their breasts—with warring precision. They plunge their swords and cause bloody wounds in each other, making red blood flow through the armor. They search out armor holes, cut through the harnesses, knock away each other's weapons and riddle the other with wounds.

The two camps, lined up, look on, in doubt as to who will be the winner of this piteous combat.

When two boars, stung by love, clash in the forests of Dodona, they gather up the weight of their horrendous grumbling bodies, their fur stands up, they foam at the mouth, their jaws howl, and with fury they run their horns into the enemy's neck,[25] they bloody each other's bellies. And the shepherd who looks on from a hill hides out of fear; he signals with hands and head to his dog, for whom he worries, to remain quiet.[26]

In just such a way, the two warring men battle one-on-one with ferocious valor. They attack each other, they rush blows of their swords' point and shaft into each other, they lop off many a blade and much chain mail. They hammer at each other's body, storming at the steel like two smiths whose wheeling arms beat iron on an anvil, which winces under the blows, and who end up bent over and breathing difficultly, out of breath.[27] Or else, like one also sees hail crash down on the roofs of houses, when angry Jupiter rages against nourishing Ceres in summertime; or when he pounds on the head of Bacchus, the good father.

[25] Line 1129: Compare this description (lines 1126–29) with Ronsard, *RL* 8:69, lines 477 et seq. See also Balibé 1975: 271.

[26] Dodona: place in ancient Epirus, where an oracle of Zeus was situated amidst a grove of oaks.

[27] Line 1141: This simile (1124–41) is drawn from StTheb: 11:530–40. The impact is emphasized by Garnier's use of pronominal verbs: *s'entre-alloyent* (line 1135), *se ruoyent* (line 1136), *se marteloyent* (line 1138), *se courber* (line 1141). See note to line 332.

In the end, Polynices,[28] upon whom still rain the cowardly ploys of his enemy brother, his exile shameful and all faith broken, gets mad—he has fought so long against him. [1150] He grits his teeth in rage and, making his whole body hard, he throws himself on hand and foot against his enemy, with such great violence that he thrusts six inches of his sword into his brother's gut. Steaming blood gushes out, as on an altar [1155] the blood of a lamb steams after the holy priest has dealt a mortal blow to its throat.

Eteocles paled, grew weak and was stunned to see his blood run from all this violence. He feels his forehead freeze solid with a deathly cold, [1160] his knees tremble—but still, he tries with the little energy he has left to carve matching wounds into his brother's body. He follows him and hounds him; his brother, mocking him, turns away and flees.

Eteocles grows increasingly tired and no longer has any strength [1165] to hold up his body. He loses all hope, he falls over, his weapons clash down and a horrendous darkness closes his eyes.

JOCASTA

Oh most wretched woman!

ANTIGONE

Oh most unfortunate daughter!

JOCASTA

Oh damned day!

MESSENGER

[1170] Polynices, convinced that he is the sole victor, throws down his sword and his shield, removes the sturdy breastplate from his body.[29] Then, turning his two hands and his face towards the heavens, he offers thanks to the immortal ones with happy fervor [1175] for having that day lent him their favor. He approaches Eteocles and, thinking him to be as lifeless as he appeared,[30] attempts—as the victor—to remove his armor. But, as he carelessly leans over him, [1180] kneeling on the ground and bending over his face, his brother observes him and gathers

[28] Line 1146: Statius refers to Polynices at this point only as "the exile [*exsul*]" (StTheb: 11:540). Compare, too, Garnier with Statius's additional comment that Polynices is "he whose anger is the stronger [*fortior ira*] and crime the juster [*nefas. . . iustius*]" (StTheb: 11:541–42).

[29] Line 1172: Polynice's mistake, which causes his death, is not mentioned by Seneca but by Euripides (Lebègue: 279).

[30] Line 1177: Garnier says of Eteocles merely that he makes himself appear dead ("Du tout desanimé, comme il faisoit paroistre," line 1177), whereas Statius calls this "a final trick [*fraudem. . . spuremam*]" (StTheb: 11:554).

together what remains of his strength, he fires up his heart and his tired muscles with the ancient rancor and stabs his vengeful sword into his brother's chest before [1185] vomiting out, as he dies, his criminal soul.

Polynices, feeling weak from the blow that was struck him, and his soul swimming towards the river of Forgetting,[31] said with a sob that he pushed out from his belly:

"You are thus alive, you traitor, and you still battle [1190] with crafty hypocrisy![32] Let us go, let us head off to Pluto's fields to finish our battle there."[33]

Upon these words, he fell down upon his brother's body, mixing his warm blood with enemy blood.[34]

JOCASTA

Furies,[35] rush upon me through cavernous Tainaron![36] [1195] I brought trouble to the laws of nature. I gave birth to this deadly war. I mothered these children in horrendous incest.[37]

Unfortunate me, I conceived Oedipus and with Oedipus, I took my child—Oh crime!—into my bed, [1200] my parricidal child and I kissed the hand of the man upon which spilled my husband's blood.

What else could—what else should—be born from such a repulsive union other than such repulsive fruit? They massacred each other with terrible wrath.[38] [1205] The light went out in my husband's eyes and not content merely to flee

[31] Line 1187: The River of Forgetting: the Lethe, one of the rivers of Hades. Dead souls drink of its water to forget their life on earth.

[32] Line 1191: Polynices's words (lines 1189–91) are based on those he says in Statius: "Do you live? Or does your anger still remain, surviving you, traitor, who shall never deserve the abodes of peace? Hither with me to the shades! There too I shall demand what was agreed" (StTheb: 11:168–70).

[33] Line 1189: At this point, when Polynices say to Eteocles "You are thus alive," the latter is, of course, already dead.

[34] Line 1193: The final death of the brother is based on Statius: "Saying no more, he fell and covered his brother with the weight of all his arms [*totis fratrem gravis obruit armis*]" (StTheb: 11:573). Garnier's description, with emphasis on the mixing of brotherly blood rather than on the weight of arms, translates the moment with much greater pathos. There are certain similarities between the death, here, of the two brothers and that of Antigone and Haemon in the fifth act. See note to line 2590.

[35] Line 1194: Garnier refers to the Furies with their Lat. name, *Dirae*.

[36] Line 1194: In Statius, it is Oedipus and not Jocasta who first reacts to the double deaths (StTheb: 11:580 et seq.).

[37] Line 1194: Tainaron: the entrance to Hades, situated according to mythology at Cape Tainaron, also known as Cape Matapan. See also line 1331.

[38] Line 1204: See note to line 332.

heaven's brightness, he has banished himself from Thebes and turned away from us.[39]

At this juncture, Creon, finding the throne empty, will with no trouble usurp the Agenoride scepter. [1210] And we, the weak sex, will serve under the yoke of a tyrant as slaves—unless we die. But I prefer death, even if death arrives too late to ensure happiness. Ah, how I should have died, if the heavens had allowed it, [1215] before my body was polluted by that dirty coupling with you, my offspring, with you, Oedipus, the author of the sorrows I now suffer.

But, oh my dear daughter, accompany his steps, never abandon him until his final passing. [1220] The gods will not allow that such a gracious deed go unnoticed and without proper reward. Rather, they will recognize it and your piety will flourish, immortal and celebrated.[40]

As for me, I now descend into Pluto's realm, underground, [1225] to calm the tears of our ancient misfortunes. Already for a long time I have carried in my aching breast this dagger, in order to put an end to my harsh fate.[41]

ANTIGONE

Oh gods! What do I see?

JOCASTA

A healing dagger.[42]

ANTIGONE

Healing? In what way?

JOCASTA

To leave sorrow behind.

---

[39] Line 1208: For Statius's description of Creon's ascension to the throne of Thebes, see StTheb: 11:648–55. Statius underlines the continuity between the brothers' battle and Creon's ascension: "Creon held Cadmus's power. Alas, a sorry end to the war! [*miser heu bellorum terminus!*] For him the brothers had fought [*illi pugnarant fratres*]" (StTheb: 11:650–52).

[40] Line 1223: Jocasta again underscores Antigone's piety. Prior to 1585, lines 1222–23 read "Vous aurez le guerdon de vostre pieté, / Si dessus les mortels regne la deïté" (You will have the reward of your piety, / If the goddess reigns over mortals) (Beaudin: 106), a change that Lebègue comments as follows: "En 1585, Garnier a changé un vers qui semblait mettre en doute l'existence des dieux" (In 1585, Garnier changed a verse that seemed to put into doubt the existence of gods) (Lebègue: 280). Regarding Antigone's immortality, see also lines 1619 and 1729.

[41] Lin 1227: Eng. "put an end to" renders Fr. *donter* (to tame), a term which underscores Garnier's (and Seneca's) dialogue with Stoic ideals.

[42] Line 1228: Jocasta now desires death, as did Oedipus in the first act.

ANTIGONE

Oh Jupiter! Oh heavens! What are you saying? Good gods! That you will kill yourself?

JOCASTA

What better deed can I do? What other cure is there for my pain and my excruciating sadness other than speeding up the coming of my final day, my final hour? Come, come dear Death, come help me quickly.

ANTIGONE

I will not allow you to kill yourself. This criminal blade—I should have it.

JOCASTA

No, no. I want to seek out my Laius in Erebus's silence.[43] Oh Laius, oh my husband, do not forbid that I wander in your company on the dark banks. My crime is cleansed by the sacrifice I make to you of my victim soul.

ANTIGONE

Ah, Mother.[44] For God's sake, do not leave me!

JOCASTA

My daughter, do not force my will.

ANTIGONE

It is to turn you away from a harmful plan.

JOCASTA

But it would turn me away from health-giving peace.

ANTIGONE

If ever I did something that was to your liking, if I have dedicated my heart to obeying you, and if I am a guide to my old father in his sadness, I pray you: put down this murderous dagger and purge your soul of the desire that gnaws at it. Live, Mother, live[45]—do not kill yourself.

---

[43] Erebus: the son of Chaos and the personification of darkness and shadow; refers also to Tartarus or Hades.

[44] Line 1242: See note to line 502.

[45] Line 1251: See notes to lines 502 and 1242.

JOCASTA

I retort: if ever your pitiful heart was ever pleasing to me and to your father,[46] if you have always obeyed me, then please, do not force my will at present.

ANTIGONE

Do you want me to approve of something bad?

JOCASTA

Do you want to disapprove of a plan that pleases me?

ANTIGONE

I cannot take pleasure in this deadly wish.

JOCASTA

Death and death alone can give me any pleasure.

ANTIGONE

If death pleases you so, if this frenzy is so much imprinted upon your imagination that you have to die, then I will die with you. Would you descend there, leaving me here? I will not let you do that. Rather, I will follow your Shade as its eternal companion into the somber abode.

JOCASTA

No, no. Live, my daughter. Why would you die? The gods do not aim their anger at your head as they do upon unlucky me. They will perhaps show you their clemency—as indeed they show me their rigor.

ANTIGONE

I do not wish to survive you. Rather, I wish for this dagger to pierce both our hearts, first yours, then mine.

JOCASTA

While you are in the flower of youth?

ANTIGONE

Would I leave my mother?

JOCASTA

Yet you will leave your father, sad and solitary, afflicted by incurable torment, his eyes plunged in tenebrous night?

[46] Line 1253: Eng. *pleasant* here renders Fr. *agreable*. See note to line 914.

ANTIGONE

Ah! What shall I do then? Oh, how unthinkable is this distress![47] Accompanying one means abandoning the other:[48] if I follow my mother, cutting short the thread of my days,[49] then I must leave my father wanting for help. With whom do I remain? And to whom, oh poor me, am I more obliged, to whom more subject?[50] I honor them both and to both am duty bound, but one of them wishes to die, the other to mourn his misfortune. Overwhelmed by so much sorrow, I would prefer death—and nothing, today, would please me more than death. But wait! That would increase my poor father's grief. Moreover, I would then not be able, when his hour has come, to lay him in his coffin; I would not be able, when his final words have been spoken, to close his eyelids. I must then, despite myself, survive—alas! I must outlive you, bereaved of all joy. Oh misery! Oh distress! Oh deadly fortune!

Mother,[51] my hope, you who are all that I have apart from my unlucky father, please extinguish and chase off this desire for death, which you seek out from the dagger. Death is nearby—wait for it to come to you, your soul can hardly remain in you forever. Death will arrive suddenly and your aged body will see itself effortlessly freed of torment. There is no need to hurry your hour.[52]

JOCASTA

It has already arrived! Already Death's deadly dart has lodged itself in my heart.

---

[47] Line 1276: Eng. *harsh* here renders Fr. *estrange*, which has a number of overlapping meanings. Cotgrave gives the following translations: "Strange, uncouth, unusuall; forraine, alien, outlandish; unaccustomed, unacquainted; also, harsh, rude, od (sic) (in condition, or constitution)." Although Antigone may be unaccustomed to such distress (having to chose an alliance between two close relatives), it is exactly that same situation in which Jocasta has already found herself, in being forced to choose between her two sons.

[48] Line 1277: Antigone here echoes Jocasta's earlier lament over which of Eteocles and Polynices to support. See lines 520–24. See also Lebègue: 280.

[49] Line 1278: The allusion, of course, is to the thread of life, measured out by the three Fates (Gk. *Moirae* or Lat. *Parcae*): Clotho, Lachesis, and Atropos.

[50] The term *subject* has different connotations in sixteenth-century French. Cotgrave defines the word as follows: "A subject, vassal; underling; servant [. . .] and particularly the peasant, who being bound, by his tenure, to pay scot and lot unto his Lord, is not bound to follow him in the warres without pay."

[51] Line 1293: See note to line 502.

[52] Line 1300: Antigone has already counseled her father against suicide (see line 367).

Oh god of the deep dwellings,[53] you who welcome the shades of the dead upon the banks of the Acheron, whatever their provenance, you, king of the blackened world, take my crying soul, which flees with this body the great azure vault. Take my plaintiff soul and put it to rest. It has suffered ever since it entered into me. It leaves hell as it leaves this world and seeks out repose in the Stygian waves. Come, sweet dagger, come plunge yourself into me, and chase me rapidly from this body of mine. Too long I wait, full of fear.

ANTIGONE

What do you want to do? Help! Help! She wants to kill herself! You will *not* kill yourself—I will stop you from doing that.

JOCASTA

My daughter—you cry out in vain: I will die, I will. Leave me, leave me, my death is decided. I can already see Charon's hairy head. And I see already the ghosts of Hell. I hear already the terrible voice of Tartarus's thrice-barking dog.[54]

Dagger, enter into my heart, penetrate my breast, enter into my loins, as far as the sword's handle permits. Farewell, my dear daughter. . . Now I am dying! Ah! I am dying. Catch me, I am falling.

ANTIGONE

Oh sorrow of sorrows! Oh disastrous affliction! Oh wretched queen! Oh sinister unhappiness! Oh deplorable death! Oh, Mother, why do you leave me like this?[55] Why do you die? So that I, too, die? Oh harsh destiny! Oh such cruel Fates! Ah, your eyes now swim in eternal night. Your life is extinguished and your suffering spirit now falls down into the gulfs of Tainaron.[56] Cold pallor now drains your face. You breathe no more, a deadly testimony. Oh, Mother, oh, Mother,[57] at least I should have been part of the homicidal violence of this bloody dagger.

Tear-worthy Erigone, following your harsh criticisms of your father, and after so many sacred tears that you cried sadly in the woods of Marathon, in

---

[53] Line 1302: These lines (1302–08) are among those quoted in 1946 by Thierry Maulnier, a year after he produced an adaptation of Garnier's play. In reference to them, he noted that "l'invocation d'Iocaste près de mourir est l'un des plus beaux moments poétiques de notre langue" (Jocasta's invocation, when she is near death, is one of the most beautiful poetic moments in the French language) (Maulnier 1946: 67). See also notes to lines 240 and 2183.

[54] Cerberus: the three-headed dog which guards the gates of Hades.

[55] Line 1326: See notes to lines 502, 1242, etc.

[56] Tainaron, or Cape Matapan: a cape on the southernmost point of mainland Greece. A cave situated there is supposedly the entrance to Hades. See also line 1194.

[57] Line 1334: See note to line 1326.

response to your pain, you hanged yourself with a noose.[58] Do I suffer any less pain than did Erigone? Was she, in her heart, more pitiful than Antigone? And yet, on I live, I live, but as I live I carry more pain than I would feel in death.

So, my two brothers died on the dusty ground; my mother, in my arms, was just now her own murderer.[59] My father wanders, blind, amidst rocks he cannot see, filling the air with his cries, tears, and regrets. Our race is destroyed; the Theban scepter will no longer be held by the descendants of Agenor. We have lost everything. Today—this very moment—brings total destruction to our ancient line.[60] And, wretched me, I live! Alas, yes! Alas, I do. But I wish I were already drinking from the Cocytus.[61] I survive despite myself, to bury these bodies, for fear the dogs devour them.[62] And I survive, too, in order to guide my father and to bring him comfort in his bitter sadness, to bury him with my own hands, to entomb his body as soon as death steals him away from me. Otherwise, otherwise, I am ready to die—that alone holds my death at bay.

HAEMON

What? My dear Antigone, have you given your mind forevermore to anguish because of a dreadful disaster? These beautiful eyes that I adore and which set my soul on fire, will they always douse with tears their own sweet flame?[63] What misfortune is this? What is this cadaver lying here and which you sprinkle with your falling tears? What is the purpose of this dagger you carry in your chaste hand?

ANTIGONE

Alas! It is our queen. Alas, it is Jocasta.

HAEMON

Who causes this calamity? Her two dead children, are they responsible for shortening her old days?

[58] Erigone: on discovering that drunken shepherds had killed her father, she hanged herself. Marathon: an ancient Greek city-state.

[59] Line 1345: Compare with Racine 's *Thébaïde*: "Ta mère vient de mourir dans tes bras" (Your mother just died in your arms) (line 1204).

[60] Line 1352: Racine's Phèdre will also say this (Racine, *Phèdre*, IV, 6). (See also Pinvert: 2.445).

[61] Cocytus: the "river of wailing" in the underworld.

[62] Line 1355: On Antigone's desire to bury the dead, see StTheb: 11:707–56.

[63] Line 1365: Lebègue sees here the influence of French petrarchism (Lebègue: 280).

ANTIGONE

It is the proclaimed fortune of her sons, my brothers, that planted this dagger in her breast. The blood is still wet and her spirit, now released, wanders, lamenting in gasped sobs. Am I not truly lost?

HAEMON

Alas, my dear life! You have for a long time now been pursued by misfortune. I pity your troubles. Oh, why is your suffering not within me, so that your soul would no longer be afflicted! You wound my heart with your pitiful laments. These sobbing moans each grip me so. Calm down, my soul, calm your pains. *Our tears of pain will not bring the dead back to life.*

ANTIGONE

If only I could cry so much that I could also cry out my soul, which is shaken by such an accumulation of torment!

HAEMON

May my soul also accompany it, for I never want, oh you my heart, to be far from you. As long as you live, I will live; but as soon as the hour arrives when the Fates take you away, I, too, must die. I live in you alone. Without you—this I know—without you, I will find even the sweetest pleasure bitter. If you are pained, I will be sad; if you are happy, I will be joyous.

ANTIGONE

I have lost all joy, I wish now only to live with my father in some remote cave.

HAEMON

Live in the empty deserts of sun-baked Africa, amongst the Garamantes; live in Scythia in the Hyperborean heights where raging winds bring large heaps of snow.[64] I will live there, with you. Neither heat nor cold, as long as you are there, will ever seem harsh.

ANTIGONE

Haemon, I pray you, turn your heart away from me, from poor lamenting me, all knotted up in extreme sadness. My love longs for death and the burial vault. My only desire is for a dark tomb.

[64] Garamantes: a people of Berber origin, who founded a kingdom in modern-day Libya. Hyperborea: a land, whose name means "beyond the Boreas," i.e. "beyond the north wind."

HAEMON

I should prefer that watery Triton be born upon the earth and that the wooly sheep graze in the sea—rather that than extinguishing the rage I carry in the marrow of my bones, that rage for worshipping your too beautiful beauty.[65] During the day when Phoebus walks around and at night when the heavens show their ornaments—a thousand shining stars, I have you in my soul, and always your likeness that wanders before my eyes inflicts wounds of love.[66]

ANTIGONE

And I love you, too. But my affection is now troubled by so much pain. All my mind contains is deaths and funerals.

HAEMON

But I still carry love sown deep within my entrails.[67]

ANTIGONE

How great is my affliction!

HAEMON

It is so great. *Normally, ills come upon us all at once.* *But just as one sees spring follow on from winter*[68] *and after much rain fine weather appear, so also when misfortune has long stormed around us, we must hope for better times.*

ANTIGONE

I now have only one hope. My lost joys could never—alas!—be given back to me. *When death has taken us, we cannot be reborn. We lose with no possibility of return those who head towards death.*

HAEMON

Each and everyone must die. From this shared lot the cruel Fates release no one. If your aged mother and your brothers are dead, this is just Atropos's normal doings.[69] Their day had come, like the day, perhaps, when we must all stand

[65] Triton: messenger of the sea.

[66] Line 1414: According to Lebègue, none of Antiquity's Antigones admitted feelings of love for Haemon (Lebègue: 280). This is surely open to debate. See note to line 1455.

[67] Line 1417: Compare with Garnier's *Porcie* (line 752).

[68] Line 1420: Compare with Garnier's *Cornélie* (line 351).

[69] Atropos: one of the Moirae (Parcae, Fates), she is the cutter of the thread of life.

before Minos.[70] For if Clotho so wishes it, we must immediately [1435] allow ourselves to be the spoils of death.[71]

ANTIGONE

May she hurry up and cut my life's thread,[72] for I have more than slaked my thirst for this world. It is only with much regret that I live on. And were it not for my father, I would already have planted this dagger in my heart—[1440] and I would be with you, my mother. Ah, wretched me! I have been unable, unable, to be of any help to you. I have not been able to turn away, nor divert your mind from wanting to get out of its prison. Ask Pluto that I might follow you very soon, [1445] and that here, far from you, I do not remain too long. Mother, ah, may I once again kiss these sweet eyes of yours, this mouth and this neck, which are so precious to me. It is the last time that I touch this hand. Alas! I cannot pull my mouth away from it.

HAEMON

[1450] Oh mine eyes, stop these tears and this sobbing—all they do is increase my suffering. May she, then, be carried into town, so that she may be provided, as her final rites, with a royal sepulcher. Henceforth, my heart, this is all she needs. [1405] All she now wants for is a sepulcher.[73]

ANTIGONE

Ah! Ah!

CHORUS

You are dying,[74] oh noble race,
You are dying, oh City of Thebes,
You see only death[75]

[70] Minos: the judge of the dead in the underworld.

[71] Clotho: sister of Atropos, is the Fate who spins the thread of human life.

[72] Line 1436: Lines 1434–46 and 1937 are imitated by Basscecourt in his *Tragi-comédie* (lines 1932–36). See Lebègue: 280.

[73] Line 1455: About the exchange between Antigone and Haemon, Lebègue has noted that "Garnier a eu le mérite d'inventer un dialogue de deux amoureux" (Garnier was right to invent this dialogue between two lovers), adding that "à la représentation, en présence du cadavre encore chaud de Jocaste, cet entretien fait une étrange impression" (when performed, in the presence of Jocasta's still warm corpse, this exchange creates a strange impression) (Lebègue: 280). See note to line 1414.

[74] Line 1456: This choral ode is based on Seneca's *Oedipus* (lines 110–201).

[75] Line 1458: As elsewhere throughout the play, Garnier emphasizes visuality and invites the reader or spectator to picture events (and especially the sad state of Thebes) in his mind's eye.

In your fertile countryside.[76]
Your fine hills are deserted,
Your citizens are banished—
Whose ancestors once saw,
Under Bacchus's banners,
The birth of Aurora's first rays
Shedding light onto the vanquished Indians.

They saw the odorous kingdom
Of the endeavoring[77] Arabs;
And the delicious hills
With their fragrant woods.[78]
They tamed the Sabeans
And the Nabaeteans.[79]
They saw the fine lands of the
Persians and the sprightly Parthians,[80]
And the banks of the Eritrean wave,
As well as the mountains of Gedrosia.[81]

We, the children of such noble ancestors,
Are almost all overwhelmed
By the Argians who gather
To make themselves our masters.[82]

---

[76] Line 1459: Compare with Seneca's *Oedipus*: "Thou art falling, O noble race of Cadmus, with all thy city. Rest of its tillers thou seest thy land, O pitiable [*miseranda*] Thebes" (SenOed: 110–112)

[77] Line 1467: Eng. *endeavoring* renders Fr. *industrieux*, which has a range of meanings, suggested by Cotgrave: "Industrious; diligent, vigilant; indeavouring (sic); laborious, painefull, heedie, readie."

[78] Line 1467: Compare with Seneca's *Oedipus*: "The Arabs, blest with their cinnamon groves, they saw. . ." (SenOed: 117)

[79] Sabeans: an ancient population that occupied a territory in southwest Arabia. Nabaeteans: an ancient nomadic population that spoke a Semitic language, living near the Dead Sea.

[80] Line 1467: Compare with Seneca's *Oedipus*: "[The Arabs saw] fleeing horsemen, the backs of the treacherous Parthians, to be feared for their flying shafts" (SenOed: 118–19).

[81] Parthians: name given by the Greeks and Romans to a semi-nomadic population. Gedrosia: the ancient name of Balochistan (Pakistan), where the Balochi people lived, who migrated from Persia.

[82] Line 1479: Compare with Seneca's *Oedipus*: "We, the offspring of an unconquered stock [*invictae genus*], are perishing, are falling 'neath the fierce onslaught of fate. Each hour a new train moves on to Death; the long array of a mournful band hastes to the

The grass drinks our blood;
The plain is changed into a bloodbath,
It is covered with Theban bodies.
All that might remain
Of the Dircean city
Is not enough to bury them.

Our leaders with their unconquered hearts,
Who have fallen dead before our city's walls,
Leave for future centuries
Many testimonies of their valor.
They mixed their blood
With that of the Argolide enemy,
Throwing their adventurous soul
At sharp swords,
With no fear for the numerous crowds
Of Danaans whom they fought.[83]

They were handed similar misfortune.
If they valiantly assailed us,
Our courage never lacked,
Nor did our numbed arms fail to defend us.
No more of our soldiers survive
From these wars than did
Those of the attacking army.
If they think they conquered us,
Then it was a Cadmean victory,[84]
In which the victors wail the most.[85]

Those who survived the battle
Are now laid up, wounded, in tents.

---

shades; the gloomy procession jams, and for the throng that seeks burial the seven gates spread not wide enough. The grievous wrack of carnage halts and funeral crows funeral in unbroken line" (SenOed: 124–31).

[83] Line 1495: Danaans: the Greeks.

[84] Line 1504: Cadmean victory: a victory that involves one's own ruin, after Cadmus, the founder of Thebes, who secured water for the city by sacrificing his own people. As Beaudin notes (214), the term had already been used by Jacques Grévin in his tragedy *César* (line 969).

[85] Line 1505: Here and elsewhere Garnier underscores how the cost of victory is equally high on both sides, a theme also mentioned in *La Troade* (line 358). See Jondorf 1969: 80

They are not numerous enough
To assail our walls.
Polynices quickly followed
His brother, ravished by death,
By a shared wound.
There is no madness so great
As brotherly rancor
Mixed in with covetous greed.

Act IV

Antigone, Ismene.

ANTIGONE

My dear sister, Ismene,[1] on this day fortune shows itself to be bitterly unfortunate for our race. What sorrow, I ask, could strike a man that Jupiter, from his wrath, has not already dealt us? [1520] What cruelty can there be that our eyes do not already glimpse in all these burials before our walls? We have buried Jocasta's body, but our twin brothers lie dead and tombless.[2] Let us take on the charge, my sister, of covering them with earth [1525] until they receive monuments of stone.[3]

---

[1] Line 1516: With the fourth act, Garnier's *Antigone* reaches the point where most versions of *Antigone* begin, including Sophocles's. This act and the final one follow, in a general sense, the Greek text. Garnier's use of "*chere* soeur Ismene" (*dear* sister Ismene) picks up on the fact that, in the Greek text, Antigone uses "a strengthened form of the word for sister, 'very sister,' 'sister with the same mother and father,' and an adjective implying both this joint link and also a common bond of interest through kinship" (Goldhill 1986: 90). It has been noted that this act (899 verses in length) is the longest act in all of Garnier's theater (Lebègue: 269; Gras 1965: 41).

[2] Line 1523: In Sophocles, it is Ismene who recalls the death of the two brothers (SophAnt: 11–14).

[3] Line 1525: Antigone's initial address to Isemene differs from the one in Sophocles in several respects. No mention is made of Oedipus. In Sophocles, we read: ". . .which of the evils that come from Oedipus is he not accomplishing while we still live?" (SophAnt: 2–3). In Garnier, only fortune (Fr. *la fortune*) is to blame. Sophocles, too, makes no mention in Antigone's first words (v. 1252) of Jocasta's burial. In Garnier, death of Jocasta seems a necessary event for Antigone to speak in her own voice and as a hero: "Pendant les trois premiers actes Antigone est réduite au rôle de confidente. Ce n'est qu'après la mort de sa mère qu'elle semble donner libre cours à l'ardeur héroïque qui lui fait mépriser la vie et rechercher la 'belle mort'" (1618) (For the first three acts, Antigone is reduced to the role of confident. It is only following the death of her mother that she seems to give free reign to the heroic ardor that makes her despise life and seek out a "fine death") (Federici 1975:73).

ISMENE

Creon promptly buried Eteocles, for he was seen carrying arms for our native land, and because he died for it, along with a thousand and a thousand more of Thebes's courageous young children. [1530] But he forbade that Polynices be moved from where he fell and that he be given a sepulcher,[4] as if undeserving of a grave after having waged war on the city of his birth. And Creon wants (oh cruel heart!) that sharp-beaked crows [1535] feast upon his flesh and on the other defeated men.[5]

ANTIGONE

He wants Polynices to be fodder for grazing beasts, lying there on the ground without a grave? That he not be mourned? That grumbling Charon make him wander for a hundred years without crossing the Acheron? [1540] *That is too cruel a thing. All envy and all rancor must perish when we die.*[6]

ISMENE

He threatens with death those who go against his harsh decree and who would like to bury him.[7]

ANTIGONE

Let us show our good heart, may our goodwill [1545] overcome Creon's harsh decree.

---

[4] Line 1530: In Sophocles, it is Antigone who announces Creon's edict to Ismene (SophAnt: 26–38), a situation that Garnier here reverses.

[5] Line 1535: On this image, see also lines 1724, 1834, and 2634.

[6] Line 1541: Here begins Antigone's first formulation (to Ismene) of her reasons for wanting to bury Polynices. Compare to SophAnt: 45 et seq. On Antigone's formulation in Sophocles, see Foley 2001: 174. Antigone's tone in Garnier is strikingly different from what we read in Sophocles: Antigone's first thought is not of love for her brother, but a critique of Creon's political behavior. From this point on, her arguments are of a much less private and familial nature than in Sophocles. For Antigone's other formulations, see lines 1809–37 and notes to lines 1837 and 2214.

[7] Line 1242: It can be noted that, in Ismene's summary, Creon foreground the problem of his decree (and metonymically his power in general) not being respected, of which the will to bury Polynices would thus be a particular case. In other words, we see immediately Creon's hunger for power. The Fr. text of these two lines ("Il menace de mort ceux qui contreviendront / A sa dure defense, et l'enterrer voudront") is somewhat proleptic, in that it uses the future tense ('who will go against,' 'who will want to bury')—but this is also a consequence of differences between the two languages.

ISMENE

What shall we do? The prince must be obeyed.[8]

ANTIGONE

I see clearly that fear rids you of our family's natural courage.[9]

ISMENE

Consider the danger of such an enterprise.

ANTIGONE

In such matters you are too timid. [1550] Please, think seriously about coming with me.

ISMENE

I do not want to go against the king's ordinance.[10]

ANTIGONE

Of an unjust ordinance one need not take account.[11]

ISMENE

But anyone who goes against it will receive prompt punishment.

ANTIGONE

One never sees anything great achieved without danger.

---

[8] Line 1546: Given the fact that such a line, with reference to "the prince" in general, could be easily read from an allegorical point of view, it is important to note that in the first two (1580) editions of the text, this line was in quotation marks to suggest its universality. See note to line 1609.

[9] Line 1547: Eng. "rids you of our family's natural courage" renders MFr. "vous fait degenerer." MFr. *degenerer* is rendered by Cotgrave as: "To degnerate, grow out of kind, be unlike his ancestors." Antigone's reproach thus suggests then not that Ismene is afraid and lacks courage, but that she is not living up to her family heritage. See note to line 1725.

[10] Line 1551: Eng. *ordinance* renders MFr. *ordonnance*, a term that would have had particular resonance for Garnier's readers. In Renaissance France, an *ordonnance* was a royal law of some amplitude and for general application throughout France, in opposition to a MFr. *edit* (Eng. *edict*), which would treat one particular subject, for a specific group of people or geographical area. See also lines 1740, 1804, 1875. Also to be noted here is that Creon is refered to by various titles: prince (line 1546), king (line 1551), etc.

[11] Line 1552: Antigone's opposition to that which is unjust is central to her stance in Garnier. See also line 1809.

ISMENE

Where there is danger, one must not take action.

ANTIGONE

Too cowardly is he who takes no chances.

ISMENE

I prefer to avoid harm and to have you think me a coward.

ANTIGONE

Think again: will you help me?

ISMENE

I earnestly beg you, too, to rethink.

ANTIGONE

Since you do not want to go, I shall thus go alone.

ISMENE

I fear greatly, my sister, that you will end up suffering.

ANTIGONE

Come what may—I am determined.

ISMENE

I would go willingly if Creon should wish it.

ANTIGONE

I do not want to betray the Manes of my brother.[12]

ISMENE

He is my brother, too, but I can do nothing.

ANTIGONE

And why not?

ISMENE

Because of Creon, whom I fear.

---

[12] Line 1564: Manes (or *Di Manes*): chthonic deities that represent the souls of the deceased. This is the closest that Garnier's Antigone gets to defending her act as a private gesture, echoed further in line 1597.

ANTIGONE

He cannot stop such holy acts.

ISMENE

Think, my sister, of our weak sex, unskilled for this world's perilous designs.[13] Consider our age and think also that we are all who remain of Agenor's line. We are helpless. The ancient goodwill of our citizens changed with the change in ruling power: Creon is obeyed. He, a tyrant,[14] longs to uproot completely our ancient name. *We must follow the will of the powerful, to which we are bound. Doing more than one can will be judged to be madness.*[15]

ANTIGONE

Move not, then, my sister, venture nothing. Remain alone at home in calm repose. *I* will not allow for a greedy she-wolf to feed at will upon the body of my brother.[16] I will bury him, even if I have to suffer violent assaults and a hundred cruel deaths in all my limbs. There is no affront I will not suffer if suffer I must for such a sacred act. Once I have done it, I will feel no grief at being placed with him in the same coffin.[17] You, live in peace. Live happy always.

ISMENE

I would do like you, but I am too fearful.

---

[13] Line 1568: Ismene's gendered comments here are based on her words in Sophocles: "Why, we must remember that we are women [γυναῖχ'], who cannot fight against men, and then that we are ruled by those whose power is greater, so that we must consent to this and to other things even more painful!" (SophAnt: 61–64).

[14] Line 1574: Jondorf has commented: "It is tempting to see this [lines 1573–74] as a Machiavellian interpretation of Créon's behavior (the new prince exterminating the old ruling family); but when Etéocle and Polynice had killed each other, Créon, Jocaste's brother, had little choice but to claim the throne, and this attack can be seen as a flash of bitterness at the destruction of Ismène's own family rather than a serious argument against Créon" (Jondorf 1969: 103).

[15] Line 1577: This general statement is based on Sophocles: ". . .I shall obey those in authority; for there is no sense in actions that exceed our powers" (SophAnt: 65–69).

[16] Line 1581: Lines 1580–81 are imitated by Basscecourt in his *Tragi-comédie*, lines 1779–80. (Lebègue: 281).

[17] Line 1587: Antigone's acceptance of death as a necessary consequence of her actions and the promise of eternity with her brother in the tomb take on a different light here compared to Sophocles's text. In Sophocles, Antigone cries out "I am his own and I shall lie with him who is my own" (SophAnt: 73). Here, death is much more something to be stoically endured and accepted, rather than welcomed. Less emphasis, too, is placed on *philia*.

ANTIGONE

This fear stems from your lack of a courageous heart.[18]

ISMENE

That is not where my fear comes from.

ANTIGONE

Then, from where, I beg?

ISMENE

From a weak nature that worships the laws.

ANTIGONE

What an excuse! Fine, then. Do nothing, I am going to bury him.

ISMENE

Good gods, where are you going? You cause me to go pale. Not a hair on my head does not stand up in fright.

ANTIGONE

I am going to bury my brother Polynices.[19]

ISMENE

At least, be careful not to be found out.[20] For my part, I will tell no one.

ANTIGONE

Tell everyone, I want it to be known. *One who does not do wrong need not hide.*[21]

ISMENE

How you burn to do wrong!

ANTIGONE

Whether it is wrong or right, Polynices will receive funeral rites.

---

[18] Line 1590: Anticipates line 1916.

[19] Line 1597: See note to line 1564.

[20] Line 1598: Various verses (1598–99, 1606, 1608–09) here are imitated from Baïf's translation of *Antigone* (Lebègue: 281).

[21] Line 1601: In Sophocles, Antigone's words are much more specific to the context: "Ah, tell them all! I shall hate you far more if you remain silent, and do not proclaim this to all!" (SophAnt: 86–87). Garnier has Antigone speak more universal truths.

ISMENE

Yes, if you are able—but it is not an easy thing.

ANTIGONE

I will spare no effort—and I will, moreover, be pardoned.

ISMENE

That which we cannot achieve, we should not undertake.[22]

ANTIGONE

We must undertake all that is right by law.

ISMENE

Law means observing the king's orders.[23]

ANTIGONE

One must always do right, even when the king forbids it.[24]

ISMENE

But he has declared Polynices an enemy.

ANTIGONE

Indeed, after he grabbed hold of the scepter.

ISMENE

I pray you: abandon this dubious enterprise for one who lives no more.

ANTIGONE

How exasperating you are! Leave me, I pray you, to my temerity. Your words do nothing but annoy me. My plan is praiseworthy and no other harm can come from it save seeing myself freed from my sorrows by a fine death, which from the dark tombs will cause my name to pass into future centuries.[25]

---

[22] Line 1606: See note to line 1598.

[23] Line 1608: See note to line 1598.

[24] Line 1609: In the 1582 edition of the play, this line is in quotation marks to underline its universality. See also note to line 1546. These lines (1606–09) contrast with the equivalent passage in Sophocles. In Sophocles, Ismene condemns Antigone for the impossible (SophAnt: 90) and for pursuing hopeless ends (SophAnt: 92). Here, the discussion is also markedly political in nature, related to the connection between rights and rulers. Pinvert called this line (1609) a "réplique précornélienne" (proto-Cornelian line) and pointed out its absence in Sophocles (Pinvert: 2.445)

[25] Line 1619: Regarding Antigone's immortality, see also line 1223.

ISMENE

Go, then, with God. May good fortune guide you and make your sacred mission go well.

CHORUS

Heaven withdraws from us[26]
Its anger—
It now favors us.
We must, for such benevolency
Toward us,
Make sacrifices to the Immortal Ones.

Of our walls heaven took care
When needed;
It held out its hand.
Our city would not exist
At present
Had they not defended it.

Who could ever as a
Warrior
On the destroyed wall,
Have killed Capaneus
Without the arm
Of Rhea's thundering son?[27]

Under the shield that protected him,
He mocked
The flames and flying arrows
That launched from all around
Our soldiers
At his glistening armor.

As he passed them he
Cut them down

[26] Line 1622: The choral ode draws loosely on SophAnt: 100–61. The most notable change is in addressee: Sophocles addresses the ode to the sun and to Zeus ("Beam of the sun, fairer than all that have shone before. . .. For Zeus detects the boasts of a proud tongue. . ."); whereas Garnier addresses his to heaven ("le Ciel"). As Beaudin notes (218), Garnier also puts emphasis on the notion of providence.

[27] Capaneus: one of the seven against Thebes, an ally of Polynices, struck down by one of Zeus's lightning bolts. Rhea: mother of Zeus.

Like a wild boar that crosses
Through mutinous squadrons
Of dogs
That he fells and knocks down;

Or he is like, in a meadow that is
Brightly flourishing,
The reaper who cuts down the grass
And who gathers the fallen crops
From the ground,
Forming many a sheaf.

When Jupiter notices him
Destroying
Thebes, ready for its misfortune,
He took his red thunderbolt in hand and
Rapidly
Smashed it upon his head.

On seeing Amphiaraus, too,
Pitiless,
Putting us under deadly attack,
Jupiter, to protect us,
Sent him
Rapidly down into hell.

Thus, it was the guardianship of the
Good protective gods[28]
And not human courage which
Has kept us safe at present,
Supporting
The poor City of Thebes.

From the gods one always finds
Help:
They preside over battles,
They steer off the violent assaults
Of the strongest
And they protect our walls.

[28] Line 1670: Compare with Aeschylus's *Seven Against Thebes* (lines 226–34).

May they forever receive honor
For the happiness
That their grace brings us.
Each year on the return of
This date
May we make a sacrifice to them.

Our enemies, knocked down,
Frightened,
Run about, pricked by fear.
Over these harsh mounts, these
Wanderers
Leave the land stained with their blood.

They have not buried the bodies
Of their dead
So much does cold fear rush them.
They are in danger of vultures
And bears
Chewing on them with gluttonous hunger.

They march off without a flag and
Without order—
They dare not raise their heads,
Ashamed to see themselves
Be dealt
Defeat instead of victory.

Creon, the chorus of elders, the men who guard Polynices's body, Antigone, Ismene, Haemon.

CREON

Thanks to the immortal gods[29] who have taken care of us and helped us with good favor when we needed it, our broken enemies have now taken flight, leaving in shame from our destroyed land. The bloody countryside is covered with dead bodies. Cephissus's[30] sinuous banks now run crimson from the various bloods that mix together; its waves ripple with color, as does the blond hair of Ceres.

---

[29] Line 1706: Creon's initial speech (lines 1706–47) draws on SophAnt: 161–210.

[30] Line 1711: Cephissus: a river in Boeotia.

They brought in the Argolides, the troops of Megara, and the Mycenaeans.[31] The Achaean troops set up camp outside our walls and launched innumerable weapons to fill our towers with terror. Adrastus, their great king, had already promised himself that he would see his Polynices put back on his throne, so that he would govern with force and press into servitude that Ogygian people of indomitable courage.[32] But Polynices fell. His teeth biting into the dirt, he lies dead, layed out on the plain. The crows will graze on his flesh, which is not worthy of Cadmus's tomb—this wicked one has strayed from his line.[33] He has, full of fury, warred against his own people, and with fire and iron ransacked the land. His name must be dishonored for future generations and his damned body must rot without a tomb.[34]

Now I, as the closest in blood to unfortunate Oedipus, *I* come to reign in my rightful rank. I have issued a public edict that expressly forbids that wicked man from being buried. Anyone who attempts to do the opposite and who breaks my law can be sure to experience the anger of a king.[35]

I swear by the heavens that surround this earth, by this honored scepter, and by this crown, that if I see any Theban breaking this law, I will have him punished—there will be no hope for pardons, even were he my own child.[36] *An ordinance is in vain if its offenders are exempt from punishment.*[37]

I have guards seated on the surrounding hills who will keep watch over the enemy bodies night and day. As for the citizens who died and expelled all life,[38]

---

[31] Megara: a city located between Athens and Corinth. Mycenaeans: inhabitants of mainland Greece in the late bronze age.

[32] Ogygus: a native king of Boeotia. The Ogygian people thus refers to the inhabitants of Boeotia, in the region of Thebes.

[33] Line 1725: See note to line 1547.

[34] Line 1729: Compare Creon's damning of Polynices, whose dishonor must be immortal, to the notion of Antigone's piety guaranteeing her immortality. See lines 1223 and 1619.

[35] Line 1735: In Sophocles, Creon explains his actions as follows: "Eteocles, who died fighting for this city [πόλεως], having excelled in battle, we shall hide in the tomb and we shall render to him all the rites that come to the noblest of the dead below. But his brother, I mean Polynices, who came back form exile meaning to burn to the ground his native city and the gods of his race, and meaning to drink the people's blood and to enslave its people, as for him it is proclaimed to this city that none shall bury or lament, but they shall leave his body unburied for birds and dogs to devour and savage" (SophAnt: 194–206).

[36] Line 1740: This line, of course, resonates in various ways: with the fate of Oedipus, as well as with Creon's own—for by killing Antigone, he will also lose his son Haemon and his wife, Eurydice.

[37] Line 1740: See note to line 1551.

[38] Line 1744: Garnier writes literally ". . .qui ont vomy leur vie" (who have vomited out their life).

who fought with great valor for their dear land, I want them to be mourned and, with public lamentation, that they be buried and that their courage be sung.

CHORUS OF ELDERS

You want each to receive his fare wage—some for their good deeds, others for their villainy.

CREON

Every principality remains at peace[39] *when to each man is rendered that which is his.*[40] *Criminals must be punished for their crimes and good men must be rewarded by the prince. Punishment and reward are the two foundations and the firm pillars of all governments.*[41]

CHORUS OF ELDERS

Do you wish to issue any other orders?

CREON

That everyone prepare to respect my edict.

CHORUS OF ELDERS

Who will be so rash as to risk danger of death for the sake of a dead man?

CREON

There are always rebellious citizens.

CHORUS OF ELDERS

I know of none who lack proper allegiance to you.

---

[39] Line 1750: See also note to line 2091.

[40] Line 1751: One wonders to what extent Garnier here alludes ironically to Matthew 22:21 ("Render therefore unto Caesar the things which are Caesar's; and unto God the things that are God's") (King James).

[41] Line 1755: Only the 1580 editions give this line (which starts at "and the firm pillars. . .") in quotation marks—but given that the change is mid-sentence, the lack of quotation marks in later editions is more likely due to oversight than to intent. In Sophocles, Creon's self-awareness as leader was already apparent SophAnt: 175–77. Creon's statement here (lines 1750–54) draws on what the chorus says in Sophocles: "It is your pleasure, son of Menoeceus, to do this to the man who is hostile and to the man who is loyal to the city; and you have power to observe every rule with regard to the dead and to us who are alive" (SophAnt: 211–14). According to Jondorf, these lines (1748–55) suggest that, in his own way, Creon could "claim right on his side" even if he is judged to be wrong by the chorus (see Jondorf 1969: 66).

GUARD

You, advance. Advance.

ANTIGONE

I do not hold back.

CHORUS OF ELDERS

Who is the woman they hold by the arms? It is poor Antigone. Ah, the poor girl! You have readily shown too much pity.[42]

CREON

Bring her, drag her. You are good men. Where did you capture her?

GUARD

She was at her brother's side.

CREON

At the side of Polynices?

GUARD

Covering him with earth.[43]

CHORUS OF ELDERS

Obstinate misfortune devastates this house!

CREON

By command of the gods, you will die. But, tell me how you were able to find her as she performed this burial?

GUARD

We were off behind these hills,[44] for fear the smell of corpses reach our nostrils, sheltered from the wind, watching carefully to make sure that no one came along to steal this most loathsome body. We then noticed this crying girl, a metal shovel in one hand and a splendid cup in the other, approach the dead body,

---

[42] Line 1765: Antigone appears much earlier in Garnier than in Sophocles. Garnier leaves to one side the first interaction with the guard (SophAnt: 223–383).

[43] Line 1768: This initial piece of information was given in the first guard's speech, though without it being ascribed to Antigone: "Someone has just gone off after burying the body, sprinkling its flesh with thirsty dust and performing the necessary rites" (SophAnt: 245–47).

[44] Line 1772: The guard's description of Antigone's action (lines 1772–99) draws on SophAnt: 407–40.

rushing upon it in great distress, sounding a thousand regrets, a thousand piteous moans, enough to drive the wood's tigers to grief. Her moving voice of lament resonated everywhere like that of a bird numbed by sadness when, carrying back a beakfull of food to its nest, it no longer finds its small brood there.

Once she had lamented her misfortunes for some time and honored the wounds of the dead man with kisses, she sprinkled burial sacrifices, prayed to the Manes,[45] and invoked the names of the Stygian virgins. Then, having put down the sacrificial cup, she picked up the spade and scattered the driest sand upon his breast. Right away, without any further waiting, we ran up to her, so as to catch her at her crime and deliver her to your hands. But she was not frightened, she surrendered to us of her own accord, making an open confession about the funeral rites she had wished to offer the body of Polynices. I pitied her, but duty binds me to tell you what happened and not to keep it quiet.

CREON

Is it true? Did you commit this crime? Were you caught there by these guards? Lift your eyes up from the ground. Do not disguise the truth.[46]

ANTIGONE

It is true, I did it.[47]

---

[45] Line 1788: See note to line 1564.

[46] Line 1802: Garnier says literally, "Disguise nothing" (Fr. "ne desguisez rien"). Cotgrave includes for Fr. *desguiser* the meanings of "to disguise; to counterfeit, or set a false coat or glosse on; to alter, adulterate, falsifie, sophisticate." See note to line 1869.

[47] Line 1803: This is one of the most important lines of the play, wherein Antigone publicly acknowledges having broken Creon's edict. Sophocles's version reads: "καὶ φημὶ δρᾶσαι κοὐκ ἀπαρνοῦμαι τὸ μή" (SophAnt: 443), a line that has been translated in various ways. Fagles renders it as "I did it. I don't deny a thing" (Sophocles 1982: 81), Greene as "Yes, I confess: I will not deny my deed" (Sophocles 1991: 43). A more literal translation, as given by Hugh Lloyd-Jones in the Loeb edition, would be "I say that I did it and I do not deny it." Analysis of this line constitutes the heart of Butler 2000. Garnier's rendering is quite different—and, moreover, it changed between editions. In the 1585 edition (Paris: Mamert Patisson), the last prepared by the author before his death in 1590, Antigone says "Il est vray, je l'ai fait" (It is true, I did it). In the first three editions (*Antigone,* Paris: Mamert Patisson, 1580; *Les tragédies*, Paris: Mamert Patisson, 1580; *Les tragédies*, Paris: Mamert Parisson, 1582), Antigone said something different: "Ce qu'ils ont dit est vray" (What they said is true). Garnier's change—from "Ce qu'ils ont dit est vray" (What they said is true) to "Il est vray, je l'ai fait" (It is true, I did it)—is not a minor one, for even if it does not exactly reproduce the very specific phrase in Greek, wherein Antigone both refuses to be forced into an untrue speech act and fully accepts the authorship of her acts, it does tend towards asserting Antigone's control of her own speech, for she no longer just says "what they say is true."

CREON

Did you not know that a public ordinance forbade it?[48]

ANTIGONE

Yes, I knew it all too well. I was aware of it.

CREON

Who, then, made you go against this law?

ANTIGONE

God's ordinance, for he is our great king.

CREON

God does not order that laws be disobeyed.

ANTIGONE

He does indeed,[49] *when they are so full of injustice. Great God, who made heaven and earth, shaped human laws to fit his own*[50] *which he bids us to safeguard as sound,*[51] *and to reject those that go against them. No tyrant's laws must endure*[52] *when we see that they rebel against God's precepts.*[53] Both the god of hell who reigns over

[48] Line 1804: See note to line 1551. The MFr. term *edit* (Eng. *edict*) might have been more appropriate for this specific ruling given the latter's very focused nature. Creon's reference to a "publique odonnance" takes up the Greek verb κηρύσσω (to proclaim, announce, command publicly) (SophAnt: 447).

[49] Line 1809: Antigone's opposition to that which is unjust is central to her stance in Garnier. See also line 1552.

[50] Line 1811: Compare these lines (lines 1810–15) to Michel de l'Hospital in his *Harangue de St-Germain-en-Laye*, August 26, 1561: "faut considerer qu'il y a deux sortes de loyx; aux unes l'on ne peult desroger sans contrarier aux ordonnances de Dieu et celles-là demeurent inviolables" (it is necessary to consider that there are two kinds of laws: some cannot be disobeyed without going against God's ordinances—those ones must remain inviolate) (qtd. Mouflard: 1. 147).

[51] Line 1812: See line 196.

[52] Line 1814: The word *tyrant* was already used at line 1027.

[53] Line 1815: The *guillemets* around lines 1809–15, at this crucial point in the play, show that Antigone is arguing her point from a certain remove, with a goal of situating her stance within a more general political ideal. Judith Butler has argued that, in Sophocles, Antigone's law "appears to have but one instance of application" and that it is "a law formulated precisely through the singular instance of its application" (i.e. to the case of her brother) (Butler 2000: 10).

Shades[54] and he who presides over the celestial troop urge us towards human piety—whereas you order nothing but inhumanity.

No, no, I do not have such high regard for your laws that to obey them I would commit a crime, and violate the sacred precepts of the gods, precepts naturally imprinted within our hearts. They last eternally in man's essence and we are born to protect them from the cradle on. Should I have corrupted them? Should I. . . should I have had so little esteem for them because of your authority?[55] You will have me killed, I was sure about that, but fear of death means nothing in my position. In my extreme grief, death is all I want. *Whoever suffers greatly longs for the coffin.*

What, Creon? Should I have violated nature's laws and allowed my own brother to become food for the wolves because he remains unburried, as it is ordered? My brother, my own blood, born from the same womb? I would have offended the gods who are favorable to the dead, I would have made them pitiless against me.[56]

---

[54] Line 1816: It is not clear why Jacques Morel made the following comment about lines 1809–16: "L'*Antigone* de Garnier [. . .] pense que les lois humaines ne sont pas en droit différentes des lois divines 'ancrées' au cœur de tous les hommes; obéir aux 'préceptes sacrés,' c'est obéir *a fortiori* à la loi de l'état" (Garnier's *Antigone* [. . .] thinks that human laws are not, in law, different from those divine laws anchored in the hearts of all men; obeying 'sacred precepts' is obeying *a fortiori* the law of the state) (Morel 1991: 365). It would seem rather that Antigone is arguing for the absolute difference and incompatibility between divine and political laws. For another perspective on the piety evoked here, see Lebègue 1990: 81.

[55] Line 1827: Here, Antigone stands up against unjust laws, opposing the edicts of Creon and divine laws. In Sophocles, Antigone justifies her position by stating not just that the laws were not proclaimed by Zeus, but also (a) that Justice (Δίκη) did not ordain such things for men; and (b) that, in her opinion, a simple mortal like Creon would be unable to topple such unwritten laws: divine ordinances (θεῶν νόμιμα) are necessarily, for Sophocles, "unwritten" (ἄγραπτα) (SophAnt: 451–52). These laws are eternal and unchanging: "For these have life, not simply today and yesterday, but forever, and no one knows how long ago they were revealed" (SophAnt: 456–57). The law is divine and/because it is unwritten—divine laws "require no promulgation" (Brague 2007: 22). Antigone's defense of her claim is very specific to Athenian notions of religion, society, and politics. Antigone is sometimes thought to be the mouthpiece of a law and authority alternate to Creon's, the unwrittenness of that in the name of which she speaks is surely essential. For sure, "the distinction [between written and unwritten laws] was hazy in Athenian legal discourse," such that "written laws [. . .] were, for the most part, known in oral form" and yet "'the unwritten laws' were a category within actual Athenian legal practice"—Aristotle advises litigants to have recourse to unwritten laws should they fail to find appropriate written ones, giving moreover Antigone as the example (Wohl 2009: 126).

[56] Line 1837: Here concludes Antigone's second formulation (lines 1809–37) of her justification for burying Polynices. This second formulation ties together the refusal of

CHORUS OF ELDERS

This poor Antigone disobeys in her misery. Her heart is too lofty for her condition.

CREON

The power of the king tames rebellious hearts and submits them to the laws they ignore.

Not only does this woman break my forbiddance, but, as if breaking it were a holy act, she takes glory from it and with reckless audacity she maintains that she did right, even to my very face. She mocks my power and is of the open opinion that, out of some vain respect for those kings that came before, she is not bound by it; and, further, that the treason she exhibits towards me must go unpunished.[57] But, even though she is the sister and daughter of kings, born to my sister under marital law, I will have her killed, and her sister with her if I find her sister to be part of the plot. Bring her here! For when I saw her just now, I believe her mind was taken with some big thought, so anguished did she seem. *Often our secret is visible and gives itself up.*

ANTIGONE

You can, at most, have me killed.

CREON

And indeed, nothing more do I plan to do.

ANTIGONE

Why do you wait so long? What makes you delay?

CREON

It will happen when I desire, for nothing keeps me from it.

ANTIGONE

I am impatient for that death that is my destiny.

CREON

It will not keep you waiting much longer, it is coming.

---

injustice already performed in the first defense to the Christian notion of *pieté* (line 1818). Political and religious notions are thus bound together. See also notes to lines 1541 and 2214. See also Patin 1873: 2.286–88 and Pinvert: 2.446.

[57] Line 1849: Garnier does not render Creon's celebrated retort: "Indeed, now I am no man, but she is a man, if she is to enjoy such power as this with impunity" (SophAnt: 484–85). See note to line 2043.

ANTIGONE

I will die outside the law for a glorious deed.

CREON

[1865] You will rightly die as a daring and courageous woman.[58]

ANTIGONE

There is no one who would not have committed this same crime.

CREON

Yet, no one did it.

ANTIGONE

If they could speak freely, they would praise my deed.[59]

CREON

Who would stop them from speaking without disguise?[60]

ANTIGONE

[1870] The fear of upsetting a king too cruel.

CREON

Why do you not fear upsetting him, as they do?

ANTIGONE

For I do not fear death, the remedy to my wretched sorrow.

CREON

Your disdain for death causes you to do wrong.

ANTIGONE

It is not wrong to bury one's dead brother.

---

[58] Line 1865: Creon's condemnation, that Antigone will die as "une audacieuse" has various strands. The MFr. term *audacieux/audacieuse* has various meanings, both positive and negative, as Cotgrave notes: "Bold, stout, hardie, aduenturous, hazardous, couragious (sic), full of mettall, stomacke, valour; also, audacious, daring, saucie, malapert, presumptuous; rash." See also lines 1984 and 2052 (and notes).

[59] Line 1868: Garnier reworks Sophocles: "I would say that all these men would approve this, if it were not that fear shuts their mouths" (SophAnt: 502–05); and "These men too see it; but they curb their tongues to please you" (SophAnt: 508). Garnier ties this in with his anti-tyrannical position (line 1870).

[60] Line 1869: Here Eng. *disguise* renders MFr. *feintise*. See note to line 1802.

CREON

You have, in burying him, transgressed my edicts.[61]

ANTIGONE

But the laws of nature and of the gods are stronger.

CREON

You did not honor your other brother in a similar manner.

ANTIGONE

You took care of my other brother.[62]

CREON

And if I hadn't?

ANTIGONE

Then I would have buried him, too.

CREON

Polynices waged war on and sacked his homeland.

ANTIGONE

The wrongdoing originated in his native land.

[61] Line 1875: See notes to lines 1551, 1740, 1804. The choice of Fr. *edits* (Eng. *edicts*), in the plural, might be considered somewhat surprising here.

[62] Line 1878: Antigone's defense of her position, which privileges God's law over that of Creon, and which makes God's law the only source of authority for earthly justice is close to the underlying point of Théodore de Bèze's *Du droit des magistrats* (first published 1574) and which begins: "Il n'y a autre volonté que celle de vn seul Dieu qui soit perpetuelle & immuable reigle de toute justice. C'est donc luy seul auquel nous sommes tenus d'obeir sans aucune exception" (There will be no other will than that of God alone, which will is an eternal and unchangeable rule of all justice. It is thus he alone whom we must obey without any exception) (Bèze 1579: 3). De Bèze also raises the question of whether individuals should abide by the rulings of princes: "quant a l'obeissance deue aux princes, s'ils estoyent tousiours la bouche de Dieu pour commander, il faudroit aussi dire sans exception qu'on leur deuroit obeir tout ainsi qu'a Dieu: mais [. . .] trop souuent, ceste condition y doit estre apposee, Pourueue qu'ils ne commandêt choses irreligieuses, ou iniques" (as for the obedience owed to princes, if they always spoke God's words in their commandments, it would also be necessary to say without exception that princes should be obeyed as God—but too often this condition must be added: as long as they order nothing unreligious or iniquitous) (Bèze 1579: 3).

CREON

And he brought here our deadly enemies.

ANTIGONE

Each is allowed to defend his rights.

CREON

I will defend my rights against you who rebel.

ANTIGONE

I have done nothing that was not due to natural love.[63]

CREON

One should not love a public enemy.

CHORUS OF ELDERS

Here comes Ismene.

CREON

Where is she?

CHORUS OF ELDERS

She is coming. Her face is drowned by waves of tears, which wash the color from her cheeks. Ah, dear girl, I am afraid.

CREON

The snakes and plagues arrive—which I loved more dearly than my children. Did you consent to this burial?

ISMENE

I am the one who first thought of it.[64] If there is sin, if there has been a crime, then punish me and me alone, for I alone did it.

ANTIGONE

No, no, she is lying, she is innocent of this and must have no part of my punishment. She knew nothing of it, do not believe her.

ISMENE

I went there with her, following her step by step.

---

[63] Line 1885: The sense of "natural love" is given earlier, line 1876.

[64] Line 1893: Ismene makes a similar claim in SophAnt: 536–37.

ANTIGONE

Had I told her, she would have denounced me.

ISMENE

On the contrary. Without me, she would not have gone there.

ANTIGONE

Creon, her courage is not strong enough.

ISMENE

It is I who pushed you not to fear death.

ANTIGONE

She wants to steal part of the glory that I have won.

ISMENE

You want to steal from me the glory I deserve.[65]

ANTIGONE

All this she says in order to die.

ISMENE

But all this you say in order to save me.

ANTIGONE

And why, without merit, do you wish to follow me?

ISMENE

And why do you wish to force me to live?

ANTIGONE

Wish rather, my sister, that your fine days be lengthened.

ISMENE

Why, then, do you wish to cut yours short?

ANTIGONE

Unlike you, I do not throw myself at torture.

---

[65] Line 1905: According to Pinvert, "Dans cette scène, Garnier, à la différence de Sophocles, a cru devoir donner aux deux sœurs un égal héroïsme" (In this scène, Garnier, unlike Sophocles, thought it necessary to give the two sisters equal heroism) (Pinvert: 2.446).

ISMENE

Your threw yourself at it by burying Polynices.

ANTIGONE

I preferred dying to failing in the duty that we who live owe to those who have died. But you, for lack of courageous heart, did not dare follow me.[66]

ISMENE

Oh how difficult it will be if I must outlive you.

CREON

I believe this girl's mind is troubled.

ISMENE

A mind, oh Creon, filled up with bitterness is not calmed by that—this is certain.

CREON

You have lost your mind if you chase after punishment.

ISMENE

Without her,[67] I can only live in displeasure.

CREON

As for her, soon death will take her in its grip.

ISMENE

She whom you promised to your son?

CREON

Her punishment will not be slowed because of that.

ISMENE

And for your son's wellbeing, do you have no further worry?

CREON

I will find somewhere else a wife for my son.

---

[66] Line 1916: This line echoes back to line 1590. See also line 83.

[67] Line 1922: Taking into account both French and Latin syntax, there is perhaps slight ambiguity in the Fr. text, whene Ismene says that "sans elle, je ne puis vivre qu'en desplaisir" (Without her/it, I can only live in displeasure)—*elle* might refer to either Antigone, or to punishment. The ambiguity is cleared on the following line (*elle* must refer to Antigone).

ANTIGONE
See, my dear Haemon, how much you are valued!

CREON
There will be no wife where there is crime.

ISMENE
The only crime she committed was being pious Antigone.

CREON
All she did was attack my authority.

ISMENE
Do you want to deprive him of such a dear partner?[68]

CREON
Yes, even if she were his heart and his soul mate.

ISMENE
She is a daughter, a sister, and a descendant of kings.[69]

CREON
Were she to descend from the gods, she is subject to the laws.

ISMENE
She is engaged to your son.

CREON
She will be wed in Pluto's kingdom.

ISMENE
Oh criminal cruelty! Oh proud viciousness!

CREON
Be careful not to seek out similar misfortune.

---

[68] Garnier writes "une si chere amie," *amie* meaning both lover and friend in the sixteenth century.

[69] Line 1934: There is perhaps a slight play on words here. Garnier calls Antigone here a Fr. "niepce de Rois," which can mean either "descendant of kings" or "niece of kings"—and Creon is, of course, Antigone's uncle.

ISMENE

I do not fear the unjust wrath of a tyrant.

CREON

Take them both, take these two vipers and shut them away. I will make them feel how much one regrets angering me.

CHORUS OF ELDERS

Here is poor Haemon, your noble son,[70] who darkens with sorrow the appearance of his bright face. He appears to be sad and to have, when one sees him sigh, a heart so doleful. This is doubtless the effect of excessive love, of seeing his sweet fiancée wronged. He pities her. As I hear him suffering so much, I think that he cannot bear his sadness.

HAEMON

Why do you die, you who are my life? Why are you, my soul, stolen away? Away from my heart that lives only on your sweet flame?[71] Why do you die without me? Why does death lead you off to Pluto's realm and yet I do not go with you? Why do I live without you, why is my crying soul absent from you, separated from you? No, no, I do not know. Whoever kills you will join my death together with your own.

[70] Line 1944: Garnier begins this choral ode with reference to Haemon, corresponding to SophAnt: 626–30. Garnier does not reproduce the first part of Sophocles's ode, which begins "Fortunate are those whose lifetime never tastes of evil!" (SophAnt: 583), in particular about the ruin of the Labdacids: "From ancient times I see the troubles of the dead of the Labdacid house falling hard upon one another. . ." (SophAnt: 594 et seq.).

[71] Line 1952: In Sophocles, Haemon first addresses his father, not Antigone (SophAnt: 635 et seq.). There, Haemon emphasizes right away that his loyalties lie with his father: "Father, I belong to you, and you keep me straight with your good judgments, which I shall follow." Pinvert comments: "C'est la seule scène du théâtre de Garnier dans laquelle deux amants se rencontrent, et ce n'est pas une scène d'amour [. . .] Garnier fait ressortir la bonté, la 'piété' d'Hémon, aux dépens de son amour. S'il apparaît à ce moment de la pièce, ce n'est pas pour opposer au découragement d'Antigone les conseils de fermeté qui sont d'usage dans de tels moments. Hémon joue, dans sa scène auprès d'Antigone, le rôle qu'elle jouait au premier acte auprès de son père. Il n'est pas jusqu'aux paroles que les deux personnages prononcent dans ces deux occasions qui ne se ressemblent [see lines 73–80, 1396–1401]" (This is the only scene in Garnier's theater in which two lovers meet—and it is not a love scene [. . .] Garnier brings out the goodness, the 'piety' of Haemon, to the expense of his love. If he appears at this moment in the play, it is not to put in opposition Antigone's discouragement and the firm advice that are usual in such moments. Haemon plays, in his scene with Antigone, the role that she played in the first act with her father. Right up to the words of the two characters are similar) (Gras 1965: 41).

CREON

My son, have you learned of the judgment made against your Antigone, which sentences her to death?

HAEMON

I have been told, father, and it grieves me most greatly.

CREON

Do you not wish to bend to my will?[72]

HAEMON

Father, I want to please you in all things. Your command reigns over my will.

CREON

That is the necessary talk: a noble child takes no pleasure in what his father forbids. That is why everyone wants children who do not arrogantly contradict their fathers — like those children one sees who take pleasure only in countering their father's desires.

Be careful, my child, that the love of a woman, a deadly poison, does not set you too much on fire. *It is an ill towards which your age is often inclined*, but you should extract that venom by means of reason. Tame this violent passion, lest it shackle your young freedom with a most reprehensible yoke. *A mean woman brings much evil to him that she clasps in the bonds of marriage.* Such is she whom I dispatch to the darkness of nightly Acheron. Do not give her your heart. Accept that she go there without you to find a new husband in place of you. She is a daring one, an arrogant girl[73] — our greatness is displeasing to her heart. *Nothing is so dangerous to the state of a great king as a proud subject, as a rebellious subject, who endlessly strives to oppose all that he decrees.*

HAEMON

That is true. *But often a subject's intention is other than we think it to be. A grave crime may be committed where no grave intention was. Most wrongs result from imprudence.* This Virgin, when she committed a crime that deserves our pity,[74]

[72] Line 1963: To establish the kind of connection between Creon and his son, Garnier uses specific vocabulary: Creon asks his son to conform himself to his MFr. *vueil* (here translated as *will*); Haemon says that Creon's *commandement* (command, laws, bidding) controls his *vouloir* (also translated *will*). This should be compared with the use of the term *volonté* (also rendered as *will*) — see note to line 388.

[73] Line 1984: See line 1865 (and note).

[74] Line 1995: Comparing Haemon's defense of Antigone here (lines 1990–2019) and in Sophocles (SophAnt: 683–723), a few key differences reveal themselves. Garnier

went against your edicts only against her will. Everyone pities her, the whole city bemoans that a royal daughter, innocent, dies, for such a beautiful act that should have been rewarded as virtuous and not be denied.

What wrong, they ask, did this poor thing do, wanting to bury the silent remains of her dead brother, after having mourned him, so that he would not be devoured by the crows or the wolves?

That is what is said about you, but you are not made to hear it—for fear of displeasing you, no one dares. *A king knows, as a rule, only what pleases, only that which is to his taste, for everything else is kept silent.* But I, who am your child, desire more than anyone that your power may enjoy long honor; I, who love you without disguise, openly I come to tell you of the rumors amongst the Ogygian people. Conform your mind to ruling reason; do not let passion take it over. Do not resemble those who, thinking they know everything,[75] refuse to receive advice from others.

It is no dishonor at all for a wise prince to sometimes learn from a lesser person and to follow his counsel, if he gives good advice, rather than being overtly obstinate or clinging to his own opinion.[76]

CREON

Do you think I want to take advice from you?[77] And at my age learn lessons from you?

HAEMON

One should not evaluate the person, but the advice offered, and depending on what it is—take it or leave it.

CREON

Fine advice: to reward a rogue.

HAEMON

I do not advise that you do well by the wicked.

---

refers to her act as "a crime that deserves our pity," whereas Sophocles spoke of "actions that are glorious." Garnier underscores, indeed, the idea of pity (lines 1994 and 1996), a work obviously close to piety (*pieté*).

[75] Line 2014: On these lines and the question of the king's authority over legislative and adjudicatory matters, see Jondorf 1969: 69.

[76] Line 2019: The multiplication of *guillemets* in the exchange between Creon and Haemon underscores that universal notions of good governance are being discussed here—it is not *just* a discussion between a father and a son.

[77] Line 2020: On the importance of this exchange between Creon and Haemon, see Introduction.

CREON

You want me to forgive this pest.[78]

HAEMON

Her crime is most minor and deserves our pity.[79]

CREON

Burying a wicked man, is that a minor matter? A public enemy?

HAEMON

True, but it is her brother.

CREON

Violating my edicts? Having so much contempt for me?

HAEMON

She did not set out to violate your laws.

CREON

I will have her suffer punishment for her pride.

HAEMON

The City of Thebes will not agree.

CREON

What do I care for opinions? Such is my will.

HAEMON

Are you not subject to the laws of the city?

CREON

A prince is not subject to the rules of his kingdom.

HAEMON

You speak of a tyrant, not of a good prince.

CREON

You want my subjects to set laws for me.

---

[78] Line 2026: Eng. *pest* renders Fr. *peste*, which Cotgrave defines as: "The plague, or pestilence; a death, contagion, infection; also, a pestiferous fellow; one that ruines, or spoyles, others."

[79] Line 2027: Eng. *pity* renders Fr. *merci*.

HAEMON

On the contrary, they must obey their kings, those kings who are their lords — they must love and fear them. But also, a king must not break public law.

CREON

He worries over a woman and serves her as needed.

HAEMON

You, then, would be a woman — because over you alone do I worry.[80]

CREON

Do you dare, wretched you, contest your father?

HAEMON

I dare, for the sake of fareness, to combat injustice.[81]

CREON

Do I seem unjust in defending my rights?

HAEMON

Unjust in proclaiming tyrannical laws.[82]

CREON

How the treachery of a woman has made you dumb.

HAEMON

Antigone deals in neither hypocrisy, nor spite.

CREON

You will not see her again, her final day is near.

---

[80] Line 2043: Garnier takes up Sophocles: "If you are a woman [γυνὴ]; because it is for you that I feel concern" (SophAnt: 741). See also note to line 1849.

[81] Line 2045: Eng. *fareness* renders MFr. équité, which Cotgrave defines as follows: "Equitie, equalitie; euennesse; uprightnesse; mitigation of rigor; moderation of humour; mildnesse, clemencie, mercifulnesse."

[82] Line 2047: Sophocles's Haemon falls short of accusing his father of tyranny. When Creon asks "Am I offending when I show regard for my own office?" (SophAnt: 744), Haemon answers not in respect of "tyrannical laws" but by stating: "You show no regard when you trample on the honors due to the gods!" (SophAnt: 745). The whole discussion, indeed, is focused on laws in Garnier (vv. 2030, 2031, 2038, 2041).

HAEMON

If she dies, she will not die alone.

CREON

And now he threatens me, what impudent daring![83]

HAEMON

I use no threats against my father and king.

CREON

Effeminate slave, if you contest me anymore I will send you grumbling down to the swamps of hell.

HAEMON

You thus wish only to talk and to listen to no one.

CREON

I take as my witness Jupiter, he who beats the Capharean rocks with his thunderbolt, that punishment will quickly track down such presumption. Go, quickly bring me this rabid beast so that before the eyes of this suitor she can have her throat cut.[84]

HAEMON

This will not happen happen: I will die a thousand deaths rather than allow that in my presence her body be violently harmed. You will not see me again. Exert your rage upon those who patiently endure your violence.[85]

CHORUS OF ELDERS

He leaves in nimble step, bitten by wrath and love. I fear greatly that he is planning some dirty trick.

---

[83] Line 2052: It is fitting that Creon accuses Haemon of Eng. *rashness* (<Fr. *audace*), echoing his accusation of Antigone, whom he called Eng. *rash* (<Fr. *audacieuse*). See line 1865.

[84] Line 2061: Garnier's MFr. *galant* (here rendered as Eng. *suitor*) translates Gk. νυμφίος (bridegroom) (SophAnt: 761), thus slightly modifying how Creon sees his son's relationship to Antigone. Cotgrave glosses *Galant homme* as "A gallant, goodlie; noble, worthie, virtuous; also, a subtill, wise, craftie, cunning, wylie, fellow."

[85] Line 2065: It is worth noting that words of the same family are used to describe both the physical punishment exerted against Antigone, and the violence of Creon's power over the citizens. In the first case, garnier writes Fr. "on outrage son corps" (rendered as Eng. "her body be violently harmed"); in the latter, Fr. "endurent tout outrage" (who. . . endure your violence).

CREON

May he do as he pleases. May he shout and storm, may he swagger with pride, may he raise up his head [2070] against me, his father[86]—whatever he does, he will not save this viper from the death for which she is destined.

CHORUS OF ELDERS

It is an honorable love that tortures his soul.

CREON

To that love he must prefer fear of his father.[87]

CHORUS OF ELDERS

There is nothing that does not surrender to passion.

CREON

[2075] But, it is to me that he owes the greatest affection.

CHORUS OF ELDERS

To what kind of death have you sentenced her?

CREON

She will be taken off to a dark desert, wild and uninhabited, and then in a hollow cave she will be holed up, alive, within the tenebrous rock. [2080] I will have food brought to her as she waits for her death and when it comes to lack, she will ask Pluto, whom she adores above all, that he grant her a gentle death. She will learn how vain it is [2085] to honor the gods of the infernal plain.

---

[86] Line 2070: Garnier has Creon say that Haemon shall not cause Antigone ("cette vipere") to be released, whereas Sophocles had said that he shall not "save those *two* girls from death" (SophAnt: 760), i.e. Antigone *and* Ismene. Garnier's play, as in other parts, here remains more focused compared to its models.

[87] Line 2072: The chorus's response here differs from Sophocles's text. Sophocles's chorus *per se* is differed in Garnier (see further on, v. 2326 et seq.). Confrontation with it, however, is still useful here: Garnier references an "honneste amour," a term that Beaudin glosses as meaning "honorable" (p. 261). Sophocles's chorus refers not to the particular love of Haemon and Antigone, nor to its honorable nature, but to love in general ("Ἔρως ἀνίκατε μάχαν. . ." [Love invincible in battle]) and to its power over individuals: "None amongt the mortals can escape you. . ." (SophAnt: 781–800). Eros and Aphrodite (SophAnt: 801) are replaced, in Garnier, by a more personal appeal to love's power, as well as to its gallant (see note to line 2061) and honorable nature.

CHORUS

The gods who, from up above,[88]
Know what our lot must be
Give us Justice
As the proper reward—
To bestow virtue
And to repress vice.

Mortals, we have nothing
On this earthy round
As useful to us
As respecting the laws
With which just kings
Govern a city.

Justice can make us
Live in a perfect age
Of happy peace:
It protects the good, but
Seizes the criminal hand
Of the villainous.

Thanks to justice, the foreigner
Has safe passage,
Thanks to justice, the sparing man can
Save his money;
And thanks to justice, the indigent is not
Oppressed by the rich.

Justice delivers to the gods
The man who is religious;
It is justice that the widow

---

[88] Line 2086: This chorus has no model in either Seneca or Sophocles. Here, Garnier writes a veritable "Hymn to Justice," somewhat in the style of his own *Chants royaux* and *Hymne de la monarchie*, and comparable, too, with Ronsard's *Hymne de la Justice*. Beaudin notes that these stanzas "peuvent être, sur le plan de la mise en scène, considérées comme des propos qu'échangent entre eux, dans leur langage simple, quotidien et pourtant poétique, les citoyens scandalisés par la décision de Créon" (might be, in a production, considered as lines exchanged between citizens scandalized by Creon's decision, in their simple language, quotidian and yet poetic) (Beaudin: p. 230). On the connections between and meaning of these texts see Charpentier 2003 and Florence Dobby-Poirson 2003, as well as Introduction.

And the orphan,
Destined to be mere spoils,
Seek out for protection.

Mothers keep safe the
Chastity of their daughters
Thanks to justice,
Which shows the debaucher
What punishing torment is
Reserved for maiden ravishers.

But crooked vice
Imitates virtue
With such close resemblance that,
Not noticing it,
We often do not see
The difference between the two.

The path of virtue is straight,
But so narrow that
Often we stray from it
Into the paths
Of the two vices that
Neighbor the straight road.

For he who time and again
With cruel laws
Governs a city,
By his harshness is more of
A criminal than he whose
Vice he punishes.

Because in taking uprightness
To the extreme
Such a man strays
As much as he who,
Dissimilar from him,
Goes beyond the opposite extreme.

Creon is very wrong
To deliver to death
This royal virgin.
He thinks that he shows

How fair is his justice
By not sparing his family.

But the crime is not such
That it should be deadly
For his daughter-in-law and his niece.[89]
He scorns the love
Of his son who complains
Of such harshness.

Antigone, the chorus of maidens

ANTIGONE

Look, citizens, you who live in Thebes, at the finale battle in all my afflictions![90] Look at my final trial, my last torture! Look how I am taken into a filthy burrow to end my days there! Look—ah, look—at the food granted for my final meals! Look at the harsh shackles that grip my two arms! Look how these torturers bury me alive! Look how they are going to wall up my body within rock for having wanted to bury my brother! A royal daughter is being handed over to hard death. I am condemned to death for no greater a transgression.[91]

CHORUS OF MAIDENS

Console yourself, oh virgin, grieve not. With courageous heart relieve your torment. As you head to the burial chamber, it will not be without praise. Your innocent death will live on, forever famous—and famous, too, will remain the glory of your piety.[92] Each year we will celebrate you as we would a goddess, and with a thousand hymns the citizens will honor your Plutonic shades.

---

[89] Creon's niece: Antigone.

[90] Line 2158: The insistence on seeing (Antigone asks the citizens of Thebes to look on at her final tourments) can be compared to earlier moments: when Thebes complained of seeing what had happened to it (line 794 et seq.); and when Polynices is asked if he, too, can stand seeing what has happened (line 830 et seq.)

[91] Line 2169: Unlike Sophocles's *Antigone* (SophAnt: 806–16), Garnier's makes no mention of the fact that she will die unmarried, although the chorus does address her as a virgin (line 2170). See notes to lines 52 and 2214.

[92] Line 2174: Although both Sophocles and Garnier refer to Antigone being praised and glorious after death—Sophocles uses the Gk. adjective κλεινός, derived form Gk. κλέος (glory) (SophAnt: 817), a typical attribute of the hero—Garnier makes it very clear that he wishes to celebrate specifically her piety (line 2174). See note to line 88.

ANTIGONE

Oh Dircean fountain![93] Oh Ismenean river! Oh meadows! Oh forests! Oh hills! Oh the bloody and purple water's edge! Oh the yellowing sun, the light of this world! Oh Thebes, my land, abundant with courageous men and now fertile with harsh cruelty, I am now compelled to leave you and your kingdom.[94]

Farewell, Thebes, farewell. The austere malady of its pale barrenness has not uglied my face. No knives are being plunged into my chest. And yet, death forces me to leave.

CHORUS OF MAIDENS

Happy is your death that ends the wretchedness that hounded all of your Labdacid fathers, down to wretched you—from the cradle to the threshold of your tomb that wretchedness has followed you.[95]

ANTIGONE

What will become now of my blind father's teary old age once separated from me? What will you do? Ah! Who will console you? Who will guide your steps and who will feed you? Ah, I know all too well that very soon as I leave my rock I will meet you, my father, in the depths of Avernus![96] You will not live long after my sad lot—news of it will hasten you toward your death. I will see you, my unhappy mother Jocasta, I will see Eteocles and Adrastrus's son-in-law who recently fell to dark Acheron and who have not yet been granted passage by Charon the ferryman.[97]

Farewell, most loved brigade. Farewell, my dear companions. Off I go to lament in the lands of darkness. I enter still alive into my tomb where my body will languish, dead and alive, removed from the living and the dead.

---

[93] Line 2178: Garnier does not render the exchange, in Sophocles, between Antigone and the chorus about Niobe (SophAnt: 823–38).

[94] Line 2183: These lines (2178–83) are among those quoted in 1946 by Thierry Maulnier, a year after he produced an adaptation of Garnier's play. In reference to them, he noted that "les plaintes d'Antigone à l'instant de son supplice, ne sont pas dans la tragédie de Garnier, indignes de son modèle grec" (Antigone's laments, at the moment of her torture, are not in Garnier's tragedy, unworthy of its Greek model) (Maulnier 1946: 67). See also notes to lines 240 and 1308.

[95] Line 2191: Given the omnipresence of the theme of justice in the play, it is perhaps unexpected that Garnier does not, here, remain closer to Sophocles's chorus, which reads: "Advancing to the extreme of caring, you [=Antigone] stumbled against the lofty altar of Justice, my child! And you are paying for some crime of your fathers" (SophAnt: 853–56).

[96] Line 2197: Avernus: the entrance to the underworld.

[97] Line 2204: Adrastrus's son-in-law: Polynices.

CHORUS OF MAIDENS

Oh cruel misfortune! Oh proud destiny! Oh the too obstinate wrath of agèd Creon! May death come quickly and may its blessed dart, right here and now, plunge into each one of us.

ANTIGONE

Here, then, is my prison, here is my home, here is my tomb where I must die! I do not wish to delay, I must enter inside.[98]

Farewell, shining sun, farewell burning light, farewell forevermore! For into this tear-soaked hollow, my final home, your light never enters. Farewell, my dear Haemon, you will see me no more, I am off into confinement within this closed chamber. Remember me, remember that death is given to me, that I am being offered to death for having been good.

You drip with tears, your eyes are drowned, cry no more for me, my sisters, cry not. Why do you sob? Why do you beat so hard and bruise your alabaster white breasts? Farewell, my dear sisters, I cause you to suffer. From you, I now long only for this final kiss. Farewell, my sisters, farewell. Too long with my pitiful complaints do I delay the death that gazes at me.[99]

CHORUS OF MAIDENS

Oh, how our days are filled

[98] Line 2214: We might have expected here the third and final of Antigone's formulations in defense of burying Polynices, as in Sophocles (SophAnt: 904–20), which Helene Foley has called Antigone's "authentic" speech (Foley 2001: 175). Perhaps borrowing from Herodotus, where Intaphrenes, given the chance of saving the life of husband, child, or brother chooses her brother, Sophocles's Antigone explains that she would never have taken on the ordeal of standing up to Creon's edict had it been for her dead child or husband: "If my husband had died, I could have had another, and a child by another man, if I had lost the first, but with my mother and my father in Hades below, I could never have another brother" (SophAnt: 909–12). This explanation is not reproduced by Garnier. See notes to lines 1541 and 1809. Antigone's final farewell in Sophocles begins by characterizing what her fate has reserved her—she is to die "un-lamented, friendless,unwedded" (SophAnt: 876). Again, her non-wedded status is foregrounded in Sophocles, but not in Garnier. See notes to lines 52 and 2169. More generally, Antigone's final lament is much shortened in Garnier. Compare Garnier lines 2192–2207 and 2212–2229 with SophAnt: 891–928.

[99] Line 2229: Antigone's final words, in Garnier, are not ones of self-justification, but of farewell—the word *adieu* is repeated again and again (lines 2215, 2216, 2218, 2226, 2228). The overall impact is surely to keep the focus on more universal questions of justice and good government as opposed to Antigone's relationship with her brother, sometimes characterized as incestuous.

With inhuman calamities![100]
Ah gods, how many encumbrances!
How much distress!

May our curly locks
Unfurl and blow about;
May we scratch our faces
Into bloody wounds;

May our bare chests
Be covered in scabs;
May blood drip from them
And fall down, drop by drop;

May endless tears
Bathe our misery;
May the tears never end
And may they stream;

May these secret mounts
Resound with sorrow
And these hornèd rocks
Ring out with continued laments.

May our sad heart
Enclose nothing but languor;
May bitter sadness
Inhabit it durably.

May the beautiful sun
Never redden on us,

[100] Line 2230: Garnier's chorus here differs from Sophocles's (SophAnt: 944–87). The latter offers a more general reflection on the power of fate, via specific examples from mythology (Danae, Lycurgus, etc.): ". . .the power of fate is strange: neither wealth nor martial valor, nor a wall, nor black ships crashing through the sea can escape it." Of Garnier's chorus, Beaudin writes that it "offre la possibilité d'une mise en scène dont la beauté plastique est suggérée par les vers 2234–45: les jeunes filles se frappent la poitrine, pleurent, dénouent leurs cheveux, déchirent leurs vêtements: il s'agit d'une belle scène de déploration dans la meilleure tradition des tragédies antiques" (offers the possibility for a production whose plastic beauty is suggested by the lines 2234–45: the young girls beat their chests, cry, untie their hair, tear their clothes up—it is a beautiful scene of lament in the best tradition of ancient tragedies) (232).

Rather: May it always
Dip its lamp in darkness.

The darkness of nights
Fits well our disquiet—
May our importunate afflictions
Take pleasure in somber nights.

Now, may the gods lead you
To those sacred places
Where piteous souls
Rest in peace.

And there may they pay you
The proper dues, which
Your noble heart deserves,
At the body of your brother.

HAEMON

You, cruel one, you have thus assaulted my love, you have, you criminal, stolen my soul from me, you have ripped out my heart, my blood, my life, you have with your austerity taken my dear love away![101] A Hyrcanian tiger would not have been so criminal, a Sarmatian, a Tartar would have had more humanity.[102] Walling up a virgin inside a hard rock, a king's daughter, my future wife! Your niece, you cruel one, whom you should cherish like your daughter, you have her killed! You have her killed, yet she is not a criminal! Her crime and her felony are having been virtuous.

Oh, you have a torturer's nature! Oh heart too barbaric, exceeding in austerity both bears and lions! At least if you had cut her throat on the battlefield,

[101] Line 2270: Haemon's speech (lines 2270–2325) is not based on Sophocles. It offers a virulent critique of Creon, attaching him by comparison (with a Hyrcanian tiger, the Sarmatians, etc.), by appealing to the idea of *philia* (with words like *niepce, fille*), by underscoring (unlike above) Antigone's virginity, by calling Creon's heart "barbarous," with terms like "tyrant" (see notes to lines 44, 196, 1027, 1814, 1868, 2047), etc. Note that Haemon's speech displaces the dialogue, in Sophocles, between Creon and Tiresias, an echo of which appears later. See note to line 2509. Pinvert has noted: "Introduite ici par raison de symétrie et pour faire pendant aux adieux d'Antigone à la vie, cette scène n'est pas dans Sophocle" (Inserted here in order to create symmetry vis-à-vis Anigone's fairwell to life, this scene is not present in Sophocles) (Pinvert: 2.446).

[102] Line 2275: Hyrcania: an area near the Caspian sea. Sarmatians: an Iranian people of classical antiquity. Tartar: a Turkic ethnic group.

rather than having her killed by raging hunger! You were not satisfied by such regular torture, you had to show yourself to be crueler than anyone.

The light from her eyes and the softness of her face were unable to break your heart's hard ice. Truly, it is filled with extreme cruelty, for it was able to hurt such extreme beauty—such beauty could have made a rock feel love, if only a rock could feel.

Ah, may her sentence be also mine! And if it is not enough to take from tyrants their accumulated torture and to apply them to me, then with decided patience I will suffer their harsh violence. Thus, if I live, she will not die, or else her death will be shared between us. I will break open the hollow rock and if anyone stands in my way and attempts to stop her being taken out, I will make them understand the rashness of wanting to stand in the way of an angry lover.

Is my soul any the less taken by love than was that noble descendant of Acrisius for Andromeda, who rushed at the sea monster and untied the maiden after he killed it?[103] My soul is more heated by love than was his, and Antigone wins out over Cepheus's daughter in chaste beauty.[104] I thus have a heart less strong, if I do not free her and save her from death.

But too long I delay, and meanwhile perhaps, as I cry out so many useless tears, the poor thing might have opened up her chest with some iron sword rather than wait for hunger, or else lacking of air she might have suffocated, or she might have cracked her head open by smashing it into a rock. There must be no delay for fear of such calamity, for my secret destiny depends on hers.

I thought myself happy that she had been given to me, that we would celebrate a blessed wedding. But if heaven does not listen to my noble wishes, we will go to be wed in the shade-filled Acheron. May that not befall us, oh gods! But allow for pity's sake that this day I take her out of her low hollow.

CHORUS

Oh severe Love,
Whose sharp arrow,
Pausing neither day nor night,[105]
Torments all souls,
You gloriously conquer
Men and gods.

No one is protected

---

[103] Line 2305: Acrisius: king of Argos and father of Perseus who found Andromeda about to be devoured by a sea-monster, and fell in love with her.

[104] Line 2309: Cepheus's daughter: Andromeda.

[105] Line 2230: This chorus is based on Sophocles, but displaced from the point before Antigone's final farewell (SophAnt: 781–800). Garnier's chorus is significantly longer than Sophocles's. See also note to line 2072.

From your childlike hand
Striking an arrow
Into the breast—
For against your assault
No strength is enough.

Monarchs so feared and
Crown-wearing kings
Are just as promptly wounded
As the ignorant masses—unless,
Perhaps, you attack the powerful
Even more readily.

Jupiter, who is the master
And father of the gods,
Who governs the land
And the heavens and the waves,
Feels this dainty child
Triumph over his heart.

Neither the dazzling thunderbolt
In his red-glowing hand,
Nor his frowning eyes
That scare heaven,
Can protect him against
The arrow of this impish archer.

To hell he descends,
Into Pluto's cruel soul
He drops down,
And there leaves a spark
Which no torture can equal
In all the infernal depths.

He conquers, under water,
The scaly troops;
He attacks, too,
The speckle-feathered birds—
The plains and the woods
Are subjected to his laws.

The forest dwellers, and
Tame and wild animals,

That live on hills, in marshes,
In valleys and thickets,
In both fields and houses, are
All burned by his firebrands.[106]

But we above all,
Human creatures, are
Exposed to his blows
And to his cruel arrows—
More often do we suffer
His trying flames.

He hides out in the eyes
Of a sweet virgin,
On her gracious brow,
On her beautiful breasts,
Or on her curly hair—
To cause a thousand deaths.[107]

But alas! It is a great pity
That he whom he besieges
With strong love
Feels such rage
That he knows no rest
As long as this illness gnaws at him.

Benumbed, he dreams only
Of that beauty he loves,
He no longer cares
For his own person.
His paternal duty
He now neglects.

He now changes temperament
And alters his nature,
He takes on strange manners
Under this tyrannical stranger.

---

[106] Line 2373: This and the previous stanza develop Sophocles: "Over the upland folds thou [Love] roam'st, and the trackless sea" (SophAnt: 782).

[107] Line 2385: Compare with SophAnt: 781: "Love who pillowed all night on a maiden's check dost lie."

His former mildness
Leaves his heart.

Do we not see Haemon,
Formerly so noble,
Now rebellious
Against his father's wishes—
Ever since this love
Took up residence in him?[108]

He cannot condone that
His Lady be so wronged;
He prefers to feel death
Within his soul.
I fear that his pain will
Bring us disaster.

[108] Line 2409: This stanza underscores Haemon's opposition to his father—he was Fr. *debonnaire* (noble, under his father's sway) and is now MFr. *contumax* (rebellious). The tone here (and in the final stanza) is different from that in Sophocles's chorus, where we read: "Mad are thy subjects all, and even the wisest heart / Straight to folly will fall, at a touch of thy poisoned dart. / Thou didst kindle the strife, this feud of kinsman with kin, / By the eyes of a winsome wife, and the yearning her heart to win" (SophAnt: 791–800).

Act V

Messenger, Chorus, Eurydice, Creon, Dorothy.

MESSENGER

How Fortune shakes, topples, and overturns human affairs—it turns them upside down.[1] *How it disturbs*[2] *everything and, mocking us, puts everything wrong-side up! For a time, it rolls proudly* [2420] *along fragile heights, then suddenly its wheel turns and it leaves the heights behind—no mortal can predict his destiny.*[3]

Here is old Creon, so happy this morning but now so unhappy. He was, without expecting it [2425] and without hoping for it, made king of a powerful city. He has at present chased off our enemies whom Polynices had gathered against us. Now, misfortune falls on his house, which equals in sadness this new happiness.[4] [2430] *For, whoever has sorrow in his mind, even if he is a great king, does not live happily.*[5]

---

[1] Line 2416: Gras notes: "Garnier fait de l'acte V [. . .] l'acte des récits, de l'émotion et des lamentations. Il termine ainsi une pièce divisée de nouveau en trois parties: 1) épisode des frères ennemis; 2) épisode Créon-Antigone; 3) punition de Créon" (Garnier makes of Act 5 [. . .] the act of narratives, emotion, and lamentation. He thus ends a play divided into three parts: 1) the episode of the enemy brothers; 2) the Creon-Antigone episode; 3) Creon's punishment) (Gras 1965: 42).

[2] Line 2418: Here, Eng. *disturbs* renders MFr. *brouille*, which word had a slightly wider set of meanings in MFr. Cotgrave translates: "To iumble, trouble, disorder, confound, marre by mingling together; to hudle, tumble, suffle, things ill-fauoredly; to make a troublesome hotchpotch; to make a hurry, or great hurliburly."

[3] Line 2422: These lines (2416–22) are similar to SophAnt: 1158–60. Beaudin (235) also suggests a possible reminiscence of Baïf's *Antigone* (lines 1277–85). Both Sophocles and Garnier share the emphasis on fortune's role in human affairs—Sophocles's messenger notes that ". . .fortune [τύχη] makes straight and fortune brings down the fortunate or the unfortunate man at all times, and no prophet can tell mortals what is ordained" (SophAnt: 1158–60).

[4] Line 2429: Compare lines 2423–29 with SophAnt: 1161–65. Garnier insists on Creon's old age, not mentioned by Sophocles. In the first act, Garnier also insisted more than Seneca on Oedipus's old age—see note to line 3.

[5] Line 2431: Compare lines 2430–31 with SophAnt: 1165–67.

You have covered the mountains with flocks and the grassy fields with wooly herds—in vain; you have gold that glistens yellow on the soft Lydian shore of the Pactolus or on the shore of the Spanish Tagus—in vain; you are master of a hundred cities and of a hundred peoples, indeed you appear as a monarch to all kings—in vain. If in your mind you do not have contentment, then your happiness will be nothing but torment.[6]

CHORUS

What bloody misfortune still torments us?

MESSENGER

Fortune beats at us—and is more bloody than ever.

CHORUS

Have new calamities befallen us?

MESSENGER

All is filled with sighs and tears.

CHORUS

Is it in the castle that this misfortune falls?

MESSENGER

Upon Creon's head this catastrophe descends.

CHORUS

Creon's? A catastrophe at his white-haired age?

MESSENGER

It is because of him, the unfortunate one, that everything has occurred.

CHORUS

What is it? Tell us now instead of keeping us in fear.

MESSENGER

Everyone is dead because of his arrogant pride.[7]

---

[6] Line 2439: Compare lines 2432–39 with SophAnt: 1168–71. Garnier's Fr. *félicité* (here rendered as 'happiness') translates Gk. ἡδονή, which LSJ defines as "enjoyment, pleasure."

[7] Line 2449: The messenger's reference to Fr. *outrecuidance* (here rendered as 'arrogant pride') marks a subtle change from Sophocles: "[Haemon] died at his own hand, in anger against his father for the murder he committed" (SophAnt: 1177).

CHORUS
Great Jupiter, who died? Who committed this murder?

MESSENGER
Haemon, poor Haemon, he put an end to his days.

CHORUS
And why? What pushed him to this? His father's wrath?

MESSENGER
He died maddened by love and anger.

CHORUS
He was totally taken by his love for Antigone.

MESSENGER
Love for Antigone and Antigone's death—both caused his ruin.

CHORUS
So the life of this poor virgin has thus been extinguished.

MESSENGER
Her death was followed by that of her Haemon.[8]

CHORUS
But I think I glimpse Eurydice emerging. Did she hear some news of her death? Or that, thanks to Fortune, she escaped?

EURYDICE
Oh Thebans, my friends, I turned away from serving the gods when a frightful noise issued from the castle—it distressed me as I heard it. I was on my way to the temple where Pallas is worshiped, but hardly had I reached the street when I hear[9] the grumblings of the terror-struck citizens, who groaned sadly about a new calamity in the royal household. On hearing this collective voice,[10] I am struck by fear and, fainting, collapse.[11] My ladies, taking me in their

[8] Line 2457: This stycomythic exchange is more developed in Garnier than in Sophocles.

[9] Line 2466: Garnier here switches tense to the present of narration.

[10] Line 2468: Garnier writes Fr. *cette voix* (Eng. *this voice*) in the singular, as if all the citizens groan as one. The word *collective* has been added to suggest this.

[11] Line 2469: Beaudin (238) suggests *rapprochement* with Baïf's *Antigone* (lines 1317–19).

arms, lift me up like a heavy load and covering my face carry me to the palace. There, shortly after having recovered from fainting and remembering anew the atrocious din, I head out, full of worry, restless to know [2475] what the misfortune is and what is going on. My chest pounds, the blood runs numb in my heart, a cold sweat dampens my face, all strength leaves me, my arm now lacks a pulse, and my knees tremble beneath my weak body.

[2480] I predict a great calamity, for this morning the white-tailed eagle above our towers sounded out long moans in its feeble voice. On our beds, I saw a thousand bloodstains—and on my clothes, too. I have since realized that these were omens of [2485] the murders of the two kings and of other bloodshed: our good citizens who died today as they fought valiantly against the Argive onslaught. But now I see that this sign shows that upon our own heads adversity will fall. [2490] I see it in the grieved faces of the people who follow me and who cry for me. I hear them mumbling about some horrible thing, about some great misfortune about which they dare not warn me. But it must be known. [2495] Tell me, I pray you, what misfortune gives rise to this clamor of lament? Tell me frankly, the burden of affliction is not new to me—new afflictions attack me endlessly.[12]

MESSENGER

I will recount everything to you, dear Lady. For what is the point of hiding such dark sorrow from you? [2500] We cannot hide it even if we try, you will still know it even if it is hidden from you—by learning of it tomorrow, your sorrow will be no less than if you learn of it today.

EURYDICE

You keep me hanging too long. Hurry, I pray you.

MESSENGER

[2505] Creon's advisers untaught him his wrath: they recommended that the oracles of the great gods, announced by Tiresias, be followed, and that funeral rites be quickly given to the body of Polynices.[13]

---

[12] Line 2497: These lines (lines 2461–97) are expanded form SophAnt: 1183–91. Compared to Sophocles's version, Garnier emphasizes Eurydices's emotions and reaction to the news.

[13] Line 2509: These lines (lines 2505–09) relate to the deleted exchange between Tiresias and Creon (see note to line 2270). Garnier's assertion that Creon has 'un-learned' his anger establishes a complex relation with how Tiresias, in Sophocles, set about offering advice to the king (SophAnt: 992–1090). There, the initial discussion turns on what Creon can learn from Tiresias, anchored to the term διδάσκω [didasko] (to instruct, to teach, but also: to explain, to show by argument and, of dithyrambic and dramatic poets, to produce a piece of poetry). And Creon, for his part, will "learn" (γιγνώσκω [gignosko]), meaning to come to perceive, to know by reflection, to distinguish, to recognize,

We were, in our sadness, heading along twisting paths covered with cavernous rocks, for the blood-stained crimson countryside is still scattered with great piles of bodies. Then, after descending to the place so deadly to the brothers, we find this poor prince lying on his back, bloody all over, all covered in dirt. We pick him up from the ground and carry him off for washing on a wide stone.

Having cleansed him with pure water and with sweet-smelling linens dried him off, we invoke Hecate, calling her by her three names, and the tenebrous Pluto and his beloved cohort, to win their favor, for fear that if we scorn their anger, it might explode right over us.[14]

To give Polynices's a tomb, to fashion for him a solitary home, we set about digging into our land, into the bosom of our ancient mother. We then lower him, covered by a shroud, into the tomb while we sound many sighs and shed many tears.[15]

When this had been done, we turn around and head back in swift step to the somber den of good Antigone, so as to release her from it[16]—Creon wishes that she suffer no more. We do not get very far when we hear a plaintive cry rise from the hateful rock. The king is completely unsettled, he grows pale and can not proffer a single world, so shaken is his soul. He steps forward, he stutters, and he shows with various gestures that he fears misfortune. He hastens us to approach this rocky lair.[17] He himself runs there right away, howls out his unhappiness before moaning, sighing, crying, running his lumpish hands through his grey hair and white beard. "Ah," he says, "how wretched! That is Haemon crying out! Go, run, dash, help, I pray you, you will not get there in time, run to the thicket and rush into the savage lair.[18] Save my child for

---

and also: to form a judgment)—it is the same verb used in the *Odyssey*, for example, to describe when Telemachus "grasps the true significance of a situation" (e.g. when Athena is disguised as Mentes at *Od* 1.420).

[14] Line 2523: Compare with SophAnt: 1199–1200.

[15] Line 2527: The description of Polynice's burial (lines 2514–27) are based largely on SophAnt: 1196–1204.

[16] Line 2529: Eng. *den* renders MFr. *taniere*, an arresting word choice. Cotgrave shows the variety of meanings: "A denne, caue, burrow; the lurking hole of a wild beast." The term captures both the physical space (for the hollowed-out cave indeed is like a den), but also depicts an Antigone whose wild rashness (see line 1865) has been shut away like a wild animal. See also line 2538 and note.

[17] Line 2538: The term used to describe Antigone's cave is no longer MFr. *taniere* (see line 2529 and note), but MFr. *antre* (here rendered as Eng. *lair*), which Cotgrave defines as follows: "A caue, denne, grot, cauerne, hole, or hollownesse, under the ground." MFr. *antre* is used again at line 2545.

[18] Line 1545: See note to line 2538.

me! Save my child for me![19] My Haemon, alas, it is he, him I hear, it is his voice, I can hear it." Upon this, everyone gets moving, everyone runs, everyone rushes to the mossy rock. [2550] Each wants to arrive before the others, to have the honor of being the first to enter and to rescue Haemon.

Now at the cave, we find that it has been broken into—there is an opening just big enough for entering. We descend inside and look all around. [2555] We see Antigone in a far corner, spread out on the floor, on her front, her throat gripped by a noose made of the locks on her head tied into a thousand knots. And next to her is Haemon who cries while holding her in his arms. He laments her death and, leaning over her, moans out sobs. [2560] By name, he accuses the cruel gods and the cruel Fates, he damns and spits hate at his father's rigor, his arms writhe. He calls out to his virgin lover and, even though she is dead, he speaks with her and calls her his lover, his life, his soul. [2565] He laments his sorrow in this love, which remained pure until the end.[20] Right away Creon arrives. Having seen Haemon, Creon exhales long sighs, moved all the way down to his lungs. As if crazed, with a dead voice, trembling and panting, he spoke in this way.

[2570] "What are you doing, my son? Why are you so lost? Come back, my friend,[21] leave behind your anger. I pray you humbly, forgive my error, forgive me, you who are my heart, forgive me, you who are my life. Please, on this count, forgive my error. I [2575] will accept and suffer any punishment you may order for me."

Haemon stares at his father with a wild gaze and, mad at his words, he gives him a sideways glare. He becomes mad and, without responding a word, he sighs up a sob from deep in his entrails [2580] and at the same moment takes up his scimitar. Creon, frightened, steps back quickly and leaves the cave. Haemon, in great fury, stabs the drawn cutlass into his side.[22]

---

19 Line 2546: This chiastic line can potentially be read in two ways. The MFr. is "Sauvez moy mon enfant, mon enfant sauvez moy," which most obviously means "Save my child for me, save my child for me" (the inversion of word order having no impact on meaning), but also (if we take account of word order, "Save my child for me; my child, save me," in which Creon would be calling out for Haemon to save him by not being dead—and thus freeing Creon of his guilt.

20 Line 2565: Eng. "pure until the end" renders MFr. *chaste*, literally Eng. *chaste*, but also "pure, undefiled; inuiolated, not distained with filfth, or any (unlawfull) Venerie" (Cotgrave). Haemon is lamenting Antigone's passing and his love for her, which was never consummated. The tenses have been modified for English usage.

21 Line 2571: Eng. *my friend* renders MFr. *mon amy*, a term here used affectively and whose meanings were wider in the Renaissance, ranging through friend, lover, and companion. The progression in these lines from "my son" to "my friend" is notable.

22 Line 2583: Eng. *scimitar* renders MFr. *cimeterre* (line 2580), while Eng. *cutlass* renders MFr. *coutelas*. The former is "A short, curved, single-edged sword, used [especially by] Turks and Persians" (OED); whereas the latter is "A short sword with a flat wide slightly curved blade, adapted more for cutting than for thrusting" (OED). Gar-

EURYDICE

Ah! What do I hear! I who suffer, what do I hear!

CHORUS

Crazed like a Bacchante,[23] who flees to the heights of Mount Cithaeron to celebrate the cult of that god who conquered India, Eurydice heads off, distraught. Finish, messenger, this woeful speech.[24]

MESSENGER

As soon as the sword was lodged in his wretched side, he fell down upon the Virgin[25] and spattered her with blood. He said his final farewell, then kissed her lips. His face turned pale and his legs grew stiff, his life and his love were lost to the air.

CHORUS

Oh unfortunate pair of faithful lovers, who never deserved to suffer such fatal torment! The Fates will, with the Stygian waves, extinguish the wedding torches of their fatal marriage. Now rest, children, in eternal peace. Hold on to your sweet love forevermore.

But, why is it that the queen left so quickly when she learned of Haemon's harsh fate, without sadness, without lamentation—yet her heart felt itself overcome by such grief?

MESSENGER

I am astonished by that. I think however that she wanted to repress the pain that gnaws at her, and not to display it in public in front of everyone. I also think that she will expel her grief and her anger alone in the castle, her tears

---

nier uses the terms interchangeably. These lines are based on SophAnt: 1209–43. Major changes include: Garnier heightens the portrait of Creon's despair, but deletes certain aspects. On these verses, Beaudin notes (241) that lines 2570–75 "pourraient être dits, lors d'une représentation, en coulisse, par le roi lui-même" (could be spoken, during a production, off stage, by the king himself).

[23] Line 2585: Garnier advances the departure of Eurydice, allowing her time to arrive at the palace and time, too, for Dorothy to journey in the opposite direction (Lebègue: 285).

[24] Line 2588: Garnier's reference to Eurydice being like a Bacchante, headed off to Mount Cithaeron is not in Sophocles, who writes: "The lady [γυνὴ] has departed, before uttering a good or bad word" (SophAnt: 1244–45). Compare with Garnier's references to Agave. See notes to lines 28, 480, 586, 1087.

[25] Line 2590: Garnier writes MFr. *Vierge* (Eng. *Virgin*) with a capital letter, as if to liken Antigone (and her attendant piety) to the Virgin Mary. The mixing of blood here (as Haemons bleeds over dead Antigone) is reminiscent of the mixing of blood (Eteocles's and Polynices's) at the moment of their death. See lines 1192–93.

unseen. *He who laments wholeheartedly laments alone.* I do not believe that, because of all this pain, she will harm herself however. She is too restrained and too wise.

CHORUS

I really know nothing of this, but this sad silence seems like an omen of incurable misfortune. *Oh how redundant, in true grief, is lament.*

MESSENGER

Let us enter into the city. There we may learn if pain forced her to make an attempt on her life.

CHORUS

Let us go. But is this not unlucky Creon?

MESSENGER

It is he. That old man so obstinate.

CHORUS

He laments a corpse that is carried before him.

MESSENGER

It is Haemon, removed from the stinking cave.

CHORUS

Creon alone is the cause of so cruel a misfortune, but I fear that still other misfortunes will tumble down on our heads.

CREON

Oh three and four times over my life is wretched! Oh old age that is anguished and a servant to disaster! Oh detestable crime! Oh monstrous offense! By my own cruelty I have killed my own child! Ah, executioner of my own blood! A savage tiger does not treat its young as I treat my family. I feed on murder and still my hunger for inhumane carnage can not be satisfied. I make war on the dead—my mad rage assaults my own kind even after death. Not contented by just his death, I wanted to offer up dead Polynices to the crows and to the flesh-eating wolves. I walled up Antigone in a dark cave—instead of offering her a pious funeral and deserved glory.

I buried alive my sister's daughter and I am the murderer of my own son.

CHORUS

Too late you learn of your incurable offense. Vain are the tears, vain the repentance. You cry out these moving laments for nothing. *About what has happened, the decision is already made. God himself would not be able, even though he governs everything, to make it so that what has been done can be undone.*

CREON

Alas, this I know, to my own great chagrin. Incurable is my anguish, incurable my wrong. Alas, how my old age is weighed down by misfortunes! How much anguish fills my soul, how afflicted it is.[26]

DOROTHY

Oh tearful Creon, a swarming abundance of murders more and more overwhelms your house.[27]

CREON

What other wretched events can still befall me that fickle fortune has not already made me suffer?

DOROTHY

The queen has killed herself and with her red blood her chamber is now washed—it looks like a pond.[28]

CREON

Oh cruel Acheron and its implacable depths, which engulf and swallow all between your gaping banks, why do you want to claim me, who am already claimed?[29] Why have I not descended into Orcus, instead of filling my house with blood and carnage, pushing down my ill-fated family before me?[30]

---

26 Line 2649: These lines (lines 2624–49) are based on SophAnt: 1261–76.

27 Line 2650: This character, Dorothy (MFr. *Dorothee*), is of Garnier's own invention. The name derives from Gk. Δωϱοθέα, composed of δῶϱον (gift) and θεός (god), which also gave the names Theodore, Theodora, etc. Beaudin notes (243) that Dorothy is "une servante (ou une suivante de la reine)" (a servant [or maid to the queen]) who here takes on the role of the palace's messenger to underline the accumulation of catastrophes. One could note that MFr. *Dorothee* could also be (like Anne, for example) a masculine first name in the Renaissance. Beaudin's explanation is however the most likely.

28 Line 2655: Compare with SophAnt: 1283.

29 Line 2658: Creon's line might have reminded Renaissance readers of a proverb: "On ne doit point querir brebis qui se veut perdre [:] A wilfull sinner must not be reclaimed" (Cotgrave, entry "Perdre.")

30 Orcus: god of the underworld, here a metonymy for hell.

Ah, poor unfortunate one, poor king, unlucky king, what deceptive happiness is this royal crown! No sooner had I put it on than a terrible storm of disastrous misfortune came down upon my head.

My Eurydice is dead! And, wicked one, because of you! Other than myself, I must accuse no one. Because of me, my niece died for a praiseworthy act. Because of her, my Haemon, and becaue of Haemon, Eurydice. Thus of so many deaths, I am the only cause. I alone, too, must carry the guilt and the grief. My Eurydice is dead, Eurydice, my soul! Oh bloodthirsty one! Oh doomed Lady! Let us go, let us run to see her.

DOROTHY

Do not hurry so — you will not bring her back to life by hurrying. To your great pain you will see the poor thing all too soon, ready to be lowered into the silent tomb.

CREON

Oh, good gods, what shall I do? Could any calamity match my present misfortune? What can remain for me? What remains for my old age if it is not to steep in extreme distress? I have murdered my child whom I hold in my arms, and my loyal spouse I have driven to death. Oh, mother too pitiful! Oh, son too noble! O me, source of the trouble, obstinately severe! Oh too cruel Destiny! Oh cruel lot that with my austerity smothers niece, wife, and child!

DOROTHY

She died suddenly. She collapsed on the altar, her stomach punctured by a criminal dagger. But before she expelled her sad soul, with her two eyes open but already dulled at the edges, with her face washed of its youthful pink, she uttered a stern prayer to her former husband: she implored her Manes three times against you;[31] and she made an oath with all of Hell's Furies, so that this double murder[32] be avenged against you in Acheron's depths with a hundred and a hundred torments.

CREON

Oh poor me, oh wretched me, alas my heart trembles! I can feel my blood freezing up from mortal fear. Why does someone not come and plunge a sharp sword into my chest, or cut my throat? Steal me away from here, throw me some-

[31] Line 2694: See note to line 1564.

[32] Line 2697: Eng. *murder* here renders MFr. *parricide,* used by Garnier in this instance to refer not to the murder of a father, but to murder in general, a usage noted by Cotgrave who defines the term *parricide* (here referring to the person, not the act) as meaning "A Parricide; murtherer (sic) of his own father; also, any heinous murtherer." See also line 2725.

where else, somewhere where I might cry inside some far-off rock. I am like those whom the sepulcher encloses, so much do sorrow and misfortune mortally destroy me.

Come, Death, come, with your severe frown, terrible Death, come and steal me away from here. May this day turn out to be my last. May this day drown my crime and my suffering in the depths of the Acheron. Or rather, not my crime, alas! For indeed I must carry it down there with me and show it to Minos, in order to receive the punishment that is deserved by the bitter violence of my inhuman soul.

CHORUS

Cease these laments now, abandon this useless grief, and make sure their bodies are enclosed in coffins.

CREON

I cannot let you go, my sweet children, in order to bury you properly in a worthy grave, even though I killed you with my severity, madly irritated as I was against your sacred love. You neither, my dear spouse. Alas this same misfortune and this same crime spilled your blood! Mother, you were unable, your heart too assaulted, to outlive your child murdered by my rigor. And yet I, the murderer, live on. Clotho extends my days — I am a murderous husband, uncle, and father.[33]

Where shall I turn my eyes? To what place, unlucky me, must I retire to flee my pining sorrow? You see, poor Creon, wherever you go, you see the funerals of impious murders. Your child, cut down by your sword, lies here; killed in your house, your wife also lies here. Everything overflows with tears, grief, and laments. By fortune your joy is extinguished.

Oh rigorous and unavoidable Destiny! Oh great immortal gods! Oh father Jupiter! Put an end, I pray you, to my pain and to my life, may Eurydice's death be followed by my own.[34]

[33] Line 2725: Eng. *murderous* here renders MFr. *parricide* (adj.). See also above, line 2697. Robert Garapon has underscored the importance of the line: "*Parricide*. . . Le grand mot est dit: c'est Créon dorénavant qui remplace Œdipe et hérite de sa malédiction" (*Parricide*. . . This all-important word is said — he now replaces Oedipus and inherits his curse) (Garapon 1989: 39).

[34] Line 2737: Gras's comments regarding Creon's lamentations are particularly pertinent: "Les lamentations de Créon ont été allongées par Garnier qui renchérit sur Euripide. Garnier aime ces scènes où l'on disserte longuement sur les malheurs après qu'ils [sont] arrivés [. . .] Les lamentations de Créon et surtout la façon qu'il a de récapituler à plusieurs reprises la suite de malheurs que sa rigueur a causés, terminent la pièce comme celles d'Œdipe l'avaient commencée. Tous deux n'ont devant les yeux que désolation à la suite de leurs crimes, tous deux, n'ont plus qu'à déplorer leur destin, tous deux ont cru

CHORUS

Your losses, your misfortunes, that which you have suffered, *derive from your scorn for the great god of hell.* [2740] *You must honor him and be sure never to deprive anyone of the right to a proper burial.*[35]

THE END

agir délibérément alors qu'ils n'étaient que les instruments de la fatalité, tous deux enfin ont ce dernier sursaut de révolte contre les dieux impitoyables" (Creon's laments have been extended by Garnier, who goes further than Euripides. Garnier likes these scenes where misfortunes are discussed at length a long time after they happen [. . .] Creon's laments and especially the way he recapitulates several times the accumulation of disasters to which his rigor has given rise, end the play just as Oedipus's accumulated disasters began it. Both [Creon and Oedipus] have only desolation before their eyes, following their crimes; both can now only deplore their destiny; both thought they were acting deliberately whereas there were, in fact, just the instruments of fate; both, finally, have a last-minute revolt against the ruthless gods) (Gras 1965: 43).

[35] Line 2741: The final conclusion can be compared to what we read in Sophocles (SophAnt: 1347–53): "Good sense [φϱονεῖν] is by far the chief part of happiness [εὐδαιμονίας]; and we must not be impious [ἀσεπτεῖν] towards the gods. The great words of boasters are always punished with great blows, and as they grow old teach them wisdom." Gk. φϱονεῖνi is the same term once used by Tiresias in his attempt to teach Creon how to behave, in the dialogue deleted by Garnier. See note to line 2509. Garnier does not pick up directly on Gk. ἀσεπτεῖν (< ἄσεπτος), which LSJ and ML defines as "unholy."

Appendix
The Choral Odes

The table on the next page summarizes the main choral odes throughout the play's five acts. In addition to these, *Antigone* contains a number of other shorter interventions by the choir, all of which are (like the main body of the play) in alexandrines (for example at 4:1747, etc.).

Act	Lines	Topic	Chorus Identity	Line form	Rime	Primary model(s)
Act 1	403–67	"Prayer to Dionysos" (includes call for Dionysos to save Thebes from civil strife)	The Theban Chorus.	Thirteen five-line stanzas of octosyllabic verse	AABBA	Seneca, *Oedipus* (lines 403–508); Sophocles, *Antigone* (lines 1115–52)
Act 2	596–655	The "Calamities of Thebes," for which ambition has most often been responsible.	The Chorus. (?)	Ten six-line stanzas of heptasyllabic verse.	AABCCB	Seneca, *Oedipus* (lines 715–43)
Act 2	936–83	The (Fickle) Power of Fortune, esp. on kings. Emphasis on the price paid by the citizens and on the ravages of civil war.	The Chorus. (?)	Eight six-line stanzas of octosyllabic verse.	AABCCB	Seneca, *Agamemnon* (lines 56–106)
Act 3	1456–1515	The Destruction of Thebes.	The Chorus. (?)	Six ten-line stanzas of octosyllabic verse.	ABBAC-CDEDE	Seneca, *Oedipus* (lines 110–201)
Act 4	1622–1705	An ode of thanks to heaven, for heaven's protection of the city.	The Chorus. (?)	Fourteen six-line stanzas; the 1st and 3rd, and 4th and 5th lines are hexasyllabic, enclosing the trisyllabic verses (2nd and 4th).	AABCCB	Sophocles, *Antigone* (100–61).
Act 4	2086–157	A "Hymn to Justice."	The Chorus. (?)	Twelve six-line stanzas hexasyllabic verse.	AABCCB	No primary models. Replaces Sophocles's "Hymn to Love." Indirect influence of Ronsard's "Hymne de la Justice."
Act 4	2230–69	A lament on misfortune and sadness.	The Chorus of Young Women.	Ten stanzas of four-line hexasyllabic verse.	AABB	Replaces Sophocles's chorus on the power of fate.
Act 4	2326–415	A "Hymn to Love," detailing love's power.	The Chorus. (?)	Fifteen stanzas of six-line hexasyllabic verse.	ABABCC	Sophocles, *Antigone* (lines 718–800)

Bibliography

1. Modern Editions of Robert Garnier (by date)

Garnier, Robert. *Les Tragédies*. Ed. W. Foerster. Heilbronn. 1882–83. [Based on the 1585 *Tragédies*]

———. *Hymne de la monarchie*. Ed. Henri Chardon. Mamers: impr. de G. Fleury et A. Dangin, 1905.

———. *Œuvres Complètes*. Ed. Lucien Pinvert. Paris: Garnier, 1923.

———. *Poésies diverses*. Ed. Raymond Lebègue. Paris: Belles-Lettres, 1949.

———. *La Troade* [and] *Antigone*. Ed. Raymond Lebègue. Paris: Belles Lettres, 1952.

———. *Antigone*. Ed. Jean-Dominique Beaudin. Paris: Champion, 1997.

———. *Two Tragedies: Hippolyte* and *Marc Antoine*. Ed. Christine M. Hill and Mary G. Morrison. London: University of London, Athlone Press, 1975.

———. *Théâtre Complet IV: Marc Antoine*. Ed. Jean-Claude Ternaux. Paris: Classiques Garnier, 2010.

2. Sixteenth-Century Editions of Garnier's *Antigone* or Complete Works (selection)

Garnier, Robert. 1580. *Les Tragédies de Robert Garnier*. Paris: Mamert Patisson, 1580. [Bibliothèque de la Comédie française, fonds Rondel; Bibliothèque de l'Arsenal, B.L. 9687.]

———. *Antigone ou la Pieté*. Paris: Mamert Patisson, 1580. [BnF Rés Yf. 3951. Bibliothèque de l'Arsenal, B.L. 9686.]

3. Other Primary Sources

Alamanni, Luigi. *Tragedia di Antigone*. Ed. Francesco Spera. Turin: RES, 1997.

Baïf, Jean-Antoine de. *Antigone*. Ed. Simone Maser. In *La Tragédie* à *l'*époque *d'Henri II et de Charles IX*. Première série, vol. 5, 1573–75. Paris: PUF and Florence: Leo S. Olschki, 1988.

Bèze, Théodore de. *Du droit des magistrats sur leurs subjets: traitté très nécessaire en ce temps, pour advertir de leur devoir, tant les magistrats que les subjets : publié par ceux de Magdebourg l'an M D L & maintenant reveu & augmenté de plusieurs raisons & exemples*. S.l.: s.n, 1579. [Gallica]

———. *Abraham sacrifiant*. Ed. Keith Cameron, Kathleen M. Hall and Francis Higman. Geneva: Droz, 1967.

Boullé, Jean, ed. *La Tragédie au XVIe siècle* [An Anthology]. Paris: Larousse, 1948.

Buchanan, George. *Medea Euripidis poetae tragici Georgio Buchanano Scoto interprete*. Paris: Vascosan, 1544.

———. *Tragedies*. Ed. P. Sharratt and P. G. Walsh. Edinburgh: Scottish Academic Press, 1983.

Demosthenes. *Against Meidias, Androtion, Aristocrates, Timocrates, Aristogeiton*. Ed. and trans. J. H. Vince. Cambridge: Harvard University Press, 1935.

Du Bellay, Joachim. *La Deffence, et illustration de la langue françoise*. Ed. Jean-Charles Monferran and Ernesta Caldarini. Geneva: Droz, 2007.

Euripides. *Phoenician Women*. Trans. Richard Lattimore. Chicago: University of Chicago Press, 1959.

Grévin, Jacques. *Théatre complet et poésies choisies*. Ed. Lucien Pinvert. Paris: Garnier, 1922.

———. *César*. Ed. Ellen S. Ginsberg. Geneva: Droz, 1971.

Homer. *Odyssey*. Trans. A.T. Murray, rev. by George E. Dimock. Cambridge: Harvard University Press (Loeb), 1995. 2 vols.

Horace. *Odes*. Trans. and ed. David Mulroy. Ann Arbor: University of Michigan Press, 1994.

Jodelle, Etienne. *Œuvres et mélanges poétiques*. Paris: Chesneau et Patisson, 1574.

———. *Cléopâtre captive*. Ed. Keith Cameron. Exeter: University of Exeter, 1979.

———. *Cléopâtre captive*. Ed. Françoise Charpentier, Jean-Dominique Beaudin, and José Sanchez. Mugron: Editions José Feijóo, 1990.

L'Hospital, Michel de. *Œuvres complètes*. Ed. P.-J.-S. Duféy. Paris: A. Boulland, 1824–1825. 4 vols.

La Boderie, Guy Le Fèvre de. *La Galliade, ou De la révolution des arts et sciences*. Paris, G. Chaudière, 1578.

La Péruse, Jean de. *Œuvres poétiques*. Ed. Gellibert des Seguins. Geneva: Slatkine Reprints, 1969.

———. *Médée*. Ed. James A. Coleman. Exeter: University of Exeter Press, 1985.

La Porte, Maurice de. *Les Epithetes (1571)*. Ed. François Rouget. Paris: Champion, 2009.

La Taille, Jean de. *De l'art de la tragédie*. Ed. Frederick West. Manchester: Manchester University Press, 1939.

———. *Saül le furieux. La Famine, ou les Gabéonites. Tragédies*. Ed. Elliott Forsyth. Paris: Didier, 1968.

———. *Saül le furieux, La famine ou les Gabéonites*. Ed. Catherine Moins. Paris: Editions du Temps, 1998.

———. *Saül le furieux*. Ed. Jean-Yves Boriaud. Paris: Ellipses, 1998.

L'Estoile, Pierre de. *Registre-Journal du regne de Henri III. Tome III (1579–81)*. Ed. Madeleine Lazard and Gilbert Schrenck. Geneva: Droz, 1997.

Montaigne, Michel de. *Les Essais*. Ed. Pierre Villey and Verdun-L. Saulnier. Paris: PUF, 1965.

Muret, Marc-Antoine. *Juvenelia*. Ed. Virginia Leroux. Geneva: Droz, 2009.

Pibrac, Guy Du Faur. *Les Quatrains; Les plaisirs de la vie rustique et autres poesies*. Ed. Loris Petris. Geneva: Droz, 2004.

Plato. *Laws*. Cambridge: Harvard University Press (Loeb), 1961. 2 vols.

Propertius. *Elegies*. Ed. and trans. H. E. Butler. London: William Heinmann (Loeb), 1916.

Racine, Jean. *Les Œuvres de Jean Racine*. Ed. Paul Mesnard. Paris, 1912.

Ronsard, Pierre de. *Œuvres Complètes*. Ed. Paul Laumonier. Paris: Didier/Nizet (STFM), 1937–83. 20 volumes.

———. *Œuvres Complètes*. Ed. Jean Céard, Daniel Ménager, and Michel Simonin. Paris: Gallimard (Pléaide), 1993–94. 2 vols.

Seneca. *Hercules furens; Troades; Medea; Hippolytus; Oedipus*. Ed. and trans. Frank Justus Miller. London: William Heinemann (Loeb), 1917.

———. *Hercules; Trojan Women; Phoenician Women; Media; Phaedra*. Ed. and trans. John G. Fitch. Cambridge: Harvard University Press (Loeb), 2002.

———. *Oedipus; Agamemnon; Thyestes; Hercules on Oeta; Octavia*. Ed. and trans. John G. Fitch. Cambridge: Harvard University Press (Loeb), 2004.

Seneca (Sénèque). *Tragédies*. Trans. François-Régis Chaumartin. Paris: Les Belles Lettres, 2002.

Sophocles. *The Oedipus at Colonus of Sophocles*. Ed. Sir Richard Jebb. Cambridge. Cambridge University Press, 1889.

———. *The Three Theban plays*. Trans. Robert Fagles. New York: Penguin Books, 1982.

———. *I: Oedipus The King, Oedipus at Colonus, Antigone*. ed. and trans. David Greene. Chicago: Chicago University Press, 1991.

———. *Antigone; Women of Trachis; Philoctetes; Oedipus at Colonus*. ed. and trans. Hugh Lloyd-Jones. Cambridge: Harvard University Press (Loeb), 1994.

Statius. *Thebaid*. ed. and trans. D.R. Shackleton Bailey. Cambridge: Harvard University Press (Loeb), 2003. 2 vols.

Tahureau, Jacques. *Poésies*. Paris: Cabinet du Bibliophile, 1870.

4. Secondary Sources

Appiah, Kwame Anthony. "Thick Translation." *Callaloo* 16, 1993: 808–19.

Arcellaschi, André. *Médée dans le théâtre latin d'Ennius* à *Sénèque*. Rome: Ecole française de Rome, 1990.

Augé-Chiquet, Mathieu. *La Vie, les idées et l'œuvre de Jean-Antoine de Baif.* Paris: Hachette, 1909.

Bacon, H. H. "The Chorus in Greek Life and Drama." *Arion* 3, 1994–95: 6–24.

Balibé, Jacques. "Quelques aspects du pathétique dans les 'Juives' de Robert Garnier." In *Actes du colloque Renaissance-classicisme du Maine*. Paris: Nizet, 1975, 57–75.

———."Ronsard et Robert Garnier." In *Ronsard et la Grèce. Actes du colloque d'Athènes et de Delphes. 4–7 octobre 1985*. Ed. Kyriaki Christodoulou, Paris: Nizet, 263–75.

Balmas, Enea. *Un poeta del rinascimento francese. Etienne Jodelle*. Florence: Leo S. Olschki, 1972.

Banachévitch, Nicholas. *Jean Bastier de la Péruse (1529–44). Etude biographique et littéraire*. Geneva: Slatkine Reprints, 1970.

Barbier, Pierre. *Le Théâtre militant au XVIe siècle*. Geneva: Slatkine, 1970.

Barchiesi, A. "L'Incesto e il regno." In *Seneca: Le Fenicie*. Ed. A. Barchiesi. Venice: Marsilio, 1988, 9–39 and 101–9.

Barnavi, Élie. *La Sainte Ligue, le juge et la potence: l'assassinat du président Brisson: 15 novembre 1591*, Paris: Hachette, 1985.

Barrangerab, Milly S. "Les Atrides: Ariane Mnouchkine's Dance of Death." *Text and Performance Quarterly* 14:1, 1994: 77–85.

Beauchamp, Virginia Walcott. "Sidney's Sister as Translator of Garnier." *Renaissance News* 10:1, Spring,1957: 8–13.

Bellenger, Yvonne, ed. *Le Théâtre biblique de Jean de la Taille*. Paris: Champion, 1998.

Bennett, Lyn. *Women Writing of Divinest Things: Rhetoric and the Poetry of Pembroke, Wroth and Lanyer*. Pittsburgh: Duquesne University Press, 2004.

Berman, Antoine. *L'Epreuve de l'étranger*. Paris: Gallimard, 1984.

Bernage, S. *Etude sur Robert Garnier*. Geneva: Slatkine, 1970.

Bernstein, Jane A., ed. *Guillaume Costeley: Selected Chansons*. New York: Garland, 1989.

Bethune, Robert. "Le Théâtre du Soleil's *Les Atrides*." *Asian Theatre Journal* 10:2, Autumn 1993: 179–90.

Bever, Jean. "Un précurseur méconnu de notre théâtre classique: Robert Garnier (1545–1601) [sic]." *Revue de France* 6, 1925.

Bloom, Harold. *The Anxiety of Influence. A Theory of Poetry*. New York: Oxford University Press, 1973.

Braden, G. *Renaissance Tragedy and the Senecan Tradition*. New Haven: Yale University Press, 1985.

Brague, Rémi. *The Law of God. The Philosophical History of an Idea*. Trans. Lydia G. Cochrane. Chicago: University of Chicago Press, 2007.

Brereton, Geoffrey. *French Tragic Drama in the 16th and 17th Centuries*. London: Methuen, 1973.

Bryant-Bertail, Sarah. "Gender, Empire and Body Politic as Mise en Scène: Mnouchkine's *Les Atrides*." *Theatre Journal* 46:1, March 1994: 1–30.

Buck, Robert J. *A History of Boeotia*. Edmonton: University of Alberta Press, 1979.

Burgess, John F. "*Pietas* in Virgil and Statius." *Proceedings of the Virgil Society* 11 1971–72: 48–61.
Buron, Emmanuel. "La renaissance de la tragédie, ou le spectacle ed la parole: vie et parole dans les tragédies de Jodelle." In *L'Inscription du regard. Moyen Age-Renaissance*. Ed. Michelle Gally and Michel Jourde. Fontenay-aux-Roses: ENS, 1995, 125–68.
Burton, R. W. B. *The Chorus in Sophocles's Tragedes*. Oxford: Clarendon Press, 1980.
Butler, Judith. *Antigone's Claim*. New York: Columbia University Press, 2000.
Buttay-Jutier, Florence. *Fortuna: Usages politiques d'une allégorie morale* à *la Renaissance*. Paris: PUPS, 2008.
Caigny, Florence de. *Sénèque le Tragique en France (XVIe-XVIIe siècles). Imitation, traduction, adaptation*. Paris: Classiques Garnier, 2011.
Calame, Claude. *Choruses of Young Women in Ancient Greece: Their Morphology, Religious Role, and Social Functions*. Trans. Derek Collins. Lanham: Rowman and Littlefield, 2001.
Calder III, William M. "The Size of the Chorus in Seneca's *Agamemnon*." *Classical Philology* 70:1, Jan 1975: 32–35.
———. "Seneca's *Agamemnon*." *Classical Philology* 71:1, Jan 1976: 27–36.
Calin, W. "Ronsard and the Myth of Justice." *Degré Second* I, July 1977: 1–11.
Capitani, Patrizia de. "La storia, luogo privilegiato della tragedia: l'esempio di Robert Garnier." *Studi di letterartura francese* 18, 1990: 275–90.
Cartier, Alfred. "Les idées politiques de Théodore de Bèze." *Bulletin de la Société d'histoire et d'archéologie de Genève* 12, 1990.
Chardon, Henri. *Robert Garnier. Sa vie, ses poésies inédites*. Geneva: Slatkine, 1970.
Charpentier, Françoise. *Pour une lecture de la tragédie humaniste*. Saint-Etienne: Publications de l'Université Saint-Etienne, 1979.
———. "Naissance de la tragédie poétique en France: Jodelle, La Péruse, Jean de la Taille." In *Par ta colère nous sommes consumés*. Ed. Marie-Madeleine Fragonard. Orléans: Paradigme, 1998, 73–86.
———. "Tragédie et monarchie." In *Cité des hommes, cité de Dieu, Mélanges Daniel Ménager*. Geneva: Droz, 2003: 140–52.
Christin, Olivier. *La paix de religion. L'autonomisation de la raison politique au XVIe siècle*. Paris: Seuil, 1997.
Cioranescu, Alexandre. *L'Arioste en France: des origines* à *la fin du XVIIIe siècle*. Paris: Editions des presses modernes, 1939.
Coffey, Michael, and Roland Mayer. *Seneca: Phaedra*. Cambridge: Cambridge Greek and Latin Classics, 1990.
Coleman, Robert. "The Role of the Chorus in Sophocles's *Antigone*." *PCPS*, 1972: 3–27.
Compagnon, Antoine. *Chat en poche: Montaigne et l'allégorie*. Paris: Seuil, 1993.

Crouzet, Denis. *La sagesse et le malheur: Michel de l'Hospital, Chancelier de France.* Seyssel: Champ Vallon, 1998.

———. "A Law of Difference in the History of Difference: The First Edict of 'Tolerance'." In *Religious Difference in France.* Ed. Kathleen Perry Long. Kirksville: Truman State University, 2006, 1–18.

Csapo, Eric and William J. Slater. *The Context of Ancient Drama.* Ann Arbor: University of Michigan Press, 1995.

Cullière, Alain. "La mort du comédien Adrian Talmy (1603)." *BHR* 65:3, 2003: 601–12.

Dale, A. M. "The Chorus in the Action of Greek Tragedy." In *Collected Papers.* Ed. A. M. Dale. Cambridge: Cambridge University Press, 1969, 210–20.

Daubresse, Sylvie. "Le Parlement de Paris et l'édit du 17 janvier 1562." In *Revue Historique*, 300:3, July-September 1998: 515–47.

Dauvois, Nathalie. "Enonciation lyrique, énonciation tragique, dans *Saül le Furieux*." *Littératures* 39, 1998: 31–44.

Davies, John Kenyon. *Wealth and the Power of Wealth in Classical Athens.* Salem: Ayer, 1984.

Davis, P. J. "The Fabric of History in Statius's *Thebaid*." In *Studies in Latin Literature and Roman History.* Ed. Carl Deroux. Brussells: Latomus, 1994: 7.464–83.

Delmas, Christian. *Tragédie de l'*âge *classique (1553–1770).* Paris: Seuil, 1994.

Derrida, Jacques. "What is a 'relevant' translation?" Trans. Lawrence Venuti. In *The Translation Studies Reader. Third Edition.* Ed. Lawrence Venuti. New York: Routledge, 2012, 364–88.

Dhuga, U. S. *Choral Identity and the Chorus of Elders in Greek Tragedy* Plymouth: Lexington Books, 2011.

Dobbins, F. "Music in the French Theatre of the Late Sixteenth Century." *Studies in Medieval and Early Modern Music.* Ed. Iain Fenlon. Issue of *Early Music History* 13, 1994: 85–122.

Dobby-Poirson, Florence. "Autour des Hymnes: la postérité de Ronsard dans l'*Hymne de la monarchie* de Robert Garnier." In *Cité des hommes, cité de Dieu, Mélanges Daniel Ménager.* Geneva: Droz, 2003, 281–89.

———. *Le Pathétique dans le théâtre de Robert Garnier.* Paris: Champion, 2006.

Duron, Jean. *Regards sur la musique—la naissance du style français: 1650–1673.* Ed. Jean Duron. Wavre: Mardaga, 2008.

Emeline, D. "La mort dans les tragédies de Robert Garnier." *Mélanges Jean Larmat, Annales de la Faculté des Lettres et des Sciences Humaines de Nice* 39, 1982 and Paris: Belles Lettres, 1983, 321–34.

Esposito, Stephen. "The Changing Roles of the Sophoclean Chorus." *Arion* 4.1, 1996: 85–114.

Faguet, Emile. *Essai sur la tragédie française au XVI*[e] *siècle.* Paris: Hachette, 1883. (Repr. Paris: Fontemoing, 1912.)

Fanlo, Jean-Raymond. "Figures de la souveraineté dans le théâtre de Garnier: *Hippolyte* et *Les Juives*." *Littératures* 43, Fall 2000: 56–69.

Fantham, E. "*Nihil iam iura naturae valent:* Incest and Fratricide in Seneca's *Phoenissae*." In *Seneca Tragicus: Ramus Essays on Seneca Drama*. Ed. A. J. Boyle. Victoria: Berwick, 1983, 61–76.

Federici, Carla. *Réalisme et dramaturgie: étude de quatre écrivains, Garnier, Hardy, Rotrou, Corneille*. Paris: Nizet, 1974.

Ferrari, Silvio. "Les choeurs d'Hippolyte." [*Tragedia e sentimento del tragico nella letteratura francese del Cinquecento*] *Studi di letteratura francese* 18, 1990: 83–97.

Foley, Helene. *Female Acts in Greek Tragedy*. Princeton: Princeton University Press, 2001.

———. "Choral Identity in Greek Tragedy." *CP* 98, 2003: 1–30.

———, ed. *Reflections of Women in Antiquity*. New York: Routledge, 2005.

———, and Erin B. Mee, eds. *Antigone on the Contemporary World Stage* Oxford: Oxford University Press, 2011.

Ford, Philip. *Ronsard's* Hymnes. *A Literary and Iconographical Study*. Tempe, AZ: Medieval & Renaissance Texts & Studies, 1997.

Forsyth, Elliott. *La Tragédie française de Jodelle* à *Corneille (1553–1640)*. Paris: Nizet, 1962.

Frank, Marica. *Seneca's* Phoenissae. *Introduction and Commentary*. Leiden: Brill, 1995.

Frappier, J. "L'inspiration biblique et théologique dans *L'Hymne de la justice*." In *Mélanges d'histoire littéraire de la Renaissance offerts* à *Henri Chamard*. Paris: Nizet, 1951: 97–108.

Frese, Mary Ann. *The Search for Modern Tragedy: Aesthetic Fascism in Italy and France*. Ithaca: Cornell University Press, 2001.

Frisch, Andrea. *Forgetting Differences: Tragedy, Historiography, and the French Wars of Religion*. Edinburgh: Edinburgh University Press, 2015.

Frost, J. *Etude analytique et critique sur le théâtre de Robert Garnier*. Bielefeld: J. D. Küster Wittwe, 1867

Gambier, Paul. *Au temps des guerres de religion. Le Président Barnabé Brisson, ligueur, 1531–1591*. Paris: Perrin, 1957.

Ganiban, Randall Toth. *Statius and Virgil: the Thebaid and the Reinterpretation of the Aeneid*. Cambridge: Cambridge University Press, 2007.

Garapon, Robert. 1989. "L'*Antigone* de Robert Garnier et la légende d'Oedipe." *Edipo in Francia, Studi di Letteratura francese* 15, 1989: 33–39.

Gardner, C. P. *The Sophoclean Chorus: A Study of Character and Function*. Iowa City: University of Iowa Press, 1987.

Godt, Irving Godt. "Guillaume Costeley." In *The New Grove Dictionary of Music and Musicians*. Ed. Stanley Sadie. London: Macmillan, 1980.

Goetsch, Sallie. "Playing against the Text: *Les Atrides* and the History of Reading Aeschylus." *TDR* 38.3, 1994: 75–95.

Gohin, Ferdinand. "Le lyrisme dans les tragédies de Garnier." *La Muse française*. 1925: 120–31.

Golder, Herbert. "Geek Tragedy?: Or, Why I'd Rather Go to the Movies." *Arion* 4:1, Spring 1996: 174–209. (1996a)

Goldhill, Simon. *Reading Greek Tragedy*. Cambridge: Cambridge University Press, 1986.

———. "Collectivity and Otherness—The Authority of the Tragic Chorus: Response to Gould." In *Tragedy and the Tragic Greek Theater and Beyond*. Ed. M. S. Silk. Oxford: Clarendon Press, 1996, 244–56.

———, ed. *Performance Culture and Athenian Democracy*. Cambridge: Cambridge University Press, 1999.

———. *How to Stage Greek Tragedy Today*. Chicago: University of Chicago Press, 2007.

———, and Robin Osborne, eds. *Art and Text in Ancient Greek Culture*. Cambridge: Cambridge University Press, 1994.

———, and Edith Hall, eds. *Sophocles and the Greek Tragic Tradition*. Cambridge: Cambridge University Press, 2009.

Gould, John. "Tragedy and the Collective Experience." In *Tragedy and the Tragic Greek Theater and Beyond*. Ed. M. S. Silk. Oxford: Clarendon Press, 1996, 217–43.

Gourcuff, Olivier de. *Un Ami de Ronsard: Robert Garnier*. Limoges: Dumont, 1924.

Goyet, Francis, ed. *Traités de poétique*. Paris: Livre de Poche, 1990.

———. *Audaces de la prudence: littérature et politique aux XVIe et XVIIe siècles*. Paris: Classiques Garnier, 2009.

Grant, David. "With Les Atrides in Lemetre's Kingdom. Les Atrides by Ariane Mnouchkine." *Theatre Ireland* 29, Autumn 1992: 12–15.

Gras, M. *Robert Garnier, son art et sa méthode*. Geneva: Droz, 1965.

Greene, Robert et al. *The Princeton Encyclopedia of Poetry and Poetics*. Princeton: Princeton University Press, 2012.

Griffin, Miriam. "Philosophy, Cato, and Roman Suicide: I." *Greece and Rome* 33, 1986: 64–75 and 72–75.

Griffiths, R. *The Dramatic Technique of Antoine de Montchrestien*. Oxford: Oxford University Press, 1970.

Grimal, Pierre. *Dictionnaire de la mythologie grecque et romaine*. Paris: PUF, 1996.

Guastella, Gianni. "Virgo, Coniunx, Mater: The Wrath of Seneca's Medea." *Classical Antiquity* 20:2, October 2001: 197–220.

Hall, Edith. "Is there a *Polis* in Aristotle's *Politics*?" In *Tragedy and the Tragic: Greek Theater and Beyond*. Ed. M. Silk. Oxford: Oxford University Press, 1996, 295–309.

Hall, Kathleen M. "Introduction." In Etienne Jodelle, *Cléopâtre captive*. Ed. Kathleen M. Hall. Exeter: University of Exeter, 1979.

Hannay, Margaret P., ed. *Mary Sidney, Countess of Pembroke*. Burlington: Ashgate, 2009.

Hegel, G. W. F. *Hegel's Aesthetics: Lectures on Fine Art*. Trans. T. M. Knox. Oxford: Clarendon, 1975.

Heller, Henry. *Iron and Blood: Civil wars in Sixteenth Century France*. Montreal: McGill-Queen's University Press, 1991.

Henrichs, Albert. "'Why should I dance?': Choral Self-Referentiality in Greek Tragedy." *Arion* 3, 1994–95: 56–11.

———. "Dancing in Athens, Dancing on Delos: Some Patterns of Choral Projections in Euripides." *Philologus* 140, 1996: 48–62.

Henry, Denis, and Elisabeth Henry. *The Mask of Power: Seneca's Tragedies and Imperial Rome*. Chicago: Bolchazy-Carducci, 1985.

Houellemare, Marie. *Politiques de la parole: Le Parlement de Paris au XVIe siècle*. Geneva: Droz, 2011.

Javitch, Daniel. "The assimilation of Aristotle's Poetics in sixteenth-century Italy." In Glyn Norton (ed.), *The Cambridge History of Literary Criticism*. Cambridge: Cambridge University Press, 1999, vol. 3, pp. 53–65.

Jondorf, Gillian. *Robert Garnier and the Themes of Political Tragedy in the Sixteenth Century*. Cambridge: Cambridge University Press, 1969.

———. *French Renaissance Tragedy. The Dramatic Word*. Cambridge: Cambridge University Press, 1990.

Jouanna, Arlette et al, eds. *Histoire et dictionnaire des guerres de religion*. Paris: R. Laffont, 1998.

Julleville, Petit de L. *Le Théâtre en France, histoire de la littérature dramatique, depuis ses origines jusqu'à nos jours*. Paris: A. Colin, 1892.

Kambitis, Jean, ed. *L'Antiope d'Euripide*. Athens, 1972.

Keller, Abraham-Charles. "Michel de l'Hospital and the Edict of Toleration of 1562." In *Bibliothèque d'Humanisme et Renaissance*, 14:2, 1952: 301–10.

Kingdom, R. M. "Les idées politiques de Bèze d'après son 'Traitté de l'authorité du magistrat." *BHR* 22, 1960: 565–69.

Kreyder, Laura. "Sur la dramaturgie de Jean de La Taille: L'Art de la tragédie". In *Le Théâtre biblique de Jean de la Taille*. Ed. Yvonne Bellenger. Orléans: Paradigme, 1998, 125–52.

Kulcke, Otto. *Seneca's Einfluss auf Jean de La Péruse's* Médée *und Jean de La Taille's* la Famine, ou les Gabéonites. Greifswald: Druck von F. W. Kunike, 1884.

Lackerstein, Debbie. *National Regeneration in Vichy France: Ideas and Policies, 1930–1944*. Burlington: Ashgate, 2012.

Lafeuille, G. *Cinq hymnes de Ronsard*. Geneva: Droz, 1973.

Laguardia, David P. and Cathy Yandell, eds. *Memory and Community in Sixteenth-Century France*. Aldershot: Ashgate, 2015.

Lamb, Mary Ellen. "The Myth of the Countess of Pembroke: The Dramatic Circle." *Yearbook of English Studies*, 11, 1981: 194–202.

Lanson, Gustave. "Etudes sur les origines de la tragédie classique en France." *RHLF* 1903: 177–231 and 413–36.

———. *Esquisse d'une histoire de la tragédie française.* New York: Columbia University Press, 1920. (Repr. New York: AMS Press, 1966.)

Laudun d'Aigaliers, Pierre de. *L'Art poëtique françois.* Ed. Jean-Charles Monferran. Paris: STFM, 2000.

Lazard, Madeleine. *Le théâtre en France au XVIe siècle.* Paris: PUF, 1980.

———, ed. *Autour des Hymnes de Ronsard.* Geneva: Slatkine, 1984.

———. "Du public italien au public français: épîtres dédicatoires et prologues de Pierre de Larivey." In *L'Ecrivain face* à *son public en France et en Italie* à *la Renaissance.* Eds. Charles Adelin Fiorato and Jean-Claude Margolin. Paris: Vrin, 1989, 253–64.

Lazaridès, Alexandre. "Les Atrides." *Jeu: Revue de théâtre* 65, 1992: 210–14.

Lebègue, Raymond. "L'unité de lieu dans l'*Antigone* de Robert Garnier." *Revue du Seizième siècle* XI, 1924: 238–51.

———. *La Tragédie religieuse en France; les débuts (1514–1573).* Paris: Champion, 1929.

———. *George Buchanan, sa vie, son œuvre, son influence en France et au Portugal.* Coimbra: Coimbra Editora, 1931.

———. *La Tragédie française de la Renaissance.* Brussels: Office de Publicité, 1944.

———. "L'influence du théâtre néo-latin sur le théâtre sérieux en langue française." *Humanisme et Renaissance* 6:1, 1939: 41–47.

———. "Tableau de la tragédie française de 1573 à 1610." *BHR* 5, 1944: 375–93.

———. "Notes sur le vocabulaire de Garnier." *Le Français moderne* XVII, 1949: 165–81.

———. "La représentation des tragédies au XVIe siècle." In *Mélanges Chamard.* Ed. R. L. Graeme Ritchie. Paris: Nizet, 1951, 199–205.

———. "Les représentations dramatiques à la cour des Valois." In *Les fêtes de la Renaissance.* Ed. J. Jacquot. Paris: CNRS, 1956, 85–90.

———. "Les Guerres civiles de Rome et les tragédies de R. Garnier." *Association Guillaume Budé. Congrès 1973.* Paris: Belles Lettres, 1975: 2.556–60.

———. "Tradition et nouveauté dans le théâtre de Robert Garnier." *Actes du colloque Renaissance-Classicisme du Maine. Le Mans 1971.* Paris: Nizet, 1975, 283–89.

———. "Jean de la Taille." In *Le Théâtre biblique de Jean de la Taille.* Ed. Yvonne Bellenger. Orléans: Paradigme, 1998, 13–65.

Lestringant, Frank. "Robert Garnier." In *Dictionnaire des littératures de langue française.* Paris: Bordas, 1984, 869–72.

———."Pour une lecture politique du théâtre de Robert Garnier: le commentaire d'André Thevet en 1584." In *Parcours et rencontres, Mélanges de langue, d'histoire et de littérature françaises offerts* à *Enea Balmas.* Paris: Klincksieck, 1993, 1.405–22.

Lexicon Iconographicum Mythologiae Classicae. Zurich: Artemis Verlag, 1981.

Lewis, Charlton T. and Charles Short. *A Latin Dictionary*. Oxford: Clarendon Press, 1879.

Levy, Kenneth J. "Costeley's Chromatic Chanson." *Annales Musicologiques* 3, 1955: 213–63.

Liddell, Henry George and Robert Scott. *An Intermediate Greek-English Lexicon*. Oxford: Clarendon Press, 1900.

Lovatt, Helen. *Statius and Epic Games: Sport, Politics and Poetics in the Thebaid* Cambridge: Cambridge University Press, 2005.

Marti, B. "Seneca's Tragedies. A New Interpretation." *TAPhA*, 1945: 216–45.

Mastronarde, D. J. "Knowledge and Authority in the Choral Voice of Euripidean Tragedy." *Syllecta Classica* 10, 1990: 87–104.

Mathieu-Castellani, Gisèle. "La notion de genre." In Guy Demerson (ed.), *La notion de genre à la Renaissance*. Genève: Slatkine, 1984, pp. 17–34.

Maulnier, Thierry. 1946. "L'*Antigone* de Robert Garnier." *La Revue de Paris*. June 1946: 62–69.

Mazouer, Charles. "La vision tragique de Robert Garnier dans *Hippolyte, La Troade* et *Antigone*." *Studi di letterartura francese* 18, 1990: 72–82.

———. "Les tragédies bibliques sont-elles tragiques?" *Littératures classiques* 16, March 1992: 125–40.

———. *Le Théâtre français de la Renaissance*. Paris: Champion, 2002.

Mazzola, Elizabeth. *Favorite Sons: The Politics and Poetics of the Sidney Family*. New York: Palgrave Macmillan, 2003.

McFarlane, I. D. "George Buchanan and France." *Studies in French Literature Presented to H. W. Lawton*. Manchester: Manchester University Press, 1968.

———. "George Buchanan and European Humanism." *The Yearbook of English Studies*, 15, 1985: 33–47.

McGowan, Margaret M. *The Vision of Rome in Late Renaissance France*. New Haven: Yale University Press, 2000.

McNelis, Charles. *Statius's Thebaid and the Poetics of Civil War*. Cambridge: Cambridge University Press, 2007.

Meyers, Penelope F. "(De)Allegorizing Antigone: A New Reading of Jean Anouilh's *Antigone* and Athol Fugard's *The Island*." BA Thesis, Barnard College, 2011.

Millet, Olivier. "De l'erreur au péché: la culpabilité dans la tragédie humaniste du XVIe siècle." *Travaux de littérature* 8, 1995: 57–73.

———. "Exposition au malheur et politique-spectacle: les 'grands hommes' dans la tragédie humaniste de la Renaissance." *Travaux de littérature* 18, 2005: 105–21.

Morel, Jacques. *La Tragédie*. Paris: Armand Colin, 1964.

———. *Agréables mensonges. Essais sur le théâtre français du XVIIe siècle*. Paris: Klincksieck, 1991.

Mouflard, Marie-Madeleine. *Robert Garnier 1545–1590* (La Roche-sur-Yon: Impr. centrale de l'Ouest, 1961–1964). 3 vols.

Nelli, R. "Remarques sur le vers heptasyllabique français et occitan." *Mélanges offerts* à *Rita Lejeune*, 1968.

Noirot-Maguire, Corinne. "Conjurer le mal: Jean de la Taille et le paradoxe de la tragédie humaniste." *EMF* 13, 2010: 121–43.

Pack, R. "On Guilt and Error in Senecan Tragedy." *TAPhA* 71, 1940: 360–71 and 367–68.

Patin, Henri Joseph Guillaume. *Etudes sur les tragiques grecs*. Paris: Hachette, 1873.

Petris, Loris. *La Plume et la tribune: Michel de L'Hospital et ses discours (1559–1562), suivi de l'edition du* De initiatione Sermo *(1559) et des* Discours *de Michel de L'Hospital (1560–1562)*. Geneva: Droz, 2002.

Pickard-Cambridge, Arthur Wallace.*The Dramatic Festivals of Athens*. Oxford: Clarendon Press, 1953.

Pocock, Gordon. *Corneille and Racine: Problems of Tragic Form*. Cambridge: Cambridge University Press, 1973.

Prah, N. T. "The Stoic Base of Senecan Drama." *TAPhA*, 1948: 1–11.

Pratt, Norman T. *Seneca's Drama*. Chapel Hill: North Carolina University Press, 1983.

Prescott, Anne Lake. "Mary Sidney's 'Antonius' and the Ambiguities of French History." *The Yearbook of English Studies* 38:1/2, 2008: 216–33.

Purkis, Helen C. "Choeurs chantés ou parlés dans la tragédie française au XVIe siècle." *BHR* 22, 1960: 294–301.

Purkiss, Diane, ed. *Three Tragedies by Renaissance Women*. London: Penguin, 1998.

Quainton, Malcolm. *Ronsard's Ordered Chaos*. Manchester: Manchester University Press, 1980.

Rigal, Eugène. *Esquisse d'une histoire des théâtres de Paris, de 1548* à *1635: Hôtel de Bourgogne et Marais*. Paris: A. Dupret, 1887.

———. *Alexandre Hardy et le théâtre français* à *la fin du XVIe et au commencement du XVIIe siècle*. Paris: Hachette, 1889.

———. *Le théâtre français avant la période classique*. Paris: Hachette, 1901.

———. "La mise en scène dans les tragédies du XVIe siècle." *RHLF* 12, 1905.

Roberts, Josephine A., and James F. Gaines, "Kyd and Garnier: The Art of Amendment." *Comparative Literature* 31:2, Spring 1979: 124–33.

Rohou, Jean. *Tragédie classique (1550–1793)*. Paris: Seuil, 1996.

Sainte-Beuve, Charles-Augustin. *Tableau historique et critique de la poésie française au XVIe siècle*. Paris: Charpentier, 1828.

Saulnier, Verdun-Léon. "Un ami inconnu de Robert Garnier, le poète Estienne Gasteuil." *Revue universitaire* LXI, 1952: 88–94.

———. "Etienne Gasteuil, apologiste de Robert Garnier." *Bulletin du Bibliophile et du bibliothécaire* 3, 1959.

Schanzer, Ernest. "*Anthony and Cleopatra* and the Countess of Pembroke's *Antonius.*" *Notes and Queries* 201, 1956: 152–54.

Schlegel, August Wilhelm von. *Course of Lectures on Dramatic art and Literature. Trans. John Black.* New York: AMS Press, 1973. (Translation of: *Vorlesungen* über *dramatische Kunst und Literatur I.* Leipzig, 1846.)

Searles, Colbert. "The stageability of R. Garnier's *Tragedies.*" *MLN* 1907: 225–29.

Solomon, Jon. *The Ancient World in the Cinema.* New Haven: Yale University Press, 2001.

Soulié, M. "Ronsard et la Bible." *Europe* 691–92, November-December 1986: 70–78.

Staley, Gregory Allan. *Seneca and the Idea of Tragedy.* Oxford: Oxford University Press, 2010.

Stegman, André. Ed. *Edits des guerre de religion.* Paris: Vrin, 1979.

Steiner, George. *Antigones.* New Haven: Yale University Press, 1996.

Stone Jr., Donald. *French Humanist Tragedy.* Manchester: Manchester University Press, 1974.

Street, J. S. *French Sacred Drama from Bèze to Corneille: Dramatic Forms and their Purposes in the Early Modern Theatre.* Cambridge: Cambridge University Press, 1983.

Tadic-Gilloteaux, Nicole. "Sénèque face au suicide." *L'Antiquité classique* 32, 1963: 541–51.

Taplin, Oliver. "Review: Putting on the Dog. Les Atrides by Ariane Mnouchkine." *Arion* 4:1, Spring 1996: 210–15.

Tarrant, R. J. "Senecan Drama and Its Antecedents." *HSCP* 82, 1978: 213–63.

Ternaux, J. C. "Un aspect de l'âge d'or chez Ronsard: *L'Hymne de la Justice* et *L'Hymne de Henri II.*" In *Millenarismo ed* èta *dell'oro nel Rinascimento.* Ed. Luisa Secchi Tarugi. Florence: Franco Cesati, 2003, 163–73.

Thibodeau, Martin. *Hegel and Greek Tragedy.* Trans. Hans-Jakob Wilhelm. Plymouth: Lexington Books, 2013.

Truchet, Jacques. *La Tragédie classique en France.* Paris: PUF, 1975.

Usher, Phillip John. "Introduction." In Ronsard, *The Franciad (1572).* Ed. and trans. Phillip John Usher. New York: AMS Press, 2010.

———. "Tragedy in the Aftermath of the Saint Bartholomew's Day Massacre: France's First *Phèdre* and the Hope for Peace." In *Romance Notes,* 52:3, 2012: 255–62.

———. "Prudency and the Inefficacy of Language: Re-politicizing Jean de la Péruse's *Médée* (1553)." In *Modern Language Notes* (MLN), 128:4, September 2013: 868–80.

———. "Tragedy and Translation." In *Companion to Translation Studies.* Ed. Catherine Porter and Sandra Bermann. Oxford: Wiley-Blackwell, 2014: 467–78.

———. "Courtroom Drama during the Wars of Religion." In *French Renaissance and Baroque Drama: Text, Performance, Theory*. Ed. Michael Meere. Newark: University of Delaware Press, 2015, 139–52.

Waller, Gary F. *Mary Sidney, Countess of Pembroke: A Critical Study of her Writings and Literary Milieu*. Salzburg: Institut für Anglistik und Amerikanistik, Universität Salzburg, 1979.

Walsh, George B. *The Varieties of Enchantment: Early Greek Views of the Nature and Function of Poetry*. Chapel Hill: University of North Carolina Press, 1984.

Weber, Henri. *La Création poétique au XVIe siècle*. Paris: Nizet, 1956.

Weinstein, Leo. *The Subversive Tradition in French literature*. Boston: Twayne Publishers, 1989.

Wilson, P. *The Athenian Institution of the Khoregia: The Chorus, the City and the Stage*. Cambridge: Cambridge University Press, 2000.

Winkler, Martin M., ed. *Classical Myth and Culture in the Cinema*. Oxford: Oxford University Press, 2001.

Witherspoon, Alexander MacLaren. *The Influence of Robert Garnier on Elizabethan Drama*. New Haven: Yale University Press, 1924.

Wohl, Victoria. "Sexual Difference and the Aporia of Justice in Sophocles' *Antigone*." In *Bounded by the City: Greek Tragedy, Sexual Difference, and the Formation of the Polis*. Albany: SUNY Press, 2009, 119–48.

Wygant, Amy. *Medea, Magic, and Modernity in France. Stages and histories, 1553–1797*. Aldershot, England; Burlington, VT: Ashgate, 2007.

Wyke, Maria. "Are You Not Entertained?: Classicists and Cinema." *International Journal of the Classical Tradition* 9:3, Winter 2003: 430–45.